@ Roho Publishing. All rights reserved. Printed in the United States.

ISBN: 978-09894338-8-4

Cover Design: Jenna Stanbrough

Book Layout: Jenna Stanbrough

Front Cover Photo: Cheryl Treworgy- PrettySportyPhotos

Roho Publishing

4040 Graphic Arts Rd

Emporia, Kansas 66801

www.rohopublishing.com

About Roho Publishing

When Kip Keino defeated Jim Ryun in the 1968 Olympic Games at 1500 meters he credited the win to "Roho." Roho is the Swahili word for spirit demonstrated through extraordinary strength and courage. The type of courage and strength that can be summoned up from deep within that will allow you to meet your goals and overcome the challenges in life. Roho Publishing focuses on the spirit of sport and is designed to inspire, encourage, motivate and teach valuable life lessons.

Dedication

I would like to thank my daughter, Jenna Stanbrough, for her invaluable help in the creation of this book. She has been an integral part in editing, designing and creating the final product.

A special thanks goes to my family. My mom and dad supported me in my desire to be an athlete. My wife, Wendy has encouraged me throughout my career. My three daughters, whom I was fortunate enough to coach all three in cross country and track, and who are lifetime cross country and track and field fans.

I would also like to thank the athletes whom I have had the privilege to coach over the years. With these athletes I have "practiced" many of the mental drills in this book and hopefully developed mental skills that not only improved athletic performance, but also improved each one as a person. Each of these individuals have taught me much about the qualities to be successful in life – good character, integrity, a strong work ethic, dedication and perseverance.

Preface

The potato races at the county fair were fun! To balance your potato on a spoon and run as fast as you can, periodically stopping to put the potato back on the spoon was a simple but encouraging introduction to my beginning sports experiences. Not only was it enjoyable, but being able to finish ahead of the pack gave me confidence. I look back at the county fair potato race as one of my first introductions to sports psychology.

My first organized sports experience was in the 6th grade with my first physical education class and my first exposure to an organized school athletic team. I loved it! I loved the feeling of movement and the self-satisfaction from participation in the challenge. It was then that I decided I wanted to coach and teach physical education. I have been fortunate to live the dream, because that is still what I want do and what I still get excited to do almost 50 years later!

Although I didn't realize it at the time I had several sport psychology experiences through the years. When I competed on the $6^{th}, 7^{th}$, and 8th grade track and field teams the varsity was determined by weight limit. My 6th and 7th grade years, I fell below the 90 pound limit and was junior varsity. At the beginning of my 8th grade track season, I was excited I had beefed up and broken the 90 pound barrier and expected to make varsity. However, to my dismay, they moved the weight limit to 100 pounds and I remained junior varsity. As a junior varsity competitor, I excelled in many events and that was the start of my track and field career.

In high school I continued to work hard and grow in confidence. By my senior year, I was undefeated at my specialty, the 800 meter run, and entered the state meet with a goal of winning. But the unexpected happened. At the beginning of the final lap I was tripped and fell down. When I got up, my competitors were far up the track. I took off sprinting and caught them all by the beginning of the straightaway, only to tie up and get passed, ending up in fifth, half a second from the win. It was a valuable lesson in sport psychology that the unexpected often happens. If I would not have panicked and sprinted, I still could have won, but I knew nothing of mental plans at that time.

Having never run cross country in high school it was a very challenging experience to run cross country in college. However, I had the goal of using my cross country experiences to be a better 800 meter runner, and the process worked out well as I competed at the national level in track and field and improved immensely as a cross country runner.

In graduate school at the University of Oregon, I was exposed to some of the top runners in the world that I competed and trained with. I was also fortunate to study with Olympic coaches. Those experiences have been invaluable in trying to understand how to improve performance both from a physical and mental aspect.

When I became a head collegiate cross country and track and field coach, I began to understand the use of mental skills and drills to improve performance. I started using then it with my college athletes and in my third year our team finished second in the national meet. I was just getting into implementing mental skills with the team and they bought in. Over the course of the season they continued to improve physically and mentally and overachieved with their second place national finish. I was sold on the value of mental skills and continued to implement it into practice and competition.

After spending a few years in administration I decided I like coaching people better than writing reports. So I got back into coaching at the high school level and placed a high priority on the mental game. It became an important part of our program. Was it successful? I would like to think so as we became consistent placers at the state meet, finishing in the top two teams at the state meet five years in a row, and winning a state title. But, more importantly the athletes were telling me how they could use their newly acquired mental skills to be better academically, they had more self-confidence and they felt more comfortable approaching and meeting challenging situations. Their mental skills were helping them in other areas of their lives and it was making a positive difference in their lives!

For over 30 years, I have taught at the college level and incorporated mental skills and drills into my teaching and development of young coaches. As director of the Emporia State Coaching Education Program, I get very excited when I see young, future coaches learn about mental skills. Many are similar in their experiences to what mine were. They were not previously exposed to a systematic mental skills program in their athletic experiences. Although most coaches and athletes agree that the mental side is very important, they do not engage in mental skills training. No, it is not that they are bad coaches or bad athletes, or bad people. It's just that they have not been exposed to a mental skills training program. All coaches would like mentally skilled athletes, but many don't have the knowledge to implement mental skills training. Athletes would like to be mentally skilled, but lack the knowledge of mental skills training. This book is for athletes and coaches that want to improve the mental game. It is not meant to replace the coach, but to help the athlete and coach develop mental skills that take their game to the next level.

Many books talk in theory and state the mental game in general terms. This book attempts to bridge the research and knowledge that is the basis of sports psychology and uses easy-to-use activities that can be implemented by the athlete or coach without a high knowledge of sports psychology.

Throughout the book you will find numerous activities and ideas. Three things are very important in this mental skills process: (1) the mental part is a skill and therefore should be trained similar to the physical part, (2) individuals are different and are encouraged to try the different activities and suggestions to see what works best, and (3) the development of mental skills takes time, so be patient and put in the work.

If you are an athlete, I am excited that you have chosen to improve your mental game and take your performance to the next level. If you are a coach, congratulations, you have the most influential occupation in the world. By learning about and implementing mental drills you will be embarking upon a fruitful journey to improve mental skills and make a positive difference.

Mental Skills and Drills for Track and Field

Table of Contents

Preface		1
Chapter 1	Introduction to Mental Skills	5
Chapter 2	Finding Your Optimal Arousal Zone	21
Chapter 3	Goals	39
Chapter 4	Self-Talk	61
Chapter 5	Imagery	75
Chapter 6	Focus	91
Chapter 7	Introduction to Mental Plans	105
Chapter 8	Sprints	115
Chapter 9	Hurdles	123
Chapter 10	Middle-Distance/Distance	131
Chapter 11	Relays	139
Chapter 12	High Jump	147
Chapter 13	Long Jump	155
Chapter 14	Triple Jump	163
Chapter 15	Pole Vault	171
Chapter 16	Shot Put	179
Chapter 17	Discus	187
Chapter 18	Javelin	195
Chapter 19	Activity Forms	203
Resources		209
About the Author		211

Chapter 1

Introduction To Mental Skills

As a track and field athlete you put in numerous hours of training to prepare your body. You run, jump or throw more in one season than most people do in a lifetime. You train week after week to the point of exhaustion. You train diligently. You are supremely aware of your body. You train to become fast, strong and powerful! You train hard, running, jumping, or throwing to be the best you can be. But are you doing everything you can to be the best you can be?

In track and field, there are no teammates to blame, no coach to run your race, no hiding behind excuses of cold weather, hot weather, unkind wind, a slow track, or jostling competition.

Athletes often train the physical component with a well-planned, systematic program that focuses on the physiological aspects, yet the mental training tools have not been provided and practiced. Mental skills training are often not an important component of training because few athletes and coaches are formally exposed to mental skills and drills.

How important is the mental side of track and field? How ironic that both athletes and coaches consider mental skills to be an extremely important part of high performance, but yet do not take the time to learn and develop a systematic program to develop the mental skills.

The mind controls the body, and as an athlete you want control over what your physical energy can create. Only when you have a fully prepared mind can you reach your full potential and perform at your peak. Like physical training, mental training must be practiced on a consistent basis. *Mental Skills and Drills for Track and Field* has been designed to prepare you mentally to practice and compete to your potential. It supplies mental skills and drills that will allow you to develop your mental skills and become a better athlete. Only you can make the decision to commit to the mental program to improve.

How important is the mental side of track and field? Complete *Activity 1.1 How Much of Athletics is Mental?* to determine what importance you place on the mental component of track and field.

Activity 1.1
How Much of Athletics is Mental?

What percentage of your performance is mental? _____

What percentage of your performance is physical? _____

What percentage of your time do you spend training for the mental side? _____

What percentage of your time do you spend training for the physical side? _____

Many coaches and athletes believe a large percentage of their performance is mental but they don't train for the mental side. Could this be you?

Think of how many times your performance suffered from a lack of confidence, focus or determination.

Do you believe that mental training could improve your game? How could it improve it?

Although it is hard to place an exact percentage that the mental part plays in track and field, we can agree that it is an extremely important part of the game. Would you take a week of practice off and show up on game day ready to play without any physical practice? Sounds funny doesn't it? However, many athletes are told to get psyched up and be mentally tough for the big competition, yet the athlete may not have the training tools to accomplish that task because they have not practiced it.

In surveys conducted of Olympic Track and Field athletes, 99% of the athletes engaged in mental training. In comparison to the average high school athlete, 90% do not engage in mental training. Which group would you like to be in? What is the one thing the Olympic athletes have in common? They prepare their minds as well as the body to perform at the highest level. In fact, the physical preparation sets the stage and the mental preparation allows them to achieve optimal performance

Many people believe that mental toughness is a genetic quality. Either they are fortunate to have been born with mental toughness or not. Contrary to what some might think, a person is not born with mental toughness. Mental abilities can be learned and developed just as physical skills and strength can be learned and developed.

Another potential reason why mental skills training is not an important component of training is that few athletes and coaches are ever formally exposed to them. Coaches and athletes are very knowledgeable about the physical skills, technique, strategies of their sport, and strength and conditioning. However, little education and training is available for coaches and athletes in the areas of mental training—unless they seek it out on their own.

Think about when you performed your best. Wouldn't it be nice to be in the flow all the time? A mental skills training program that is consistently practiced over time can lead to an increased chance of performing in the flow. Two major goals of mental skills training are to learn and implement skills to: (1) make high-level performance more consistent, and (2) enhance performance by allowing you to reach more of your potential.

Complete *Activity 1.2 Most Memorable Performance* to recall a memorable performance and examine how you felt that day.

Activity 1.2 **Most Memorable Performance**
Think of one of your best performances ever. It may be in track and field or it could be in something else, such as singing or giving a speech. Recall a time when you felt so good and everything came together perfectly. Recall it in as much detail as possible.
Where were you?
What were you doing?
How did you feel?
Why do you think you performed so well that day?

Similarities between physical strength training and mental strength training

1. Planned systematic approach
   Mental skills training should be integrated into your program on a regular, on-going basis. How effective would a strength training program be if you did it one or two times during the preseason and then never did it again? Mental skills training is not a one-time magical program, but it must be implemented and integrated throughout all the training periods to be maximally effective.

2. Proper progression
   Mental skills training is best developed through proper progression. The beginning stage includes awareness, progresses to education, and then must be implemented into practice and competition, then evaluated. Would you start off your weight training program by maximally lifting the day before a game expecting to be suddenly physically strong? Unfortunately, many coaches and athletes expect immediate help in the mental areas without going through the preliminary stages to build a strong foundation in mental skill development.

3. Initial decrease in performance
   When you begin a strength training program, your muscles breakdown at first in order to build themselves up later. The initial stages of a mental training program may often see a decrease in performance. With mental training, performers may have some initial difficulties as they learn and change mental habits. These frustrations may cause athletes to consider quitting the mental skills training program. However, once skills become habits, they will be much easier to use. It is recommended that mental skills training be initiated in the off-season or early in the pre-season so skills can be well learned during the season.

4. Delayed observable benefits
   Physical strength gains are seldom observed until 4-6 weeks of training. Similarly, mental skills may not have an observable immediate impact. Athletes should be encouraged to continue practice and developing skills on a systematic basis and be patient in obtaining the desired results.

5. Individualized
   Athletes begin their physical training at different levels of physical or mental strength. A specific mental training program should be specifically designed to meet the needs of the individual. The focus should be on personal mental strengths and areas for improvement.

6. Takes work and effort
   Just like strength training, mental skills training is not a miracle solution. Mental training cannot be expected to produce instant success. Mental training does not guarantee success. It does, however, greatly improve the odds of being successful. The best approach combines physical practice, mental practice, strength training, and proper nutrition for best results. Find a balance that you feel comfortable with.

Evidence that Mental Skills Training Works

Implementing an effective mental skills training program can be a very challenging task. Athletes and coaches who consider using a mental training program often have questions such as, "Am I convinced that mental training is worthwhile?" "What elements do I include in the program?" "What type of encouragement and support is needed to develop mental skills?" As an athlete, you may not believe in the importance of mental skills training and may need to be convinced of its importance. Mental skills training is most effective when there is a commitment and belief on the part of the athlete, and a commitment to practice and apply the mental skills, and the belief that the mental skills and drills will contribute to development and enhanced performance.

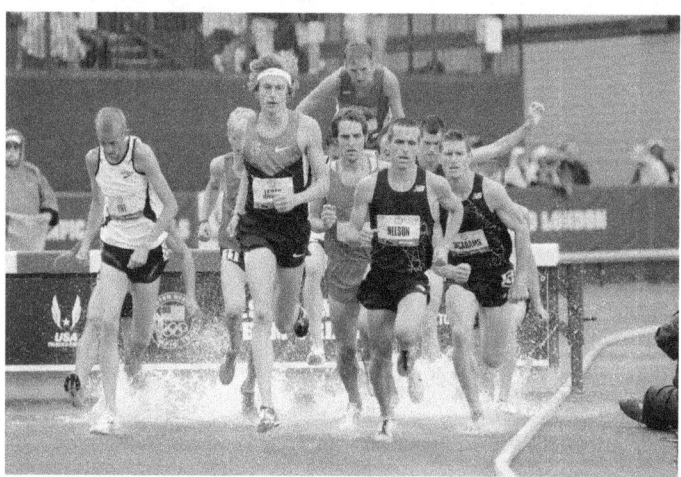

My favorite activity for demonstrating evidence of the mind-body connection for mental skills training is *Activity 1.3 Chevreul's Pendulum.* Try Chevreul's pendulum and you will be amazed with the mind-body connection.

Activity 1.3 **Chevreul's Pendulum**
Objective: To demonstrate the link between the body and the mind.
Directions: Take a 6" piece of string and tie a small weight on it. It can be something like a key or a nail. Hold the string between your forefinger and thumb with the elbow supported on the table. The weight should be steadied to be motionless with your other hand. Hold the string so the key is above the table. Now remove your hand that is steadying the weight. Focus on the weight and see it going back and forth, sideways. See the weight move from one side of the paper to the other side, back and forth. Then, see the weight stop and move toward you and away from you. See it as it comes toward you and then away from you, toward you and away from you. You may be surprised to see the weight actually moving.
What happened? The mind is sending the message through the nerves for the muscle to contract. The muscles are contracting but the contraction is so small that the string and weight have to be used to magnify the movement so that it can be visually seen. When you actually see the movements occur it is a strong visual of the mind-body connection where just thinking about the movement causes muscle contraction.

Just by thinking about it, the mind is sending the message through the nerves for the muscle to contract. When you actually see the movements occur it is a strong visual of the mind-body connection where just thinking about the movement causes muscle contraction.

Although it is easy to touch your muscles that move, as hard as we may try, it is impossible to touch the thoughts in your mind. The Chevereul's pendulum activity is a powerful demonstration of a mind-body connection.

Mental skills training is often misunderstood and viewed as a reaction to a problem. In fact, an effective mental skills training program is proactive and tries to prevent problems before they happen.

Take *Activity 1. 4 Mental Skills Training Quiz* to see what you know about mental skills training.

Activity 1.4 **Mental Skills Training Quiz**		
True or False		
1. T F	Athletes are born (innate) with strong mental skills.	
2. T F	Mental skills training works immediately.	
3. T F	Mental skills training is too time consuming.	
4. T F	Mental skills training is only for psychological whackos.	
5. T F	Mental skills training is only for elite athletes.	
6. T F	Mental skills training is about performing miracles.	
7. T F	Mental skills training guarantees a top performance at the right time.	
8. T F	Mental skills training works by simply reading about it.	
9. T F	Mental skills training is a substitute for physical conditioning and technique training.	
10. T F	Mental skills training will not turn a loser into a winner.	

Myths of Mental Skills Training

To better understand mental skills training, let's take a further look at mental training myths.

1. **Athletes are born (innate) with strong mental skills.**

Just like some athletes are born genetically with more physical talents than others, some athletes are born with more mental skills ability than others. The statement that there is little you can do to improve mental toughness is a myth. Just like the physical skills that can be improved through training, so too can the mental skills be developed through training. Motivation, staying relaxed, maintaining concentration and confidence are all mental skills that can be learned through a systematic mental skills training program. Mental training can help athletes achieve peak performance results far beyond what they ever thought possible.

2. **Mental skills training works immediately.**

A big myth about mental skills training is that a big speech or a single session devoted to the mental game just before the competition will jump start the athlete for a greatly improved performance. We have evidence that with numerous hours of physical practice, athletes can perform a skill automatically with conscious thought. The same is true for mental skills training. Some benefits can be realized with time and effort to be successful. Just like physical training, the higher the degree of performance desired, the more rigorous is the work needed in the mental skills program.

3. Mental skills training is too time consuming.

One of the biggest roadblocks to coaches not implementing a mental skills training program is because of the time factor. Athletes and coaches feel they barely have time to work on the athlete's physical skill and do not have time to focus is on the mental game. Just like the development of the physical component of athletes, the development of the mental game takes time also. When first beginning a mental skills program, working 15-20 minutes a day over several days per week has been proven to be effective. If 15-20 minutes cannot be allotted, five to 10 minutes a day can be beneficial. Athletes should be given "homework" that they do on their own to start developing and refining their mental skills. Once the athlete understands the basics of mental skills training, it should be integrated into practice, taking little additional practice time. Athletes will be able to use the mental training tools such as relaxation, energization, achieving the proper arousal zone, concentration, imagery, positive self-talk and goal setting to enhance practice sessions.

4. Mental skills training is only for psychological whackos.

The great majority of athletes at the top level use some form of a systematic mental skills training program and have no deep-rooted psychological problems. There has been a long-time stigma associated with sport psychology, that those who need to work on their mental game or are associated with seeing a "shrink" are weak. Because of this stigma, some athletes feel reluctant to work on their mental game in case they are labeled as a head case. Good mental skills training programs are proactive instead of reactive. The purpose of a systematic mental skills training program is to prevent problems from occurring (proactive) instead of having to react to problems when they occur.

5. Mental skills training is only for elite athletes

Any level, age, gender, and sport can benefit from the discipline of sports psychology and mental training skills. Mental skills become increasingly important as the level of competition increases. However, as athletes move up in competitiveness, they become more homogeneous in terms of physical skills. Any small difference in mental factors makes a large difference.

Performance will progress faster in young, developing athletes who are provided with a systematic mental skills program. The optimal time for beginning MST is when athletes are first beginning their sport. An early foundation in MST lays the foundation to help athletes develop to their full potential.

6. Mental skills training is about performing miracles.

Athletes should have realistic expectations of what mental skill training can and cannot do. Some athletes expect top results with a minimal effort. After a few sessions of mental skills training, some athletes want to quit because a miracle has not happened. However, athletes would not expect to become great after a week of physical training. It takes years of physical training to reach ones potential. Mental skill training is highly beneficial when one has put in the necessary time and effort. Just like physical training, mental skills training will help athletes perform at or near their performance capabilities only with consistent practice.

7. Mental skills training guarantees a top performance at the right time.

No method of training or technique can guarantee 100% that an athlete will create a top performance at exactly the right time. There are too many factors other than the psychological component that come into play. However, a systematic mental skills training program increases the odds that an athlete will perform at a peak level more consistently. Research has shown that an athlete with mental skills can reduce anxiety and use learned mental skills to properly concentrate and perform at their highest level under pressure.

8. Mental skills training works by simply reading about it

Just as you are reading this now, you are gaining an understanding of mental skills. Understanding the concepts of mental skills training is important and may help performance, but only reading about it will not be enough to help an athlete consistently perform under pressure. Mental training skills need to be practiced, incorporated into practice, and used in actual competitions and mastered.

9. Mental skills training is a substitute for physical conditioning and technique training

Despite the benefits derived from mental skill training, it cannot overcome poor technique and physical conditioning. Mental skills training supplements mental training, it is not a replacement for it. Mental training can never completely take the place of hard work and dedication, top physical conditioning, physical skills, and strategic mastery of athletics.

10. Mental skills training will not turn a loser into a winner

Labeling people as losers or winners is not a positive and beneficial practice. Numerous individuals and teams that have struggled to have success have improved with the help of a systematic mental skills training program. Many athletes may consider themselves losers because of a lack of self-confidence. Using mental tool such as positive self-talk, relaxation, and energization will help athletes think positive and view themselves as a winner.

Activity 1.5 Walk The Plank is designed to look at how a positive mindset and a negative mindset have two complete views in how to achieve a task.

Activity 1.5 **Walk the Plank**
Part 1: Place a board (2 inch x 4 inch approximately 4-6 feet long) on the ground. Who would like to walk the plank? If you feel it is too dangerous to walk across the board, are too nervous or scared of walking across the board as it lays on the ground, you are not required to walk across it. Go ahead and try walking the plank if you dare.
For thought: Did you walk across the plank? How did you feel as you walked across the plank? Was it hard? Was it easy? Were you scared or nervous?
Part 2: Imagine the same plank (board) placed between two tall skyscrapers. The plank is placed out one window on the 100th floor to the adjoining skyscraper window on the 100th floor. The plank links the two skyscrapers. Underneath the plank, 100 floors down is the ground. Who would like to walk the plank now?
For thought: Would you walk across the plank 100 stories high? What were your thoughts in making that decision?
Wrap up: When the plank is on the ground, it is easy to walk over the plank. You feel confident of your abilities to walk the plank and your self-talk is confident. When the plank is placed 100 stories high, thoughts turn to the negative consequences. What would happen if I fall? I would be flattened like a pancake when I hit the ground. Your mind has changed from thinking of the positive side of performance to the negative consequences of failing. What has changed in this scenario? The board has not changed. The mind has changed from a positive outlook to a negative outlook. This exercise illustrates the importance of positive thinking and self-confidence in achieving a successful performance.

Complete *Activity 1.6 Fight or Flight Response,* which provides another example of the mind-body connection.

Activity 1.6 **Fight or Flight Response**
Imagine that you and your buddy are hiking in the wood when you are suddenly confronted by a mean, hungry grizzly bear. What do you do? You don't have time to sit down and think about it. Actually, you only have to outrun your buddy!   You have two choices: fight or flight. You can try to outrun the bear (or your buddy) or you can choose to fight the bear. When confronted by an emergency, the body has a natural response by the autonomic nervous system.
What does your body automatically do to prepare for the action of running away from the bear or fighting it?   1.
2.
3.
4.
5.
Your body immediately responds physiologically Your heart rate soars, your breathing goes up, your pupils dilate, and your hormones are called in to action! You may even pee your pants!
This is an automatic response where what is perceived by your mind is immediately acted upon by the body. This mind-body connection is referred to as the "fight or flight" system.

Will you have time to sit down on the stump and ponder your next move when you encounter the bear? Of course not, you must react immediately. When you mind perceives the situation, your body automatically responds physiologically. This is an automatic response where what is perceived by your mind is immediately acted upon by the body. This mind-body connection is referred to as the "fight or flight" system. But remember, when faced with this situation, you may not have to outrun the bear if you can outrun your buddy!

The evidence is starting to pile up that there is a mind-body connection. Another powerful example of how we think and how the body responds to our thoughts is demonstrated in *Activity 1.7 Mugger or Jogger*.

Activity 1.7 **Mugger or Jogger**
You are traveling and staying out-of-town. You go out for a walk, but end up getting lost. It becomes dark and you end up in bad part of town where the streetlights are out. It is a cold night and the wind is blowing. As you try to make your way back to where you are staying, you start to become uneasy with your unfamiliar surroundings. Suddenly, you hear footsteps behind you. Hearing the footsteps, you begin to pick up your pace, walking faster, but the footsteps are getting closer and closer. You walk even faster, but the footsteps continue to get closer. Someone is behind you and getting closer and closer to you. Who is behind you?   How do you react?   If you said a mugger was behind you, the fight or flight physiological response was starting to kick in. Your heart would begin to race, you would sweat, the hormones would be activated and numerous other physiological responses would occur to prepare your body for action.   If you said it was a jogger behind you, would you have reacted differently? If you believed it was a jogger, you would have moved aside and encouraged the runner to have a good run. The way our mind interprets the situation controls how our body responds.

Activity 1.8 Think of Pizza is a fun activity that explores the power of the mind in concentrating. In the chapter on positive self-talk, we will explore the concepts of how to talk to ourselves to become more productive.

Activity 1.8
Think of Pizza

Think of your favorite food. Think of how good it tastes. Think of how you would like to eat some of your favorite food right now. See yourself eating your favorite food. You can almost smell it and taste how good it is. It may be pizza, steak, seafood, candy, or ice cream. Do not see yourself eating any of those favorite foods.

Now I want you to completely clear your mind of your favorite food. Do not think of your favorite food. Do not think of how good it tastes. Do not think of how you would like to eat some of your favorite food right now. Do not see yourself eating the favorite food. Whether it is pizza, steak, seafood, candy, or ice cream. Do not see yourself eating any of those favorite foods.

What happened when you tried to not think of your favorite food?

You still have that image of your favorite food in your mind; I know you do. Why? The brain does not know how to process and interpret the word "don't." The brain only understands what comes after don't, which in this case is, "think of your favorite food."

In track and field, runners often tell themselves, "do not slow down" or "do not let my competitor pass me." Vertical jumpers tell themselves, "do not miss" and throwers tell themselves "do not foul."

The brain does not know how to process and interpret the word "don't." The brain only understands what comes after don't, which in this case, is 'think of your favorite food.' Specifically, in track and field, we only hear "slow down, miss, or foul."

Has this happened to you? Have you told yourself not to do something in sport and then it happens? Well, you are not alone.

Can someone really stop thinking? Can you simply clear your mind? How do you relax? When someone tells you to concentrate, focus and pay attention, what are you supposed to focus on, concentrate about, and pay attention to?

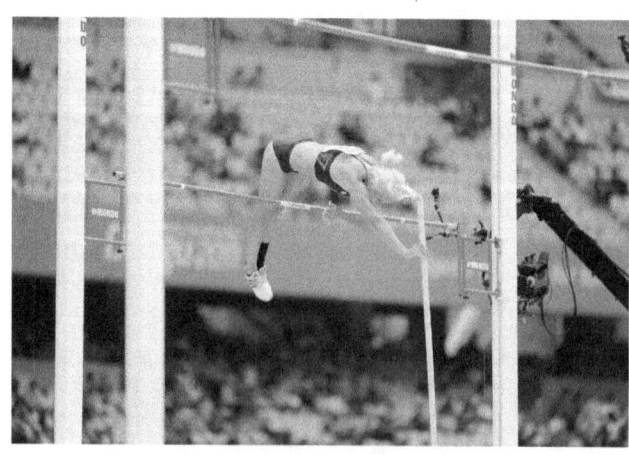

Track and Field is a physical sport. You participate in the sport because you like the kinesthetic feelings of physical movement. *Activity 1.9 Iron Arm* provides a physical example on the power of focusing on a mental thought.

Activity 1.9 **Iron Arm**
Part 1: Pair off with a partner (similar heights if possible) facing each other about an arm's length apart. Partner #1 sets an arm, palm facing up, on partner #2's shoulder. Partner #2 takes his/her hands and links them around partner #1's extended arm right above the elbow. Partner #1 is instructed to tighten his/her arm so as not to let partner #2 bend it with his/her strength downward. Let each partner take a turn in both positions before moving on.
Part 2: Repeat the scenario, but this time, have the partners imagine a strong steel bar that extends through their arm making it tight and rigid. The steel bar gives them power and makes their arm unbendable. Once this image is created, have partner #2 push down on the arm. Let each partner take a turn in both positions.
For Thought: In part 1, were you able to bend the arm of your partner? Was your partner able to bend your arm? In part 2, were you able to bend the arm of your partner? Was your partner able to bend your arm? What was the difference between part 1 and part 2? Why do you believe the difference occurred?
Wrap-up: In most cases, when the image of the steel bar is created, the arm is much stronger than when the image is not created. Just imagining the arm is an iron bar made the arm stronger. The image from the brain was transmitted to the muscles to make them stronger. Imagine how this skill could be applied to track and field help increase performance!

I mentioned earlier that it can be a hard concept to accept that mental training is valuable and worthy of your time. I hope the previous exercises have started you thinking of the value of mental skills and how you might use them to enhance your performance. You will not be alone in your use of mental skills training. Many great athletes owe a large part of their success to being mentally strong.

One of the most convincing arguments that mental skills training is beneficial is for athletes to hear or read other athletes' stories. These stories can provide that extra incentive or create an image in the athletes' minds of what is possible and what they need to be able to do to get there. There have been numerous books written by and about successful athletes that can lend some insight into how mental training plays a role in elite athletes' development.

Read *Activity 1.10 Billy Mills: Believe-Believe-Believe*, a classic story of using positive self-talk and a belief in one's self to be successful in order to establish the relationship between mental training and athletic success.

Activity 1.10
Billy Mills: Believe-Believe-Believe
Excerpt from *Motivational Moments in Men's Track and Field*, Roho Publishing

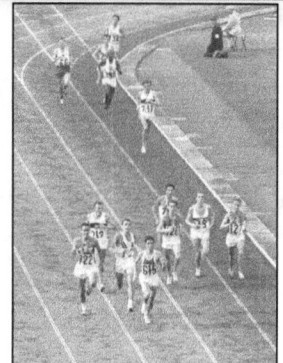

Billy Mills, a Native American (Oglala Lakota (Sioux)), was raised on the Pine Ridge Indian Reservation in South Dakota. He was orphaned at the age of 12. Mills took up running while attending the Haskell Institute in Lawrence, Kansas. He attended the University of Kansas and earned All-American cross country honors three times and in 1960 he won the individual title in the Big Eight cross country championship. Billy helped lead the University of Kansas track team to the 1959 and 1960 outdoor national championships.

After giving up running for a while, he returned to the sport to qualify for the 1964 Summer Olympics in Tokyo in the 10,000-meter run and the marathon. On October 14, 1964, 38 runners competed in the 10,000-meter final at the Tokyo Olympics. One of the starters was a virtually unknown in the track and field world. Billy Mills of the U.S. with a 10,000-meter best of 29 minutes 10.4 seconds was not expected to be a contender for the medals. However, Mills who had faced discrimination and difficult times his entire life, believed in himself. As he trained for the Olympic Games, he visualized over and over, running the race. In his mind he saw himself running with the leaders and winning! He repeated over and over to himself the affirmation: Believe-Believe-Believe.

The favorite, world-record holder Ron Clarke (Australia), led most of the way with a quick pace. With one lap remaining, Clarke had dropped all his main rivals, but he still had two athletes with him, Mills and Mohamed Gammoudi of Tunisia, both relatively unknown, and both running much faster than they ever had before. The three were hindered by lapped runners on the last lap who made no effort to let them through on the inside. In the back straight, Clarke bumped Mills, pushing him to the outside lanes and causing him to drop back about four meters. At this point, Mills focused on his affirmations: Believe-Believe-Believe, as Gammoudi and Clarke sprinted for the finish. Gammoudi had shaken off Clarke and seemed to have the race won with 50 meters to go before Mills came storming past both of them to win the gold medal. Billy's winning time of 28 minutes 24.4 seconds was a personal record by 50 seconds and a new Olympic record. The race has been called the greatest upset in Olympic history and Mill's victory remains the only Olympic 10,000-meter win in U.S. Olympic history.

Questions For Thought:
1. Why was Billy Mills race so surprising?
2. How did Billy Mills prepare himself mentally to run in the Olympic Games?
3. How can you apply the story of Billy Mills to help improve your mental skills?

Activity 1.11 Al Oerter: Competitor, is another classic story of one of the greatest Olympic athletes in history who constituently displayed mental skills to perform at his peak at the right time.

Activity 1.11
Al Oerter: Competitor
Excerpt from *Motivational Moments in Men's Track and Field*, Roho Publishing

One word best describes Al Oerter—competitor. He is the only athlete to win four gold medals at four successive Olympiads and the only athlete to set four consecutive Olympic records. At Sewanhaka High School in New York, he was a sprinter and then a miler. As he was running at practice one day, a discus landed near his feet, so he casually threw it back. His coach noticed that he threw it back farther than the discus throwers were throwing it. So, Al became a discus thrower and would set the national high school record before attending the University of Kansas, where he won two NCAA titles. While at Kansas, Al would compete in his first Olympics at the 1956 summer games in Melbourne. He was not considered the favorite, but he unleashed a throw of 184' 11" at the time, which was a career best and Olympic record.

An automobile accident at the age of 20 nearly killed him, but he recovered in time to compete at the 1960 Summer Olympics at Rome, where Oerter entered as slight favorite over teammate and world record holder Rink Babka. Babka was in the lead for the first four of the six rounds when Oerter threw his discus 194'2", setting an Olympic record and winning his second gold medal.

During the early 1960s, Oerter continued to have success, setting his first world record in 1962, becoming the first man to throw over 200 feet in the discus. He was considered a heavy favorite to win a third gold medal at Tokyo in 1964.

However, injuries plagued Oerter before the Games. He was bothered by a neck injury, and then six days before the competition, he slipped on a wet concrete discus circle and tore rib cartilage on his throwing side, causing internal bleeding and severe pain. Team doctors told him to forget the Olympics and not to throw for six weeks. He refused. "These are the Olympics," he was quoted as saying at the time. "You die before you quit." Competing in great pain, Oerter set a new Olympic standard and won a third Olympic gold medal.

Oerter returned to the Olympics in 1968 at Mexico City, but experts felt that Oerter, at age 32, was too old to win. Rising to the occasion, as he always did in the Olympic Games, Oerter released another personal record, and another Olympic record throw of 212' 6" to win and become the first track and field athlete to win four consecutive gold medals.

Al retired from athletics after the 1968 Olympics. He did make an attempt to qualify for the American team in 1980 at the age of 43, but he finished fourth, one spot from making the Olympic team. However, he did set his overall personal record of 227' 10¾" that year at the age of 43. One of the greatest competitors in Olympic history carried the Olympic flag for the 1984 Summer Olympics and the Olympic flame into the stadium for the 1996 Olympic Games.

Questions For Thought:
1. Al Oerter rose to the occasion to set a personal record in every Olympic Games he competed in. What mental attributes did Al Oerter display?
2. Oerter threw in severe pain and displayed tremendous mental toughness. On a scale of 1-10 (10 high) what is your mental toughness?
3. What are the keys, physically and mentally to maintain to perform at that high of a level?

The two previous stories are classics of Olympic Champions who demonstrated mental toughness to persevere and excel. Although these examples happened years ago, there are many current athletes who have equally compelling stories. *Activity 1.12 Lolo Jones: Backbone of Steel* tells the amazing story of Lolo Jones who overcame the odds and never gave up.

Activity 1.12
Lolo Jones: Backbone of Steel
Excerpt from *Motivational Moments in Women's Track and Field*, Roho Publishing

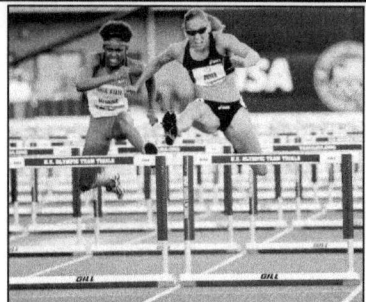

Photo by Spencer Allen

Lori (Lolo) Jones has overcome many hurdles in her life to excel in track and field. Lolo was raised by a single mother with five children while her father spent most of her childhood in prison. Her family was poor and had to move often, once even living in a church basement. As she entered high school, she parted ways with her mother and stayed with four different families throughout her time in high school. Her high school career drew the attention of Louisiana State University, where Lolo developed into one of the best collegiate hurdlers in the country, becoming a multi-time NCAA champion.

In 2004, Lolo ran in the Olympic Trials but failed to make the Olympic team. As she contemplated her future, she knew she would have to make sacrifices and work several part-time jobs in order to make it work financially. But her heart was still in track and field.

She entered the 2008 Olympic Games as a favorite and opened a slight lead in the finals of the 100-meter hurdles. With only two hurdles remaining, Lolo was just a few meters from Olympic gold. She was just a couple of seconds from accomplishing her lifetime dream. However, tragedy struck on the next to last hurdle as she tripped and stumbled, dropping to seventh place. She would have to wait four more years for another opportunity. The pain lasted for months, but Lolo would only use it for motivation to fuel the fire to overcome the hurdles to return to the Olympics.

The trip over the last hurdle at the 2008 Olympics was attributed to a spinal problem where Lolo couldn't feel her feet. The doctor said the problem was that since she couldn't feel her feet; her brain wasn't able to process where her feet were. The surgery repaired a very painful tethered spinal cord.

With the surgery only a year before the 2012 Olympics, Lolo overcame the odds to come back and qualified for the 2012 Olympic team by placing third at the Olympic Trials. Lolo Jones came all the way back to make the Olympic 100-meter hurdle final again and finished fourth against an outstanding field.

Questions for Thought:
1. Lolo overcame a difficult childhood to be successful. How can you use her story for motivation?
2. Lolo thought about giving up track at one time, but her heart was still in it. How does heart factor into success?
3. Lolo overcame the odds to return to the Olympics. What odds have you overcome?

Billy Mills, Al Oerter and Lolo Jones were very motivated athletes! Think of an athlete that you are familiar with. Maybe they are on your team or a role model or mentor to you. Complete *Activity 1.13 The Motivated Athlete,* to explore the characteristics of a motivated athlete.

Activity 1.13
The Motivated Athlete
Think of the most motivated athlete you have ever seen.
Who was it?
Why do you think they were motivated?
Were they motivated by fear?
Were they motivated by extrinsic rewards?
Were they optimistic?
What sense of purpose did they have?

I hope you recognized that among other things, the motivated athlete has focus. Motivated athletes have the ability to block out things around them to concentrate on what they need to do. They have built these skills up through practice. I hope you also mentioned they are positive and think like a winner. We all like to associate with winners. *Activity 1.14 Questions for Guest Speakers* asks you to visit with a winner and see how they think and what makes them successfully tick.

One of the best sources to demonstrate that mental skills are important for success is to have former athletes as guest speakers. These athletes should have demonstrated that they are winners through their mental toughness and their belief and approach in developing the mental game. Encouraging past athletes to speak about their journey can be a particularly meaningful experience for young emerging talent. It also provides another way for elite athletes to give back to the program and inspire others to make that commitment to excel. Often, younger athletes look upon these successful athletes as role models. Sport psychologists, mental trainers, motivation speakers, and well-known coaches, are also some individuals who can be brought in to speak with athletes about mental training. I also encourage you to interview someone who fits into the above description. Here are some possible questions to ask in your interview.

Activity 1.14
Questions for Guest Speakers
1. What role did mental skills play in your success?
2. Did you engage in mental skills training? How did you do it?
3. How much time did you devote to mental training?
4. What do you owe your success to?

To find current examples of mental training being used by athletes who are performing at the top of their game, use the media. This task can act as a springboard for discussing with athletes, either in a group or individually, the mental aspects necessary to be successful in track and field. *Activity 1.15 Media Examples* can help convince athletes to fully participate.

Activity 1.15
Media Examples
Search the media on the Internet, or newspapers and magazines for examples of mental skills used by elite track and field athletes.
Were the examples positive or negative?

You may be surprised by the number of examples that you are able to find and, in turn, this exercise may act as a source of motivation for you to begin to engage in your own mental skills training program. Every day, either online or in the sports section of most newspapers, there are excellent examples of the mental side of sport.

Before you start your program, let's find out where you are at right now on your mental game. Complete *Activity 1.16 How's Your Mental Game?*

Activity 1.16 How's Your Mental Game?					
For each question, circle the appropriate number on the scale.	Never		Sometimes		Always
1. I talk positively to myself.	1	2	3	4	5
2. A bad performance never gets me down.	1	2	3	4	5
3. I keep working even when I am physically tired.	1	2	3	4	5
4. I am excited about going to practice every day.	1	2	3	4	5
5. I always handle anxiety and pressure.	1	2	3	4	5
6. I imagine myself performing flawlessly.	1	2	3	4	5
7. I block out distractions so I can concentrate.	1	2	3	4	5
8. I handle frustration well in practice.	1	2	3	4	5
9. How often do you set goals to help you achieve?	1	2	3	4	5
10. I work with my goals on a daily basis.	1	2	3	4	5
Total Score _____					
If you scored **10-20** you are in the beginning stages of learning how to become stronger mentally. Absorb all you can.					
If you scored **21-30** you are making some headway, but still have much to learn. Jump in headfirst.					
If you scored **31-40** you are building a solid mental fitness program. Keep up the good work. Adding mental tools to your mental toolbox will take you to the next level.					
If you scored **41-50** you have a strong mental fitness profile. Congratulations! By adding more mental tools to your toolbox, think about how good your performances can be!					

The Next Step Is Yours

What factors above can you begin improving on right now? Make the decision to improve your mental skills starting right now?

After reading this chapter, I hope that you are excited about mental skills training and convinced that is works. Understanding mental skills training provides you with crucial information to becoming a better athlete or coach. You may recognize that you are already using some of the mental training tools. If so, congratulations, you are already started on your way. You may feel overwhelmed by the mental skills training process, but rest assured, the following chapters will provide mental skills information and mental drills that will allow you to become effective with mental skills training. Think of them as mental tools and as you work through this book, you will add mental tools to your mental toolbox. The main purpose of this chapter was to introduce you to mental skills training and provide evidence that it works. Enjoy the remaining chapters as you learn how to implement a systematic mental skills training program and develop specific mental training tools to take your performance to the next level.

Chapter 2

Finding Your Optimal Arousal Zone

What are the conditions that allow you to perform at your best? In Chapter 1, Activity 1.2, you thought about your best performance ever where you achieved the flow state and everything worked just the way you wanted it to. How outstanding would it be if you were able to perform consistently at that level? Although achieving the "flow" state is not guaranteed every time out, your odds are increased when you set the stage by achieving the right conditions for optimal performance.

The overall focus of this chapter is to help you determine the right conditions to achieve your optimal arousal level. With the addition of these mental tools in your mental toolbox, you will be ready to recognize when you are out of your proper arousal zone and what activities you can do to put yourself back in the zone. You will develop relaxation skills that will enable you to lower your arousal energy levels and energization skills to raise your arousal energy levels.

Track and field athletes get their energy from arousal, which is the physiological and psychological activation of the body. Arousal varies on a continuum from deep levels of sleep to the highest level of excitement. Arousal involves how much the body is activated and how that activation is interpreted. Arousal is the body's way of preparing for vigorous activity. Your arousal levels will vary at different times of the day and in different situations.

Complete *Activity 2.1 Where on The Arousal Continuum Am I?* to better understand different levels of arousal.

Activity 2.1 **Where on the Arousal Continuum Am I?**			
Place an X on the continuum line where you believe your arousal level would be for each situation.			
	Sleep		Excitement
	Low	Moderate	High
Reading this	--		
Watching TV	--		
Moments before a big track meet	--		
During a hard track workout	--		
Taking a test you are prepared for	--		
Taking a test you are not prepared for	--		

We often use the terms "psych up" to talk about raising arousal levels and "psyched out" if our arousal levels become too high. In order to perform at your best, you will need to find the right arousal level for your competitive situation.

Arousal is triggered in response to any real or perceived demand, whether physical or mental. This fight or flight response, which we talked about in chapter 1, is the body's way of dealing with real or imagined physical danger by readying itself. Arousal is also triggered by psychological demands such as preparing for a big competition.

It is important to understand that physical symptoms are normal and they signal the body's way to deal with a challenge. We often refer to this nervousness as "having butterflies." The butterflies are an important part of preparation with the challenge to get the butterflies to fly in order. Track and field athletes deal with increased arousal levels in many different ways. Some may pace, talk constantly or scream to control their arousal. Others may yawn or even take a nap. Each person responds differently. Your challenge is to find an energy arousal level strategy that works for you and then systematically implement it in practice and competition.

Yuri Hannin, a noted Russian sport psychologist, presented a theory pertaining to arousal level and performance called the Individual Zone of Optimal Functioning (IZOP) Model. The theory states that an individual has an optimal level of arousal that contributes to peak performance. This inverted U hypothesis theory states that as arousal increases from low to moderate levels, performance improves. When arousal reaches a moderate level, an athlete performs their best. However, any arousal increases above this optimal zone reduces the quality of performance. When athletes are at the low arousal end, they lack sufficient arousal physical and mental energy to perform at their best. When arousal is at the high end, athlete performance is hindered by anxiety and tenseness. The take-away point from the U hypothesis theory is optimal performance occurs when arousal levels are moderate. Each individual athlete, with the help of their coach needs to determine the level of arousal that contributes to their top performance.

Athletes often believe that that the more arousal they have, the better. However, arousal levels beyond individual optimal levels can lead to too much muscle activation and too narrow a focus, traits that will decrease performance. Later in this chapter we will focus on relaxation techniques to lower arousal levels as well as energization techniques to raise arousal levels.

Sport psychologists describe methods to obtain proper arousal levels in many different ways. Some different examples of how to achieve your proper arousal level will be presented. Try the different methods and decide which is the most effective and comfortable for you. Whichever method you use, they all have the objective of helping you achieve your proper arousal level.

Think of the arousal curve labeled with a scale of 1-9. 1 would be at the very low end of arousal and 9 is at the very high arousal level. Complete *Activity 2.2 Psych Number* to find your proper arousal level.

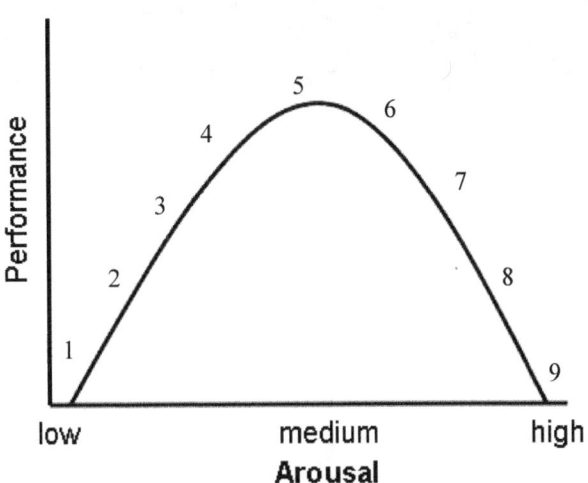

Activity 2.2 Psych Number										
Think of your three best performances. Remember how you felt before and during that performance. Rate how you felt on each variable on a scale of 1-9.										
Best Performances	**Low**									**High**
Muscle Tension	1	2	3	4	5	6	7	8	9	
Heart Rate	1	2	3	4	5	6	7	8	9	
Breathing	1	2	3	4	5	6	7	8	9	
Doubts/Worry	1	2	3	4	5	6	7	8	9	
Negative Thinking	1	2	3	4	5	6	7	8	9	
Think of your three worst performances. Remember how you felt before and during that performance. Rate how you felt on each variable on a scale of 1-9.										
Muscle Tension	1	2	3	4	5	6	7	8	9	
Heart Rate	1	2	3	4	5	6	7	8	9	
Breathing	1	2	3	4	5	6	7	8	9	
Doubts/Worry	1	2	3	4	5	6	7	8	9	
Negative Thinking	1	2	3	4	5	6	7	8	9	
Was there a difference between your best and worst performances in your ratings? What numbers do you think you performed best at?										

Recalling your best performances should give you an idea of what numbers you perform best at. These numbers would be your psych up number. Once you have determined what your psych number is, your goal will be to obtain this psych number, which represents your proper arousal level.

The Arousal Monitoring Scale in Activity 2.3 and the inverted U model uses number ratings on a 9-point scale with 5 representing the middle of the optimal energy zone. 1 to 4 represents under arousal, and 6 to 9 represents over arousal.

Activity 2.3
Finding Your Proper Arousal Level
Arousal Monitoring Scale

During practice or competition assign yourself an overall score. Over time you will discover what your number is when you are at your best and at your worst. You will find over time what your optimal arousal level will feel like.

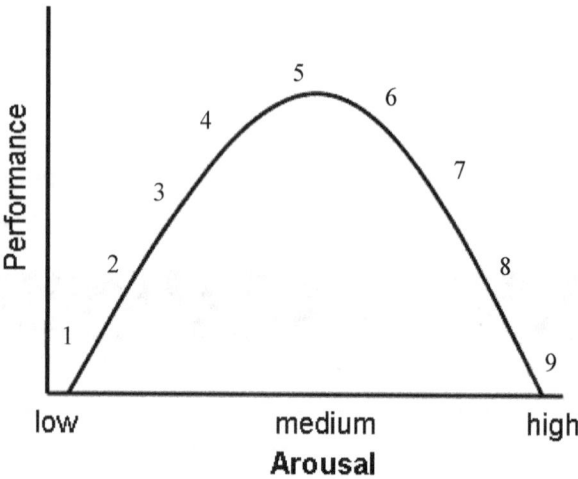

Another method to help determine your proper arousal zone uses a thermometer analogy (Laurer, Johnson). The thermometer represents the energy continuum. The low end of the thermometer is zero degrees, representing very low energy. At the high end of the thermometer is 100 degrees, representing the highest energy level you have ever experienced. Your proper arousal level is somewhere between those two extremes. Complete *Activity 2.4 Hot or Cold* to help find your proper arousal level using the thermometer method.

Activity 2.4
Hot or Cold

Using the following thermometer to rate what degree temperature you are operating for the following.

Best Performances
Temperature Range

_____

Worst Performances
Temperature Range

_____

Is there fluctuation in your performance?
Compare your better and poorer performances. What were the temperature levels?
Were there changes in preparation activities? What preparation activities led to your optimal temperature?

No matter which of the methods you use to find your arousal level, you are encouraged to keep a log of pre-performance routines and then compare this to the outcome of performance over time. Once the peak performance routines and level of arousal are determined, you should be aware of your current routines and what levels of arousal they produce. The goal should be focus on achieving your optimal arousal levels.

If you feel you are performing too tight, you should focus on relaxation. If you have trouble getting up for an explosive event such as the 100-meter dash, long jump, or throwing, you would focus on learning techniques to increase energy levels.

Activity 2.5
What does it take to be great?

Develop a list of physical and mental characteristics that you feel are essential for consistent, high level performance. Think of the ideal track and field athlete in your event. What are the mental and physical characteristics that make them ideal? Some of the characteristics you might consider would be: confident, determined, focused, positive, coachable, calm. After you have listed the characteristics, rate yourself on each physical and mental characteristic on a scale of 1-10 with 10 being high. Place your number to the right of the each characteristic.

Physical Characteristics	Your Rating	Mental Characteristics	Your Rating

---

We have covered several different assessments of awareness of your arousal level. Hopefully, you have begun to get an idea of when your peak performance occurred and what you felt like going into and during your peak performance. Now that you have become more aware of your level of arousal and where you need to be to compete for peak performance we will look at different mental skills that will allow you to achieve your optimal arousal level.

Relaxation

One of the major purposes of relaxation is to lower your arousal levels to achieve an optimal arousal state. High arousal such as high anxiety and too many distractions leads to low performance.

When we discuss the use of imagery in Chapter 6, we will further discuss how relaxation prepares the mind for imagery. The conscious (rational) mind views things as they currently are and is comfortable with the status quo. With relaxation, you will be able to use the subconscious mind and more readily accept new ideas and images.

When the sympathetic nervous system (fight or flight) is activated, you will feel anxious and show physical symptoms of stress such as an anticipatory increased heart rate and butterflies in the stomach. Although this response helps prepare us for the physical activity, it may also cause unwanted muscular tension. Relaxation helps you to decrease the unwanted muscular tension and reduce the excess activation of the sympathetic nervous system. Think of your muscles when they are not relaxed as raw spaghetti and when they are relaxed as cooked spaghetti. Relaxation also serves a key role in keeping the mind occupied.

The mind and body work together as an integrated system in order to relax. Techniques such as diaphragmatic breathing and progressive muscle relaxation are muscle-to-mind techniques. They relax the body, which in turn relaxes the mind. Techniques such as imagery and meditation, focus on calming the mind in order to relax the body and are referred to as mind-to-muscle techniques. Both approaches can be very useful to track and field athletes. A thrower may find that a breathing technique helps rid unwanted muscular tension before throwing. The tension is triggered physically but the muscle-to-mind technique also helps them relax mentally. Another thrower may use the muscle-to-mind technique of imagery relaxation by visualizing the body being calm and relaxed. The mind visualizes the relaxation and sends a message that allows the muscles to relax.

It is important to make the distinction between total relaxation and rapid relaxation. Total relaxation is a lengthier session (10-20 minutes) that focuses on relaxing completely. Rapid relaxation techniques are an abbreviated form that focuses on optimal relaxation in a few seconds. By first learning total relaxation techniques, athletes can eventually develop rapid relaxation skills and implement these into practice and competitive situations. Although you may become very proficient at relaxation skills in a quiet room with soft music laying, you must be able to transfer these relaxation skills into performance. Before the start of a race you cannot go up to the starter and request the race to be delayed so you can do a 15 minute relaxation session on the infield. Track and field athletes need techniques they can use on the fly before performing, while performing or during breaks in the competition.

There are numerous ways to relax that will be presented. Try the various relaxation activities and see which work for you. We will start by covering the total relaxation techniques. Mastery of this technique is vital in later developing rapid relaxation skills. After mastery of the relaxation techniques we will cover rapid relaxation techniques and finally, talk about the link between total and rapid relaxation techniques.

In *Activity 2.6 Bubble Blowing*, we will start with a simple technique to illustrate how breathing can relax you.

Activity 2.6
Bubble Blowing

1. Start with a bottle of bubbles.
2. Take a deep inhalation and fill your lungs of air.
3. Now as you exhale, slowly blow bubbles.
4. See how big of bubble you can blow.
5. As you get good at blowing bubbles, and more importantly relaxing as you exhale, you can try the following.
    a. Think about a worry that is bothering you and picture that you are blowing the worry into the bubble as you blow a bubble
    b. Picture the worry inside the bubble.
    c. Watch it float away and pop, carrying the worry far, far from you.
    d. Know that the worry has popped and is outside of you now, unable to bother you any more.
6. Keep blowing bubbles until you feel more calm and relaxed.

For Thought:
Do you feel more relaxed?
Do you feel less worried?
Were you able to picture your worries floating away in the bubbles?

In *Activity 2.7 Sequential Relaxation*, the focus should be on experiencing deep levels of total relaxation.

Activity 2.7
Sequential Relaxation

Assume a comfortable position and when ready, allow your eyes to close. Turn your attention to the exhalation phase of our breathing cycle… and r-e-l-a-x as you exhale… exhale and r-e-l-a-x…permit yourself to let go… and r-e-l-a-x more and more with each exhalation.

Now focus on your right foot and ankle and as you exhale notice the tension flow out of that foot and ankle… note the foot and ankle becoming slightly heavy and more and more relaxed… As you notice this allow the foot and ankle to sink down and become totally supported by the floor. As you exhale, notice a sinking down of the foot into the supporting environment.

Now focus your attention on the left foot and ankle… and allow it to let go and r-e-l-a-x with your exhalations allow that foot and ankle to become slightly heavy… and more and more relaxed with each exhalation.

Now move your focus to your right lower leg (the calf region) As you focus on this area, allow the muscles to relax… to let go as you exhale… simply allow the tensions to flow out of the lower leg as you e-x-h-a-l-e and r-e-l-a-x.

Move your attention to the left lower leg and with each exhalation, feel the muscles of the left lower leg sinking down… and becoming slightly heavy.

Move your attention to the thighs and feel that body part r-e-l-a-x as you exhale and r-e-l-a-x. Feel and experience a letting go with each exhalation.

Let the relaxation flow into the buttocks and hips… As you exhale, allow the muscles to relax and feel the buttocks sinking down into the supporting environment as you exhale.

Let the relaxation flow into the trunk area as you e-x-h-a-l-e and r-e-l-a-x. Feel the trunk sinking down and becoming slightly heavy as you feel continue to e-x-h-a-l-e and r-e-l-a-x.

Move the attention to your arms and hands, feel the relaxation flowing into the arm and hand. Feel it sinking down as you feel the gentle pull of gravity exert itself on the arms and hands.

Allow this relaxation to flow into the entire body with each exhalation. Feel sense and experience a comfortable heaviness… a general slowing down of the body… Allow the body to establish its own pace… and r-e-l-a-x as you exhale and r-e-l-a-x as you exhale.

By tightening a muscle and then releasing, you can feel the difference between tense and relaxed. Actively engaging in progressive muscular relaxation exercises effectively loosens and relaxes the muscles. Make sure not to do any movements that cause pain. If any of these exercises causes discomfort, ease up or stop to ensure that you do not cause muscle cramping or injury.

Let's start with a fun activity that will illustrate progressive muscle relaxation. These activities are very familiar to the popular foam roller exercises. You will need a foam sponge ball or a tennis ball for this activity.

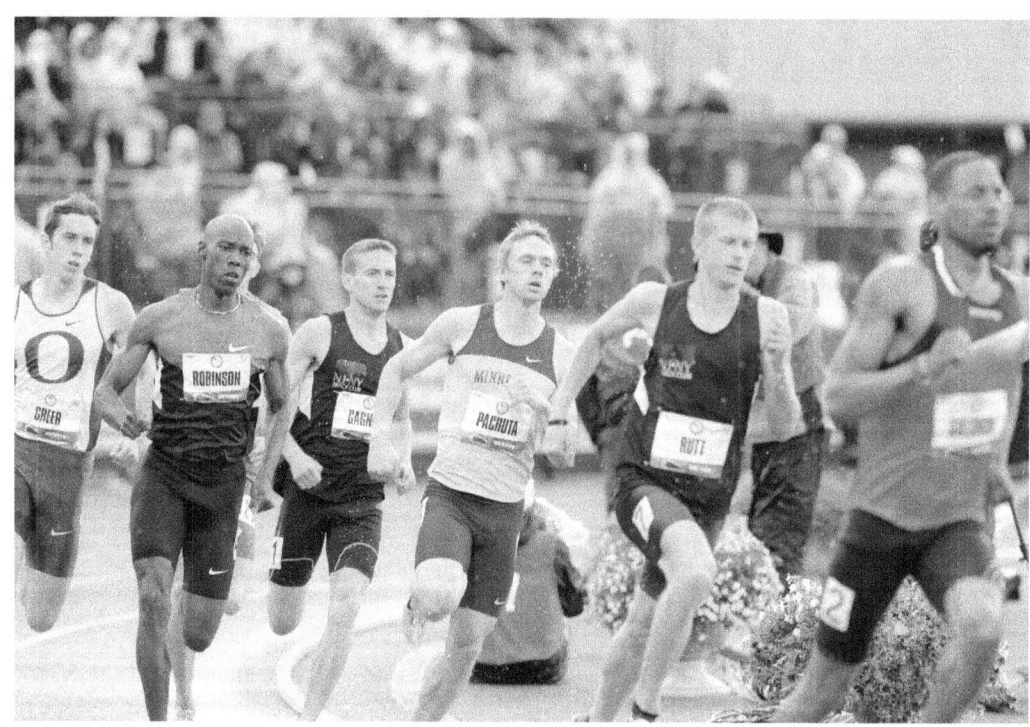

Activity 2.8
Tennis Ball Relaxation

1. Grip the ball in your hand. Squeeze the ball and hold for five seconds. As you release the tension in your grip feel the muscles relax.

2. Place a ball underneath the arch of your foot. Keep your heel on the floor and let your body weight sink in. You may want to stand next to a wall or chair for stability.
    a. Take deep breaths for 30 seconds to 1 minute.
    b. Slowly roll your foot from side to side so the ball crosses your arch. Repeat for 1 to 2 minutes
    c. Roll the ball along the length of your foot from heal to toe for 1 to 2 minutes
    d. Repeat on the other foot.

3. Knee
    a. Sit on the floor or in a chair and place the ball behind your bent knee.
    b. Attempt to contract your muscles against the ball, temporarily "squashing" the ball for a count of 10, then relax your muscles for a count of 10. Do this 8 to 10 times.
    c. Repeat on the other knee.

4. IT Band
    a. While lying on your side on the floor, place 2 balls on the outside of your thigh. Keep the balls nestled into the side of your thigh and slowly bend and straighten your knee 20 times.
    b. Move your thigh from side to side so that the balls cross the side of your thigh. Repeat for 2 minutes.
    c. Repeat on the other side.

5. Lower Back
    a. Place 2 balls vertically between your bottom and your ribs and lie down on top of them. Breathe deeply while shifting your pelvis from side to side so the balls cross your entire lower back.
    b. Move the ball more slowly in the areas where you feel stiffer, and lighten your pressure when you're near the spine so that you're not pinching the balls into your bones as you cross from right to left or left to right.
    c. Breathe deeply as you roll for up to 5 minutes.

6. Upper Back
    a. Lie down and place two balls side by side on either side of your upper back. (You can place them in a tote, stocking, or sock, if you'd like.) Interlace your hands behind your head and lift your head off the floor, bringing your chin toward your chest. Lift your bottom off the floor and take 3 deep breaths into your ribs.
    b. Keeping your breaths big and steady, roll the balls like a rolling pin up and down your upper back for 3 to 4 minutes.

These are just a few of the tennis ball activities you can do to contract, stretch and relax. I encourage you to try the tennis ball on other parts of your body to help relax.

Activity 2.9
Progressive Muscle Relaxation

1. Begin by finding a comfortable position sitting, standing, or lying down. You can change positions any time during the progressive muscle relaxation exercises to make yourself more comfortable as needed.

   The first progressive muscle relaxation exercise is breathing. Breathe in forcefully and deeply, and hold this breath. Hold it… hold it… and now release. Let all the air go out slowly, and release all the tension.

   Take another deep breath in. Hold it… and then exhale slowly, allowing the tension to leave your body with the air.

   Now breathe even more slowly and gently… breathe in…hold…out…

   …Breathe in…hold…out…

   Continue to breathe slowly and gently. Allow your breathing to relax you.

2. The next progressive muscle relaxation exercise focuses on relaxing the muscles of your body. Start with the large muscles of your legs. Tighten all the muscles of your legs. Tense the muscles further. Hold onto this tension. Feel how tight and tensed the muscles in your legs are right now. Squeeze the muscles harder, tighter… Continue to hold this tension. Feel the muscles wanting to give up this tension. Hold it for a few moments more…. and now relax. Let all the tension go. Feel the muscles in your legs going limp, loose, and relaxed. Notice how relaxed the muscles feel now. Feel the difference between tension and relaxation. Enjoy the pleasant feeling of relaxation in your legs.

3. Now focus on the muscles in your arms. Tighten your shoulders, upper arms, lower arms, and hands. Squeeze your hands into tight fists. Tense the muscles in your arms and hands as tightly as you can. Squeeze harder… harder… hold the tension in your arms, shoulders, and hands. Feel the tension in these muscles. Hold it for a few moments more…. and now release. Let the muscles of your shoulders, arms, and hands relax and go limp. Feel the relaxation as your shoulders lower into a comfortable position and your hands relax at your sides. Allow the muscles in your arms to relax completely.

   Focus again on your breathing. Slow, even, regular breaths. Breathe in relaxation…. and breathe out tension… in relaxation…and out tension… Continue to breathe slowly and rhythmically.

4. Now focus on the muscles of your buttocks. Tighten these muscles as much as you can. Hold this tension… and then release. Relax your muscles.

5. Tighten the muscles of your back now. Feel your back tightening, pulling your shoulders back and tensing the muscles along your spine. Arch your back slightly as you tighten these muscles. Hold… and relax. Let all the tension go. Feel your back comfortably relaxing into a good and healthy posture.

6. Turn your attention now to the muscles of your chest and stomach. Tighten and tense these muscles. Tighten them further…hold this tension… and release. Relax the muscles of your trunk.

7. Finally, tighten the muscles of your face. Scrunch your eyes shut tightly, wrinkle your nose, and tighten your cheeks and chin. Hold this tension in your face… and relax. Release all the tension. Feel how relaxed your face is.

   Notice all of the muscles in your body… notice how relaxed your muscles fee l. Allow any last bits of tension to drain away. Enjoy the relaxation you are experiencing. Notice your calm breathing… your relaxed muscles… Enjoy the relaxation for a few moments…

   When you are ready to return to your usual level of alertness and awareness, slowly begin to re-awaken your body. Wiggle your toes and fingers. Swing your arms gently. Shrug your shoulders. Stretch if you like.

Activity 2.10
Complete Diaphragmic Breathing

Sit or lie down in a comfortable position. Close your eyes and concentrate on taking complete breaths. Inhale through the nose, causing the diaphragm to move down. Gently place one hand on your stomach, just above your belly button, but below your rig cage. Now focus on making your hand rise and all as you inhale and exhale. You will feel the breathing as your diaphragm expand and your abdomen is pushed out. Next, as the middle portion of your lungs fill, your rib cage expands. Finally, your upper lungs fill and you feel your chest and should raise slightly. After the complete inhalation, pause and then compel a slow exhalation through the mouth. Complete 4 breaths that require you to breathe in a manner that allows you to use your full lung capacity. If you are doing this exercise properly, your hand should move up and down with each breath. Now take two - three minutes and focus exclusively on making each breath deep and complete. As you do so, be aware of how your body becomes more and more relaxed and your mind becomes calm and focused.

Activity 2.11
Slow Breathing

Sit or lie down in a comfortable position. Close your eyes and bring your attention to your breathing. Notice how it feels as you inhale and exhale. Now for the next couple of minutes, begin to change your breathing rhythm. Focus on making each breath slower and deeper than the one before until you find a rhythm that is slow, deep, and comfortable. Maintain that rhythm and notice how your breathing leaves you feeling centered and ready for any challenge you might face.

Activity 2.12
Short Version: Breathing - Relaxation

Assume a comfortable position, sitting or lying down and when ready, allow your eyes to close. Concentrate on your natural breathing rhythm. Notice how it feels as you inhale and exhale. Turn your attention to the exhalation phase of our breathing cycle. And r-e-l-a-x as you exhale… exhale and r-e-l-a-x…permit yourself to let go… and r-e-l-a-x more and more with each exhalation. As you inhale, feel the energy coming into your body and as you exhale feel the tension flowing out of your body, inhale- energy in- exhale, tension. Continue to focus on your exhalations as you exhale and r-e-l-a-x. Maintain your focus on your breathing for a few minutes. If you get distracted, notice the source of the distraction and then gently bring your focus back to your breathing. You will become relaxed and experience a state of peacefulness. When ready, stretch, and open your eyes.

Activity 2.13
Autogenic Breathing

Sit or lie down in a comfortable position. Close your eyes, take a couple of deep breaths, and focus your attention on the muscles throughout your body. As you discover tension, let it drain out of your body. Through this exercise you will be asked to focus on the bodily sensations of warmth and heaviness. These feelings occur when the body is relaxed and comfortable. Begin by focusing your attention on your breathing … (pause for 2 or 3 seconds with each). With each breath your head becomes heavier… heavier… warmer… warmer…

Now shift your focus to your arms and hands. With each breath your arms and hands become heavier… heavier…heavier…warmer… and warmer… Now concentrate on your buttock, legs and feet. With each breath your buttocks, legs, and feet become heavier… heaver…. heavier…warmer…. warmer… warmer. Now as you relax, notice your torso becoming heavier…heavier… heavier…warmer… and warmer… Be

> aware of your entire body as it becomes heavier... heavier... heavier... ...warmer... warmer... warmer... Feel how heavy your entire body has become and notice the warmth of your experience as you enjoy relaxation and peacefulness.

Rapid Relaxation and Cue Words

Once you have practiced some of the total relaxation techniques you can begin to implement the mental skills of relaxation techniques. These rapid relaxation techniques are designed to be used in just a few seconds and allow yourself to achieve the proper arousal zone during practice and competition.

During the rapid relaxation process, you should pair a cue word with your energy level in order to develop a strong association between the two. The cue word can be used to trigger the rapid relaxation response. We will cover cue words in more detail in chapter 4 on self-talk. For now, it is important to know that a cue word is a word you choose that reminds you of something to focus on. When you're nervous, your breathing speeds up and gets faster. This kind of shallow, rapid breathing will tighten your muscles and tire you out prematurely, causing you to perform poorly. To help you quickly calm yourself down under pressure you must learn to control the depth and rate of your breathing.

A simple and rapid relaxation response should be a part of every athlete's pre-performance routine. You may want to use some of the following techniques presented below. Try the different methods out and see which works best for you. Remember there is no right way to relax or one method that works for everyone and you must experiment to find a personal relaxation strategy that works for you.

Activity 2.14
Relaxing Quick Breathing

1. Inhale deeply and feel the air fill your lungs as your chest rises.
2. Exhale and blow the air out of your lungs, feeling relaxed.
3. As you exhale repeat a cue word such as "relax" to yourself.
4. Repeat two to three times.

Activity 2.15
Rapid Power Breathing

1. Blow out one noisy "whoosh" exhaling through your mouth, puffing out your checks. Blow as much air as possible out of your lungs to prepare for a deep inhalation to flood fresh air into your lungs.
2. Take a deep breath through your nose. Make it a power inhalation from your abdomen. Make sure you do not raise your shoulder or puff on your chest. Imagine the tension being pulled from your lungs by a vacuum cleaner.
3. Slowly breathe out your nose and mouth, hearing the air as it is exhaled. Imagine the tension leaving your body as you exhale. With each exhalation repeat to yourself a cue word such as "relax".
4. For just a few quick breaths, focus on inhaling energy in, exhaling tension out.

Activity 2.16
Standing Abdominal Breathing

1. In a standing position, place your hands on your sides, with your thumbs, pointing backwards and positioned in the hollow above each hip. Your fingers extend forward, resting on your abdomen and stretching just below your navel.
2. Take a deep breath and feel your abdomen swell beneath your fingers and thumbs. Make sure your shoulders do not rise and your chest does not puff out.
3. Exhale slowly and evenly until you feel your abdomen fall under your fingers.
4. Take one or two full exhalations that push the air from the bottom of your lungs.

Activity 2.17
Quick Scan and Release

1. Scan your body for any tension and then consciously release tension found in any muscles.
2. Focus on the muscles you will be using for your performance.
3. You may want to add some specific stretches to this technique so you can stretch out release the tension in the tight muscles (e.g. rolling the head in a slow circle for the neck muscles to relax).

Activity 2.18
Chill Pill

Identify three situations in which you could use a rapid relaxation response. Practice this situation now of how you would handle it. When the situation arises later in the day use the rapid relaxation technique to lower your arousal level.   Relaxation Technique Used

Situation 1
Situation 2
Situation 3

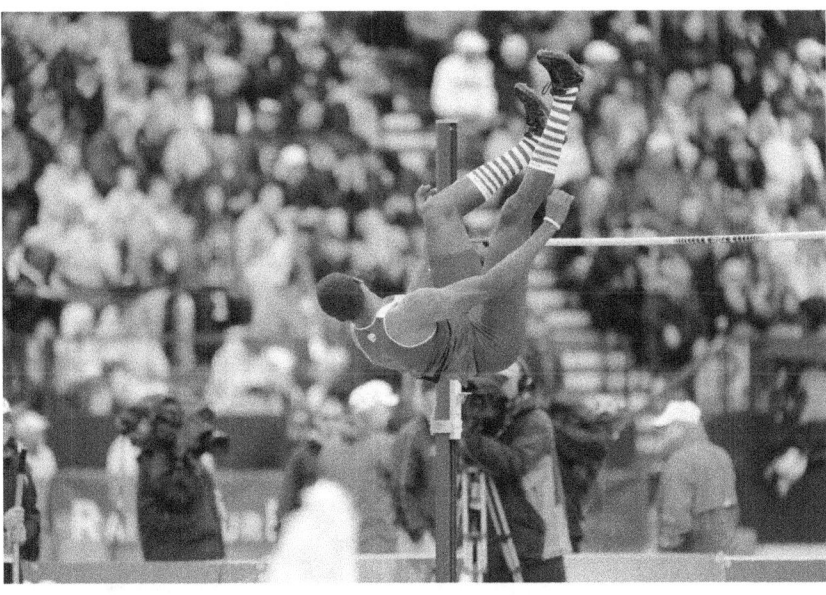

Activity 2.19
Relaxation Words

1. Pick a word that relaxes you
2. Close your eyes and focus on taking relaxing breaths.
3. With each exhalation, say your cue word.
4. Do this for one minute and then stop repeating your cue word.
5. Focus on how your body feels in this relaxed state for a few minutes.
6. Start repeating your cue word again on each exhalation for one minute.

Activity 2.20
Cued Relaxation

1. Perform a total relaxation technique that works for you.
2. Pair a cue word with the feeling of being highly relaxed.
3. Repeat your cue word after each third relaxation breath for a total of 10-15 repetitions. The cue word chosen should have a strong relaxing influence (such as relax, calm or cool).
4. Use cued relaxation to promote rapid relaxation within 5 seconds by taking 5 relaxation breaths and repeating your cue word. When you master this technique you can quickly achieve your proper arousal level within seconds.

Energization

Energization involves activating the body to prepare for optimal performance. Energization helps speed up the heart rate and breathing rate, stimulate greater blood flow to the working muscles, and enhances the activity of the mind. An athlete with high energization skills can get more out of practice, where athletes often struggle with low motivation and concentration levels. As most athletes have less of a problem with energy in competition, it does become a factor in times of fatigue, adversity, and failure. The ability of athletes to use their energization skills to get back into their proper arousal zone is key. When energy levels become low, athletes tend to lose concentration by focusing too broadly. Energization techniques help narrow the focus, reduce distractions and allow the athlete to focus on performance cues. An athlete skilled in energization techniques can call upon their skill during the later stages of competition. This ability raises confidence levels, as athletes know they can draw on this technique to control their arousal level in pressure situations.

I encourage you to try several energization techniques and choose the ones you feel most comfortable, enjoyable, and successful with. Feel free to personalize the techniques in any manner you choose to enhance effectiveness. Most track and field athletes will use multiple energization techniques.

Activity 2.21
Energizing Imagery

Close your eyes and begin to focus on your breathing. With each inhalation think of energy "coming in" and with each exhalation think of "tension out." With each inhalation, feel your muscles becoming more and more powerful. See your body as a powerful machine. Visualize performing your track and field event and performing it with high energy and power.

Activity 2.22
Music

Many track and field athletes already use music to relax and it can also be used as an energization technique. Up-tempo music provides an energizing effect. The music tends to enhance energy levels at a sub-conscious level. The rhythm of the music helps to trigger energization as the athlete plays a song mentally in their mind. A thrower might mentally replay a tune that helps him feel powerful and explosive while getting ready to throw. A sprinter might use a fast paced song. A jumper may feel the rhythm of a song on the approach. A distance runner could use an upbeat tempo to pick up the pace during a race or to kick strong to the finish.

Activity 2.23
Energy at the Top of the Mountain

Close your eyes and take several deep breaths. Feel your diaphragm expand, your chest expand, hold the breath briefly and then exhale. With each breath you relax more and more completely.

Picture yourself at the bottom of a mountain. You slowly begin to climb up the mountain, smooth and effortlessly. With each step you become more and more energized, more rejuvenated and with more vitality. As you continue to climb and go higher, you continue to build strength, power, and energy. With each step you feel the adrenaline and fuller of energy than the last step you took.

When you reach the top of the mountain, you stand on top of the world. You feel close to the bright sun, absorbing the energy. As you absorb the sun, feel the mountain tremble. As you feel the tremble, feel the energy transfer from the ground to your body, filling you full of power and energy from the feet to the top of your head. Feel the energy pulsate through your body, bringing a confident attitude. Feel the energy invigorate your legs, strength and power radiating through your feet. The waves of pulsating energy fill your lower body with strength and power, full of stamina and endurance. Your muscles tingle with energy. Feel your heart pumping oxygen to every muscle in your body.

Feel the energy spread through your upper body, pushing strength and power through your chest, shoulder, back and arms. Feel the power growing with each breathe. Every muscle fiber in your body is poised for a peak performance, just waiting for a challenge or goal to accomplish. You are totally positive, energized and ready to meet the challenge.

Count 15 breaths, each time repeating your energization cue word after each set of three psych-up breaths. As you say your cue word, focus your mind on the feelings of energization throughout your body.

Rapid Energization and Cue Words

Once you have practiced some of the total energization techniques you can begin to implement the mental skills of rapid energization techniques. Just like the rapid relaxation techniques, these rapid energization techniques are designed to be used in just a few seconds and allow the athlete to achieve the proper arousal zone during practice and competition.

During the rapid energization process, you should pair a cue word with your high energy level in order to develop a strong association between the two. The cue word can be used to trigger the rapid energization response. In chapter 4, covering self-talk, we will go over cue words in more detail. For now, it is important to know that a cue word is a word you choose that reminds you of something to focus on. If you are in an explosive jumping or throwing event, the cue word may be "explode."

Let's look at some way that we can link your total energization skills with rapid energization. Total energization is a lengthier process than rapid energization. Just like we discussed in total relaxation and rapid relaxation, we need a technique we can do in just a few seconds. Rapid energization is just that technique.

The simplest and most common form of rapid energization involves psych-up breathing.

Activity 2.23
Psych-Up Breathing

Psych-up breathing is quick, shallow breathing to quickly transport oxygen to the working muscles. A sprinter can do this technique before the start of the 100-meter dash, a thrower before stepping in the ring, and a jumper on the runway before starting the approach. The quicker breathing rhythm requires athletes to breathe shallowly with the lungs instead of with the diaphragm. The emphasis is on the inhalation phase where you should feel energy flowing in with each breath. Psych-up breathing is very effective in elevating arousal.

Once you have practiced psych-up breathing, it is time to link a cue word to it. See Activity 4.4 for some possible cue words you could use. Practice linking energization and cue words in Activity 2.24 and 2.25.

Activity 2.24
Energizing Words

1. Pick a word that energizes you.
2. Close your eyes and focus on taking energizing breaths.
3. With each exhalation, say your cue word.
4. Do this for one minute and then stop repeating your cue word.
5. Focus on how your body feels in this relaxed state for a few minutes.
6. Start repeating your cue word again on each exhalation for one minute.

Activity 2.25
Energization and Cue Words
1. Perform a total energization technique that works for you.
2. Second, pair a cue word with the feeling of being highly energized.
3. Repeat your cue word after each third psych up breath for a total of 10-15 repetitions. The cue word chosen should have a strong energizing effect (such as power, strong, or energy).
4. Use cued energization to promote rapid energization with 5 seconds by taking 5 quick psych-up breaths and repeating the cue word. When you master this technique, you can quickly achieve your proper arousal level within seconds.

Activity 2.26
Activate the Body
Another simple way to energize is to physically activate the heart rate and body by clapping your hands, jumping in place or running in place. What other quick activations could you do to energize and achieve the proper arousal zone? 1. _____ 2. _____ 3. _____

Let's conclude this chapter with the final activity that looks at how effective you have been at achieving your proper arousal level in the past. There is no score at the end, but view this as a self-discovery activity that will provide you with information to guide you in achieving your proper arousal level for future practice.

Activity 2.27
Self-Evaluation of Optimal Level of Arousal

Consider what you have done in the past to increase or decrease your own level of arousal to be able to perform at your best. Rate your effectiveness of getting into your proper arousal zone.
Use a scale of 1-10. 1=not effective, 10=very effective

How effective have you been in decreasing your level of arousal?
1. Downplay the importance of the event   1 2 3 4 5 6 7 8 9 10
2. Slow down the warm-up   1 2 3 4 5 6 7 8 9 10
3. Change your focus   1 2 3 4 5 6 7 8 9 10
4. Use total relaxation techniques   1 2 3 4 5 6 7 8 9 10
5. Use rapid relaxation techniques   1 2 3 4 5 6 7 8 9 10
6. Use cue words   1 2 3 4 5 6 7 8 9 10
7. Stretch and exercise   1 2 3 4 5 6 7 8 9 10
8. Breathing   1 2 3 4 5 6 7 8 9 10
9. Music or videos   1 2 3 4 5 6 7 8 9 10
10. Imagery   1 2 3 4 5 6 7 8 9 10

How effective have you been in increasing your arousal level?
1. Remind yourself of your goals   1 2 3 4 5 6 7 8 9 10
2. Short bursts of high intensity effort (jumping, sprinting)   1 2 3 4 5 6 7 8 9 10
3. Used cue word   1 2 3 4 5 6 7 8 9 10
4. Breathing and self-talk   1 2 3 4 5 6 7 8 9 10
5. Energizing imagery   1 2 3 4 5 6 7 8 9 10
6. Energizing verbal cues   1 2 3 4 5 6 7 8 9 10
7. Energy from the environment   1 2 3 4 5 6 7 8 9 10
8. Use total energization techniques   1 2 3 4 5 6 7 8 9 10
9. Use rapid energization techniques   1 2 3 4 5 6 7 8 9 10
10. Breathing   1 2 3 4 5 6 7 8 9 10

In this chapter we have covered what conditions should be met for you to achieve your optimal arousal levels. You have practiced both total and rapid relaxation techniques and paired them with cue words. Both of these techniques are designed to lower arousal levels and are vitally important techniques to achieve proper arousal. You have also practiced total and rapid energization skills and used cue words to associate your feelings with energization. These energization skills will help raise your arousal levels to the proper arousal level. The ability to recognize your arousal level and act to keep the proper arousal will have you well on your way to being a mentally skilled athlete.

Chapter 3

Goals

In chapter 3, we will examine the importance of goals, types of goals, go over the guidelines in setting proper goals and how to systematically implement your goals on a continual basis. Goal setting in athletics has been used since ancient times. Almost all athletes set goals, but often their goal setting process is not effective.

A goal is a specific standard or accomplishment that one strives to attain. Setting goals is easy, as it takes little effort to dream of accomplishments and triumphs. However, the term goal setting is more than just setting goals. The majority of track and field athletes have goals, but lack a systematic plan in place to reach their goals. Organizing, managing, and pursuing your goals in a consistent and dedicated manner is a much more difficult task.

Goal setting becomes an important mental skills tool to help you achieve what you want in your life. Effective goal setters establish many goals every day, all part of a well-designed plan to achieve success. Develop a goal setting mentality, a mindset in which you learn to set goals systematically in everything you do. A goal setting mentality promotes high levels of intrinsic motivation and steadily increases competence.

An important part of the initial goal setting process is understanding why you participate in the sport of track and field. Complete *Activity 3.1 Why I Participate* to review why you're in the sport of track and field.

Activity 3.1   **Why I Participate**
Think back to the first time you participated in the sport of track and field. Why did you decide to start participating in track and field?   When you first started, what did you enjoy about track and field? Think about your participation in the sport of track and field now. Why did you still participate in track and field?   What do you enjoy about track and field now?

I hope that you think track and field is fun. Fun is the number one reason athletes participate in a sport. As you develop your mental skills through the drills in this book, one of your goals should be to enjoy the sport. An increase in your mental skill levels will make the experience even more enjoyable. Work hard, be mentally strong, and enjoy what you do.

Use *Activity 3.2 Why Set Goals* to think about the important process of goal setting.

Activity 3.2   **Why Set Goals**
List three reasons why you believe it is important to set goals.   1.   2.   3.
Wrap-Up: You may have thought about the following reasons: Goals will give you purpose and direction. Well-designed goals will help motivate, promote self-confidence, and increase performance. Goals also enhance concentration and create a positive attitude.

Overwhelming evidence exists that goal setting is one of the most effective strategies available to enhance performance. The key to goal setting success lies in how you set your goals. Complete *Activity 3.3 My Goals* to start learning how to properly set goals.

Activity 3.3   **My Goals**
List four goals you have for the upcoming season. We will come back and address your goals a bit later in this chapter.   1. _____   2. _____   3. _____   4. _____

Let's examine the different types of goals. You may decide you will use a combination of the different types. Leading experts in goal setting recommend the focus be on effort, process, and performance goals as opposed to outcome goals. Let's take a look at the different types of goals.

Four Types of Goals

Outcome goals: The emphasis is on winning or beating your competitors. Most coaches and athletes set outcome goals, which are highly dependent on the quality of one's opponents, such as winning the state title. These goals are not completely under the athlete's control. These are the most common types of goals set by athletes because they are easiest to set. However, they are the least controllable goal an athlete can set.

Performance goals: The focus is on increasing personal performance. In track and field, this could be running faster, throwing farther or jumping farther or higher. Track and field is easily measured in performance statistics and we often speak of personal records (PR) or personal bests (PB).

Process goals: Process goals are based on controllable thoughts and actions related to performance execution. The main focus is on improving form and technique. To achieve outcome goals, you must achieve a series of process goals. Examples of this could be to improve stride length or technique. The destination is the outcome goal, but we must take the proper path to arrive there. When Reese Hoffa steps into the ring to win the Olympic gold medal in the shot put, he is not thinking, "I have to throw far to win." His thinking is much more focused on the process. "Stay relaxed, square, power, explode." Process goals serve as stepping stones to achieve the performance levels that will lead to desired outcomes.

Effort Goal: Focus is on the effort you will give. Effort goals are largely under one's control regardless of the competition. A beginning athlete may lose on the scoreboard but still has a chance to achieve their effort goal. If athletes are recognized for trying hard, they will likely continue. Getting athletes to understand what it means to try hard can help them throughout their life. Effort goals are motivating to all athletes, because they can control them and they can see their progress.

Activity 3.4   **What Type of Goals Do I Set**
Now, let's go back and look at what you wrote down for Activity 3.3. Identify the type of goal you wrote, as either outcome, performance, process or effort.   Goal one: _____   Goal two: _____   Goal three: _____   Goal four: _____   How would you revise your goals now that you know the types of goals and benefits of each goal?

I bet you listed at least a couple that were outcome goals. We live in a society where the focus is on winning (success) and losing (failure). Athletes often base their self-confidence on winning, therefore placing their self-confidence on an unstable foundation. This instability can become frustrating when the only criterion on how good you are is to see yourself winning or losing.

Think of the goal setting process as a continuum. Are outcome goals bad and never used? No. Athletes perform most effectively by using various types of goals and knowing when to use each type. Outcome goals can be motivating and can be used to energize athletes to work hard for major accomplishments. Performance goals are standards that athletes need to achieve in order to lead them toward their outcome goals. Process goals are critical for our actual competitive performance and should be used to focus attention on key aspects of performance and to occupy athletes' minds with relevant thoughts. Well-designed effort goals should, over time, help move you toward outcome goals. If an athlete focuses on effort goals and begins to achieve them, performance will improve and, over time, the desired outcome goal will be achieved.

**Table 3.1
Goal Continuum**

Effort Goals ---------------------- Process Goals -------------------- Performance ------------------Outcome

How do you feel competent regardless of winning or losing? Re-define success as achieving effort and process goals. Placing your focus on effort and process goals is a path that you have control over.

Table 3.2 gives examples of the different types of goals.

**Table 3.2
Goal Type Examples**

Effort	Process	Performance	Outcome
Run hard through the finish line	Obtaining the proper arousal zone	Increase leg strength by weight training	Qualify for state meet
Use a positive mental attitude at all times	Use trigger words of smooth, explode and kick	Hit take-off point on stride	Win the state title
Attack the approach every time	Visualize perfect technique prior to each jump.	Progressively increase jump heights throughout the season	Go undefeated

The most successful athletes have learned how to plan and use goal setting effectively, allowing them to become process-oriented as they compete. In order to use goal setting effectively, you should have a solid understanding of the characteristics of setting effective goals.

Characteristics of Effective Goal Setting

The acronym SMART (Smith, 1999) can be used to remember how to be smart in developing your goals.

Specific

You must identify the exact behaviors you want to engage in that will lead to success. General goals to perform well or give 100 percent fail to establish what exactly is meant to perform well or give one hundred percent.

A general goal may be, "I want to keep optimal concentration during the run." Athletes want to keep concentration and coaches yelling "concentrate" also want to see their athletes concentrate. But what should you concentrate on and how do you do it effectively? Divide the general goal into specific goals that define ways of behaving related to optimal concentration during running such as (a) use my pre-competition routine, and (b) use my cue words.

Measurable

In order to evaluate your goal setting program, goals must be evaluated. Goals in track and field can be easily quantified such as time or distance. Make sure the goal statement specifies some action that you are taking. Instead of saying "I want to concentrate consistently," you would say, "I will repeat my cue words." By making goals specific, they become more measurable. Set goals that you can clearly assess to analyze your progress.

Aggressive yet Achievable

Aggressive goals challenge you to your limits. If goals are not realistic, they do not provide direction and inspiration. In fact, they may provide the opposite. The best goals are difficult, extremely challenging, and very aggressive to inspire you, yet they must be achievable at the upper limits of your ability. These goals should push you to get out of your comfort zone.

Relevant

Relevant goals are individualized and meaningful, thus capturing attention and motivating you. You should set goals with the help of your coaches. Coaches and athletes should set relevant goals for practice as well as competition within their goal setting. Many times athletes set goals they wish to achieve in competition, but they forget that in practice and training, they make the most progress and spend the most time. Set, focus on, and evaluate both practice and competition goals as part of the goal setting process.

Time

Goals should be time bound, which means specify a target date for goal attainment. Goals that have no time frame for achievement do not facilitate focused behavior. Athletes tend to set unrealistic, dream-oriented goals when they are not required to set a time for completing the goals. With a deadline, focus sharpens and the brain kicks in the urgency of the goal. Short-term goals with deadlines can be used as stepping stones on the way to achieving an important long-term goal.

George Washington once said, "Give me six hours to chop down a tree and I will spend the first four sharpening the axe." This quote could be applied to goal setting. Spending time with proper goal setting will pay big dividends toward goal setting success.

Let's practice the SMART principle of setting goals. Although being positive is not included in the SMART principles, we will add that to strengthen our goal setting skills.

The purpose of *Activity 3.5 Writing Smart Goals* is to identify and write SMART goals. In column one are examples of errors that are often listed by athletes setting goals. In column two, use the examples given and fill in the blanks and improve the goals.

Activity 3.5
Writing Smart Goals

Column one lists a negative goal. In column two change the negative goal to a positive goal. Use the examples as a guideline.

Being Positive	
Negative Goal	**Positive Goal**
I don't want to get cut	I will make the team
I don't want to slow down	I will finish the race strong
I won't make any stupid mistakes	I will use my cue words to focus and be confident
1.	1.
2.	2.
3.	3.

Specific	
Non-Specific Goal	**Specific**
I will get more sleep	I will get 8 hours of sleep per night by going to bed at 10:00 p.m.
1.	1.
2.	2.
3.	3.

Measurable	
Non-measurable	**Measurable**
Eat less candy	I will eat the 4 servings of fruits and vegetables every day.
1.	1.
2.	2.
3.	3.

Aggressive but Achievable	
Non-Aggressive/Achievable	**Aggressive/Achievable**
I will show up at practice every day.	I will come to practice with focus and ready to get better every day.
1.	1.
2.	2.
3.	3.

Relevant	
Non-Relevant	**Relevant**
I will be the Olympic champion.	I will get better every day by working on my mental skills every day.
1.	1.
2.	2.
3.	3.

Time	
Non-Time	**Time**
I will run 4:20 in the mile.	I will run 4:20 in the mile by the end of the current track and field season.
1.	1.
2.	2.
3.	3.

Outcome goals tell you where you want to be, which can help motivate. But, on a daily basis, they do not tell you what you need to do. By changing outcome goals to process goals, you will be in control of your goal program. Complete *Activity 3.6* to *Change Outcome Goals to Process Goals*.

Activity 3.6
Change Outcome Goals to Process Goals

1. Start With an Outcome
Choose an upcoming meet, and pick a challenging but not impossible outcome goal (win, place, get a certain score or time, etc.). Write that goal down in detail here:
My outcome goal:
_____
_____

2. Moving From Outcome to Process Goals
How can you maximize your chances to achieve this goal? Write down three things (i.e. pacing, mental training, weight training, plenty of sleep) you can do in order to reach your goals. Be specific.
1. I will: _____
2. I will: _____
3. I will: _____

3. Practicing the Process and Effort Goals in Training
What can you do in practice between now and your competition to help you towards your process goals? These could include effort goals. For example, if your competition task goal is to hold a specific pace, you might focus on that pace in practice.
1. In training, I will
_____
2. In training, I will
_____
3. In training, I will
_____

I have found that when you ask athletes to write goals, they will often ask, what should I put down? Therefore, I like to provide examples. The following weekly goal-setting example illustrates what a distance runner might put down for goals. The focus is on three major goals. Under each major goal is one major affirmation that the athlete will repeat often as they visualize achieving their goal. Under each major goal is a process step that the athlete will work to attain. There is an affirmation associated with each process step. At the end of the process step line will be a series of boxes. These are commitment boxes that should be checked if the athlete accomplishes that goal. For example, if the goal for the week was to run every morning, after completing the morning run, the athlete places a check mark in a box. By the end of the week, if the athlete ran every morning, they would have seven checkmarks. If the goal is to use visualization for five minutes three times a week and that athlete accomplishes their weekly goal, there would be three checks in the row of boxes. Note that there is also a lifestyle goal, which I believe is very important. Out of the 24 hours in a day, how much time do you spend out of practice? What you do out of practice can be very important in how you perform.

As the goal setting process is a daily and weekly journey, at the end of the week, you should provide a summary of what you did well (strengths), what you need to work on, and any comments.

I recommend that you have an accountability partner. Accountability partners help encourage and motivate you, keeping you on track to meet your goals. In a weekly meeting with your accountability partner, you would both go over how you did towards meeting your goals for the previous week. After reviewing the previous week, new goals should be set for the upcoming week. The focus on the major goals may very well remain the same but the process goals or the step to attain the goal would change.

The first goal sheet includes examples of major goals, process goals, and affirmations. The second goal sheet is for you to fill in. The third goal sheet is a shorter and simpler goal form that does not include the affirmations for each process step.

Activity 3.10 is a goal sheet form that focuses on short-term goals (30-60 days or less) and long-term goals, which would be season-long goals. Activity 3.11 is the same concept as Activity 3.10, but includes a place for affirmations that are associated with each goal.

Activity 3.7 Example Goal Sheet With Affirmations

Mental Skills and Drills
Track and Field Example Goals

Goal #1

Run a 4:50 1600 or faster
Goal #1 Affirmation
I work hard toward my goals.

Steps to attain this goal:

1. Increase endurance by running 2 mornings a week
2. Workout every weekend
3. Use visualization for 5 minutes three times a week
4. Be mentally strong in practice by visualizing a good workout before practice

Affirmation for each step:

1. Morning runs make me tough.
2. I am committed to being a better runner.
3. Mental training makes me great.
4. I am prepared for a great practice effort

Goal #2

Run the 3200 meters under 10:00 minutes
Goal #2 Affirmation
I am focused on reaching my goal.

Steps to attain this goal:

1. Use affirmations during challenging periods of workouts and races
2. Set goals for my races and practices
3. Commit to reaching my practice and race goals
4. Visualize three times a week running a sub 10 3200 meters

Affirmation for each step:

I use my cue words to make me stronger.
I have a plan for success.
I am committed to my plan for success.
I am a great distance runner.

Goal #3-Lifestyle Goal

Adapt a lifestyle conducive to being a great runner.
Goal #3 Affirmation
My lifestyle makes me a better athlete.

Steps to attain this goal:

1. Get at least 8 hours of sleep every night-be in bed by 10:00 p.m.
2. Eat carbohydrates within 2 hours of each workout
3. Limit fast food to no more than three times per week
4. Practice mental training everyday

Affirmation for each step:

1. Proper sleep gives me the energy for great running.
2. I recover quickly.
3. I eat nutritiously to improve performance.
4. Mental training makes me tough.

Summary for the week:

Strengths:
_____
_____
_____

To work on:
_____
_____
_____

Comments:
_____
_____
_____

Week of _____ to _____

Name _____ Signature: _____ Date: _____

Partner Name _____ Signature: _____ Date: _____

Activity 3.8 Weekly Goal Sheet With Affirmations

**Mental Skills and Drills
Track and Field Goals**

Goal #1

Goal #1 Affirmation

Steps to attain this goal:

1. _____
2. _____
3. _____
4. _____

Affirmation for each step:

1. _____
2. _____
3. _____
4. _____

Goal #2

Goal #2 Affirmation

Steps to attain this goal:

1. _____
2. _____
3. _____
4. _____

Affirmation for each step:

1. _____
2. _____
3. _____
4. _____

Goal #3-Lifestyle Goal

Goal #3 Affirmation

Steps to attain this goal:

1. _____
2. _____
3. _____
4. _____

Affirmation for each step:

1. _____
2. _____
3. _____
4. _____

Summary for the week:

Strengths:
_____
_____
_____

To work on:
_____
_____
_____

Comments:
_____
_____
_____

Week of _____ to _____
Name _____ Signature: _____ Date: _____
Partner Name _____ Signature: _____ Date: _____

Activity 3.9 Weekly Goal Sheet without Affirmations

**Mental Skills and Drills
Track and Field Goals**

Goal #1

| Goal #1 Affirmation |

Steps to attain this goal:

1. _____
2. _____
3. _____
4. _____

Goal #2

| Goal #2 Affirmation |

Steps to attain this goal:

1. _____
2. _____
3. _____
4. _____

Goal #3-Lifestyle Goal

| Goal #3 Affirmation |

Steps to attain this goal:

1. _____
2. _____
3. _____
4. _____

Summary for the week:

Strengths:
_____
_____
_____

To work on:
_____
_____
_____

Comments:
_____
_____
_____

Week of _____ to _____	
Name _____ Signature: _____ Date: _____	
Partner Name _____ Signature: _____ Date: _____	

Activity 3.10
Short and Long Range Goals Without Affirmations

Short Range Goals (daily or 30 days or less)

I. _____
_____
_____

Three steps to attain this goal:
    a. _____

    b. _____

    c. _____

II. _____
_____
_____

Three steps to attain this goal:
    a. _____

    b. _____

    c. _____

III. _____
_____
_____

Three steps to attain this goal:
    a. _____

    b. _____

    c. _____

I am willing to make sacrifices and make the commitment to be a great runner!

_____   _____   _____
Print your Name   Signature   Date

Long Range (Season) Goals

I. _____

Three steps to attain this goal:
- a. _____
- b. _____
- c. _____

II. _____

Three steps to attain this goal:
- a. _____
- b. _____
- c. _____

III. _____

Three steps to attain this goal:
- a. _____
- b. _____
- c. _____

I am willing to make sacrifices and make the commitment to be a great runner!

_____   _____   _____
Print your Name   Signature   Date

Activity 3.11
Short and Long Range Goals With Affirmations

Short Range Goals With Affirmations

I. _____
_____

Three steps to attain this goal:

   a. _____
   *Affirmation for this goal:_____

   b. _____
   *Affirmation for this goal:_____

   c. _____
   *Affirmation for this goal:_____

II. _____
_____

Three steps to attain this goal:

   a. _____
   *Affirmation for this goal:_____

   b. _____
   *Affirmation for this goal:_____

   c. _____
   *Affirmation for this goal:_____

III. _____
_____

Three steps to attain this goal:

   a. _____
   *Affirmation for this goal:_____

   b. _____
   *Affirmation for this goal:_____

   c. _____
   *Affirmation for this goal:_____

_____   _____   _____
Print your Name   Signature   Date

Long Range Goals With Affirmations

I. _____
_____
_____

Three steps to attain this goal:

   a. _____
   *Affirmation for this goal:_____

   b. _____
   *Affirmation for this goal:_____

   c. _____
   *Affirmation for this goal:_____

II. _____
_____

Three steps to attain this goal:

   a. _____
   *Affirmation for this goal:_____

   b. _____
   *Affirmation for this goal:_____

   c. _____
   *Affirmation for this goal:_____

_____

III. _____
_____

Three steps to attain this goal:

   a. _____
   *Affirmation for this goal:_____

   b. _____
   *Affirmation for this goal:_____

   c. _____
   *Affirmation for this goal:_____

_____   _____   _____
Print your Name   Signature   Date

As you have learned, it is not simply enough to write your goals down. You must work with them on a continual basis. Table 3.3 provides recommendations and reminders on how you can focus on your goals throughout the day.

Table 3.3 **Working With My Goals**

When do I read my goals?
    a. I read my goals 9 times a day.
    b. I read my goals three times when I first get out of bed.
    c. I read my goals three times during lunchtime or before practice.
    d. I read my goals three times when I first get out of bed.
    e. I read my goals out loud if possible.
 	
Where will I place my goals at home?
    Bathroom
    Mirror
    Desk
    Bedroom
 	
Where will I place my goals when I take them with me?
    In cell phone
    On note card
    In diary

If I read my goals, and believe my goals, I will achieve my goals.

Pictures can be very powerful and some athletes are visual learners. By drawing goals, you are putting a commitment on paper. Complete *Activity 3.12 Draw Your Individual Goal* and *Activity 3.13 Draw Your Team Goal*. I recommend sharing your team goal picture with your teammates in a show and tell session.

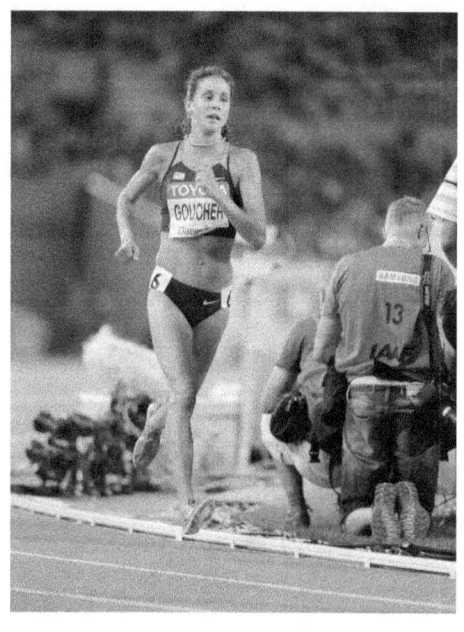

Activity 3.12
Draw Your Individual Goal

What does your goal look like? See your individual goal in as much detail as possible and then draw it. Draw yourself achieving your goal. You may want to use color to bring it to life!

Activity 3.13
Draw Your Team Goal

What does your team goal look like? See your team goal in as much detail as possible and then draw it. Draw your team achieving your team goal. You may want to use color to bring it to life!

As a coach, it is challenging to keep up with every athlete and their continual progress on their goals. One of the ideas I have found very worthwhile is to periodically have the athlete fill out a self-evaluation of their progress in the season. This evaluation can be given at various times of the season. I suggest at a minimum, do the survey at least once in the middle of the season. The purpose is two-fold: (1) it allows the athlete to think about how they are progressing and performing, and (2) it provides valuable feedback to the coach who can compare their rating of the athlete to the athlete's rating. This valuable information could be used for a coach-athlete discussion on how to continue to improve. Regardless of how many times the athlete and coach discuss the evaluation, you can use this evaluation, or make up your own to consistently evaluate your efforts and progress.

Activity 3.14 **Progress Evaluation**	
Give yourself a rating on a scale of 1-10 (with 10 being high) of how you are doing.	**Rating**
1. My performance in practice overall	
2. My performance in warm-up	
3. My performance in stretching.	
4. My performance in drills	
5. My performance in practice hard days	
6. My performance in practice easy days	
7. My performance in circuit training	
8. My attention and contribution to team meetings	
9. My encouragement of teammates	
10. My positive attitude	
11. Filling out training diaries accurately and thoroughly	
12. Use of affirmations to run better	
13. Effectively using mental training during practice	
14. Using mental training outside of practice	
15. Proper sleep	
16. Proper nutrition	
17. Good hydration practices (drinking water)	
18. Ability to push myself	
19. Contribution to team	
20. Progress toward my goal	
21. Number of times a week doing mental training	

The Road To Success

"Two roads diverged in a wood and I - I took the one less traveled by, and that has made all the difference..."
-Robert Frost

What road are you on? Training and competing in track and field is like taking a long journey towards a goal far away. As you travel, the road continually forks and you are required to decide which way to go. These forks represent all the decisions you're constantly faced with as an athlete. Some of these decisions may be:

Do I blow my training diet?

Am I really going to put in those extra hours today?

What difference could it make if I skip weight training?

Should I run hard when the coach is not looking?

Do I stay up late?

Do I do alcohol or drugs?

When you decide to take it easy when no one is around, you have made a decision to head down the road to mediocrity. This road is always the easiest to take. It requires no special talent or character. However, the easy road will lead you to performance problems.

The right road is never easy to take. It may be filled with pain, hurt, and uncomfortable feelings as you push to the limit in practice and competition. The road less traveled may include getting up early and practicing when you really want to stay in bed. It involves looking at problems and weaknesses directly rather than avoiding them.

The right road may often be the one less traveled. But what is right may not be the most popular and what is popular may not always be right. If you take the road less traveled, you will face more obstacles and challenges; however, the greater the challenge, the greater the reward.

Your goal must be big enough to choose the right road. Your goal setting program must be good enough to keep you traveling down the road less traveled. Goals can be incredibly motivating and empower us with the unstoppable power of the human spirit when we set our sights on a goal.

When you come to the fork in the road, is your goal what you want at the moment or what you want the most? Are you willing to exchange your dreams for temporary relief and comfort?

In Chapter 3, you have learned of the different types of goals, principles of setting goals, were provided with sample goal sheets, and started your goal-setting process. However, you also know goal setting is a continual process as you consistently evaluate and revise. Keep your focus on the effort and the process, which you have control over, and the performance and outcomes you desire will eventually come.

Be proud of yourself that you have made the commitment to a mindset of goal setting. Keep your goal in front of you as you follow the road less traveled. It will make all the difference!

Chapter 4

Self-Talk

After you have learned to relax, it's a good time to start developing your positive self-talk skills. Without these skills, you are prone to negative self-talk, which leads to a decrement in performance.

Generally people tend to focus on what they are doing wrong instead of what they are doing right. Consider coaches who become error correction specialists. Most of what has been modeled to us is negative, so we rapidly learn to be the same way with ourselves. Reardon and Gordin (2002) estimate that around 70% of feedback on performances is negative.

Successful athletes learn to control their self-talk so it enhances their ability to perform. Positive self-talk counteracts the mind's tendency to be negative. Positive self-talk helps you manage performance situations and puts you in control.

In this chapter, we will take a look at our self-talk. We will start off covering guidelines for establishing positive self-talk, then go over activities to positively change the way you talk to yourself.

Activity 4.1 **The Power of Being Positive**
Activity: Find a partner and face each other. Person 1 closes their eyes and extends their arms out to the side like a cross. Person 2 stands in front of person 1 and grasps the wrist of person 1. Person 2 instructs Person 1 to think of something that makes them sad and depressed. When person 2 gets this in his head, he nods his head, Person 2 then puts person 1's arms down, while person 1 attempts to keep his arms up. After the arms are pulled down, the two people exchange places and repeat the exercise. After both have completed with a sad thought, they both do the exercise with a positive, happy and energizing thought.
For thought: Compare the two different exercises. Was there a difference? What was the difference? Why did the difference occur?
Wrap-up: Normally, people are much stronger when thinking positive thoughts. The exercise demonstrates the thoughts that affect the energy level of the body and overall performance.

Activity 4.1 illustrated that more can be accomplished by using positive thoughts and often there are negative consequences associated with negative self-talk. You should develop a solid understanding of your current self-talk patterns. Once an understanding occurs, then a variety of strategies can be proactively implemented to increase the number and quality of the positive thoughts. Finally, you should be able to change negative thoughts into positive thinking.

Athletes can identify their pattern of self-talk by completing logs after practice and competition. Post practice logs can be kept daily or occasionally. Start by completing the Self-Talk Log Form for a few practices and preferably for at least one competition.

Activity 4.2
My Self-Talk Log

Select three positive and three negative situations from a practice or a competition. A positive situation is an event in which you execute correctly, show improvement, demonstrate team unity or have fun. Briefly, describe each situation and highlight the positive nature. Then record the specific positive thoughts you recalled. For example in learning a new skill it might be, "I got it!" "I want to try it again!" Repeat the process for up to three negative situations in practice or competition in which there was poor performance. Describe each negative situation and identify the specific negative thoughts you had during the experience.

My Self-Talk Log

Day _____

Positive Situations	Positive Thoughts	Effect on practice or competition
1.		
2.		
3.		
Negative Situations	Negative Thoughts	Effect on practice or competition
1.		
2.		
3.		

Wrap-up: Is your self-talk harmful or helpful?

If you are having trouble assessing positive and negative situations, then record a PMA (Positive Mental Attitude) score for each day in Activity 4.3.

Activity 4.3
My PMA Scores

Record a PMA (Positive Mental Attitude) score for each day. Rate your PMA from 1 to 10, with 1 being the most negative day of your life, 5 an average day and a 10 the most positive day of your life. The PMA score should represent the quality of the day.

	Monday	Tuesday	Wednesday	Thursday	Friday	Saturday	Sunday
Week 1							
Week 2							

What did you learn from the exercise?

Guidelines for enhancing self-talk

Concentrate on the process

Our thoughts generally focus on what needs to be done, rather than on how we are doing it. When your thoughts turn to focusing on an outcome, such as "I have to clear the high jump bar," your self-talk creates anxiety because the outcome is uncertain until the performance is over. An outcome-oriented self-talk detracts from the ability to focus on what is happening in the here-and-now process of the performance. The high jumper repeating the words "rhythm" and "flow" during each attempt is practicing positive self-talk and focusing on the process rather than the moment.

Concentrate on the present

Immerse yourself in the present and trust in your abilities. Worrying about the last negative performance or worrying about the outcome takes you out of the present moment. Jumpers telling themselves to be fast on the approach instead of telling themselves not to do what he/she did in the last attempt is concentrating on the present. We will focus more on concentration and how to increase focus in Chapter 6.

Focus on composure

Focus on what you can control (more in Chapter 6) to attain your proper level of arousal. Anxiety decreases concentration. Thinking about anxiety only increases anxiety. Focus on staying calm and keeping your composure. Believe in your ability to make it happen. If you have learned the skill of relaxation, then that is the response your body will produce, flowing the direction of your mind. You are what you think. When you think nervous, you become nervous. When you think calm, you become calm.

Try smarter not necessarily harder

Many athletes try too hard and they do not believe in their self-talk. Believing in your positive self-talk frees you to perform on auto-pilot. Use different self-talk in practice than in performance. The goal of practice is to improve, explore and identify areas to work on. Practicing self-talk may include questioning, and considering areas to change.

Competition self-talk is different self-talk because during performance, self-talk needs to be encouraging, minimal, and positive. It should contain elements of affirmation, trusting one's self and enjoying the moment. An example of positive self-talk in practice would be to focus on what it feels like to do a jump correctly. Competition self-talk would include more oriented cue words such as strong and high.

Affirmations

Once you can develop the ability to relax, it is time to move to the affirmation stage. Affirmations are powerful statements that, repeated over and over, will lead to changed beliefs. Some example affirmations are: *I am strong! I am fast! I run relaxed! I explode!*

Here are the 5 P's of Affirmations:

1. Positive
    a. All affirmations should be stated in the positive.
2. Present Tense
    a. Affirmations should be stated as "I am."
    b. "I can" or "I will" or "I'll try" is an early quit and gives athletes a way out.

3. Personal
    a. Affirmations are your words, which mean something personal to you.
4. Powerful
    a. Action words such as power, strong, explode should be used.
5. Point
    a. Be short and to the point.

Use *Activity 4.5 Effective Use of Affirmations* to develop your understanding of the effective use of guidelines.

Activity 4.5
Effective Use of Affirmations

In column 1, an example affirmation is given. In column 2, there is information on why the affirmation needs improving and in column 3, there is a re-write for an improved affirmation. Read the examples provided in 1-5 and then create your own and fill in columns 2 and 3 for numbers 6-10.

Affirmation Examples	Why it needs improving	Improving the affirmation
1. I will not slow down	Stated in negative terms	I focus on maintaining correct pace
2. I've tried in the past	Turn into present tense	I give a great effort every day.
3. Run faster	Not personal	I run faster and faster every day
4. I jump	Needs more power	I explode off the board.
5. I will get around to it	Get to the point	My training makes me powerful.
6.		
7.		
8.		
9.		
10.		

Now that you have a better understanding of the guidelines to develop affirmations complete *Activity 4.6 My Affirmations*.

Activity 4.6
My Affirmations

Fill in the following chart, listing five affirmations that might apply to your events. In column 1, list your affirmation. Review your affirmation. How could you improve it? List how you could possibly improve your affirmation in column 2. In column 3, rewrite your affirmation to make it better.

Original Affirmation	How to Improve?	Improved Affirmation

You are well on your way to developing good affirmations and improved self-talk. Now let's take a look at the difference between general and specific affirmations. Activity 4.7 gives three examples of general affirmations and three examples of specific affirmations.

In the blank space provided after the examples, list three general affirmations and three specific affirmations. If you become stumped on what affirmations to use you might want to take a look at Table 4.1, which lists several general affirmations.

Activity 4.7 General and Specific Affirmations	
General Affirmations Examples	**Specific Affirmations**
1. I am strong	1. I run off the board
2. I run with power	2. I explode out of the blocks
3. I am relaxed and focused	3. I attack the bar
Your General Affirmations	**Your Specific Affirmations**
1.	1.
2.	2.
3.	3.

Table 4.1 lists several general affirmations. More specific affirmations related to your event are found in the event-by-event chapters.

Table 4.1 General Affirmation Examples
I am **strong.**
I am **relaxed.**
I am **confident** and **ready.**
I am in **control** and **focused.**
I am physically tough and mentally **tough.**
I train **harder** and **smarter** than my opponents.
My **determination** and **drive** makes me a winner.
I accept the **challenge** and the body responds.
My enthusiastic **attitude** makes me great.
I have the **courage** to perform.
My weight training, diet, sleep, and mental training all help me to **perform** better.
When fatigue sets in, I am mentally **tough.**
My form is **fluid, smooth, controlled** and **relaxed.**
I **seize** the moment. I make my own opportunities.
I am always **positive.**
I am willing to do the **extra** things to be great.
I am **fit.**
I am a **competitor.**
My training and attitude make me **great.**
I enjoy training and reaching my **goals.**

Within each affirmation is a powerful word called the cue word. A cue word is a positive word within an affirmation that that is repeated over and over while the body is performing. Cue words can be used to help focus with applying many mental skills such as focus and relaxation while performing a physical skill. In the affirmation, "I am strong," the power word or cue word is "strong." The more often affirmations are repeated, the more noticeable the desired effect. If practiced over a period of time and incorporated into mental skill training, when you repeat the cue word, your mind draws up the image to allow your body to perform at a high level.

A cue word is a word you choose that reminds you of something to focus on. By staying focused on the cue word, the mind doesn't analyze the performance and interfere with it. The mind is only thinking of one thing at a time and the cue word has it occupied.

Example: A 400-meter runner is tying up at the end of a race and starting to slow down. Using a cue word such as "strong" and repeating the cue word over and over during last 100 meters of race, keeps the runner's mind off of focusing on pain.

Important Note: Self-talk must be practiced so habits of positive self-talk can become integrated automatically for performers.

Table 4.1 listed several general affirmations for track and field athletes. Go back and look at Table 4.1 and identify the cue words. Ok- maybe you figured it out, the cue word within the affirmation is in bold print. Within the event specific chapters later in the book, specific event affirmations are provided as examples.

The following chart lists general cue words and specific cue words. As you develop a few affirmations to use and practice, consider using some of these words. After looking at the list of cue words you could use, add five general cue words and five specific cue words.

Activity 4.8 Cue Word List General Cue Words	
Focus	Ok
Calm	Do it
Relax	Control
Tight	Confident
Add five more general cue words 1. _____ 2. _____ 3. _____	4. _____ 5. _____

Specific cue word examples	
Go	Push
Fast	Explode
Run	Catch
Swing	Cast
Up	Steady
Land	Straight
Twist	Leap
Power	Explode
Pull	Stick
Add five more specific cue words 1. _____ 2. _____ 3. _____	4. _____ 5. _____

Self-Confidence Ideas

Positive self-talk is one method to help build self-confidence. Here are several other ideas to consider as you think positive.

1. Preparation: Proper preparation gives you the right to feel confident. You should feel that you deserve to be successful because you have devoted the time and energy and work into being successful. Having a consistent pre-performance routine (which we will cover in Chapter 7) will give you consistent mental confidence.

2. Encouraging environment: When you know that others believe in you, it helps you to believe in yourself. Absorb confidence from coaches, teammates, friends, parents who believe in you. You can play your part to make others better by building confidence in others by complimenting them.

3. Own your success: When you earn it, take credit for your success. Believe that you succeeded because of your ability and effort. You weren't just lucky; you set the stage to be successful. Stay away from saying, "I got lucky." Believe that your actions caused you to succeed and it will lead to future success.

4. Model others: Our confidence can be built when we see others doing the same things, which we are hesitant about attempting. If you see someone else clearing a height in the high jump, you feel confident that you can do it. Although you can gain confidence by modeling others, you should base your overall confidence on your own personal abilities. If you are always comparing yourself to others you will likely lose confidence because there is almost always someone who is more talented than you.

5. Act confidently: Acting confidently helps you to feel more confidence. Hold your head high with good posture, smile, walk and act with confidence and soon you will feel that way.

6. Use the mental skills and drills provided in this book. The drills and skills are structured to provide success in gaining confidence as well as mental skills.
    a. Use of positive affirmations and cue words build confidence.
    b. By learning how to control your proper arousal zone you will build confidence.
    c. Use your mind to mentally recall your past successes.
    d. Use your mind to mentally visualize yourself performing successfully.

Use *Activity 4.9 Building Confidence* to reflect on your past success.

Activity 4.9 Building Confidence
Make a list of your successes with track and field and other areas. Reflect on this success and the effect that the success has had on your present level of confidence. Use this list to remind you of your talent and effort during times you are unsure of yourself.
1.
2.
3.
4.
5.

Now you are starting to understand the importance of being positive and how we can use self-talk to develop a positive mindset. The challenge is figuring out how to maintain that positive attitude and how to keep it when confronted with negative thoughts.

Mentally strong athletes reframe situations in order to perform their best. By using their mental skills, they create a positive mindset that promotes success rather than allowing the situation to dictate how they think and react. Use Activity 4.10 to reframe situations into a positive challenge.

Activity 4.10 Re-frame your Thoughts	
Take the self-defeating thoughts in column 1 that interfere with personal excellence and re-frame those thoughts in column 2. Examine the first five thoughts and use those as examples to provide five thoughts that may self-defeat you and how you can reframe those thoughts.	
Self-Defeating Thoughts	**Re-Framed Thought**
You idiot	Everyone makes mistakes
I have no talent	I can get better if I practice. Good athletes work hard to be successful.
The other athletes are better than me.	You cannot control other athletes, focus on your own abilities.
I'll take it easy today and go hard next time.	Going hard today will make it easier next time.
This hurts, is it worth it?	It hurts, but the rewards are worth it.
1.	
2.	
3.	
4.	
5.	

Activity 4.11 is similar to the re-framing thoughts activity in that it asks you to change limiting factors into strengths. In order to make those changes, add affirmations to reinforce the project.

Activity 4.11 Stinking Thinking
Limiting Factors
Write down five factors that limit you from becoming a great athlete. Example factors might be no kick, not willing to work hard, lack of mental toughness.
1. _____   2. _____   3. _____   4. _____   5. _____
Changing Limiting Factors to Strengths
For each factor listed above, write down what you could do to change the limiting factor into a strength.
1. _____   2. _____   3. _____   4. _____   5. _____

Get Rid of Limiting Factors
Take a pen or maker and cross out what you have written previously under limiting factors. Mark it out, so you cannot read it. You have taken the negative factors that limit you and eliminated them from your life. Now, let's turn our attention to the positive strengths.
Affirmations   For each of the factors listed under Changing Limiting Factors To Strengths write an affirmation that will help you to make a positive change!
1. _____   2. _____   3. _____   4. _____   5. _____
Wrap-up: You can write your limiting factors on a slip of paper. Once you have written your changed factors to strengths, you can make a ceremony out of getting rid of the stinking thinking thoughts. Wad the paper up and slam it into a trash can, or if possible and you can safely do so, burn it!

To continue to work on thinking positive, let's look at identifying the negative and positive thoughts that you have in practice, before a competition, and during a competition. Make sure you examine the differences carefully. If you do not have many positive thoughts, work on changing your negative thoughts into positive ones.

Activity 4.12 **Changing Negative Thoughts to Positive Thoughts**	
Thoughts I have in practice…	
Negative Thoughts	Positive Thoughts
1	1
2	2
3	3
What can I do to change these negative thoughts into positive thoughts?	
Thoughts I have before a track and field meet…	
Negative Thoughts	Positive Thoughts
1	1
2	2
3	3
Read your comments and form a picture of what you say to yourself. Read the positive things and relate them to your performance. How did they help you stay focused and to try harder? Did they make you feel good about your performance? Read the negative thoughts. Were there more negative thoughts than positive? When did the negative thoughts occur? What happened to your focus and your performance when you listened to them? How did they distract, limit, or defeat you?	

In Chapter 6, we will look more at how you can use cue words to re-focus. But for now, to keep developing your mental skills on self-talk, complete Activity 4.13 as an example of using cue words.

Activity 4.13 Self-Talk Exercise: Race lists several specific points in a race. List the cue words that you might use to help stay positive during the race. If you do not participate in the running events, there will be an opportunity in your event chapter later in this book that will cover specific event cue words.

Activity 4.13 **Self-Talk Exercise: Race**	
In the table below, column 1 lists specific points in the race. In column 2, provide positive cue words (such as prepared, ready, strong, control, contact, and drive) you would like to say to yourself before and during each race. See if you can come up with three cue words for each point. Take this sheet and commit your cue words to memory. When you visualize your races, try to incorporate these cue words to make the whole visualization seem more real.	
Specific Points	**Cue Words**
1 hour before the race	
5 minutes before the race	
Start	
First ¼ of the race	
Middle of the race	
The finish	

One of my favorite confidence builders is the confidence card. Actually, I like it more as a confidence re-builder. I often see athletes who work very hard in practice at improving their physical and mental skills. They are confident they have put in the work that has prepared them for a great performance. However, once they arrive at the meet, their confidence begins to quickly dwindle. Suddenly the track looks longer than 400 meters, the opponents look big and fast, and doubt begins to creep into the once-confident athletes. This is the time where the athlete pulls out their confidence card that they have prepared prior and have brought with them. By reading their card and associating it with the mental and physical work that has been practiced, confidence is restored and the athlete can re-focus.

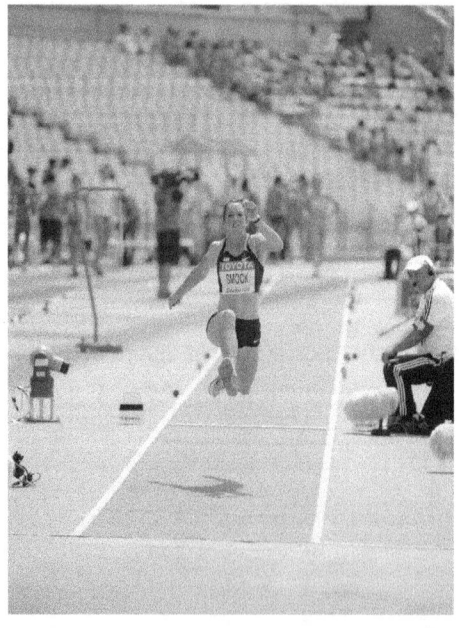

Activity 4.14
Confidence Card

Use a 3" x 5" or 4" x 6" card. Write down on the card three affirmations that give you confidence in your abilities. These should be words that you have visualized and used in practice to succeed. These are you confidence words that you believe in. When you repeat them the feelings of confidence will flow into your body.

If you wish, you can add pictures or color to your card. You might highlight cue words. You may also want to include on your card any other comments that will bring you confidence.

When you feel anxiety and nervousness before a competition or even a practice, take a couple of deep breaths to relax and then take out your card to look at. Take three deep breaths and repeat an affirmation after each one.

Example of Confidence Card:

I am PREPARED

I am STRONG

My POSITIVE attitude makes me a GREAT athlete!

I have worked hard in workouts. I have had some great practices. I will use the same confidence that I use in hard workouts to enable me to succeed today.

I will do my best.

RELAX! BELIEVE! BE A COMPETITOR! SUCCEED!

Another one of my favorite confidence builders is a power picture. A power picture combines the power of a visual image with the positive cue words that are meaningful to you. Activity 4.14 should be a fun and meaningful activity. Use a picture where you are looking good so every time you see it you feel the power!

Activity 4.15
Power Picture

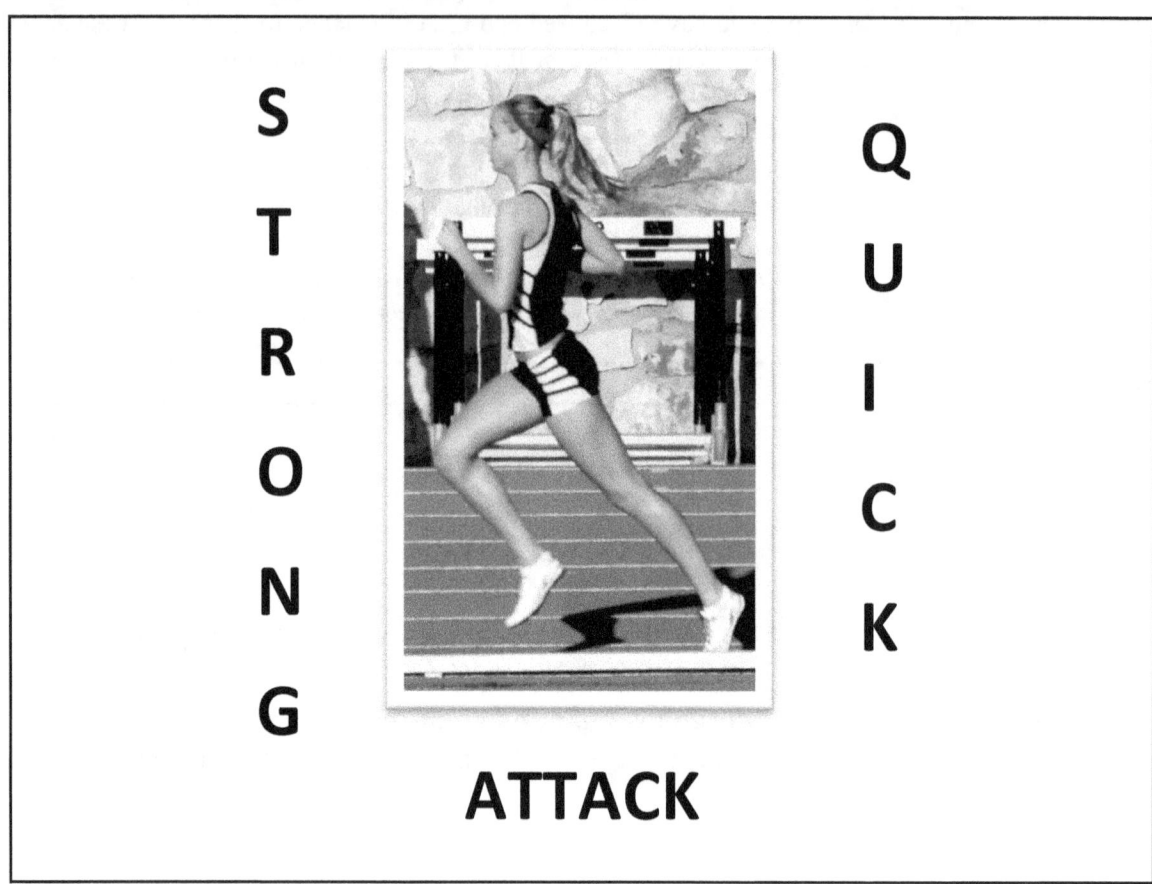

Directions:

Find a good picture of when you are competing. Make sure the picture shows you in good form and looking strong. Put the picture on a page (preferably cardstock paper). Place your cue words around the picture.

When you look at the picture with your cue words surrounding it, you should feel powerful, positive thoughts.

Activity 4.16
I'm Good At

Objective: To realize you are good at many things.

Directions: List 10 things that you are good at. These can be athletic on non-athletic related. After you get 10, go for 20!

1.	11.
2.	12.
3.	13.
4.	14.
5.	15.
6.	16.
7.	17.
8.	18.
9.	19.
10.	20.

For Thought:
Was it difficult to come up with 20 things you are good at?
Why or why not?
Did you find yourself writing down athletic things you were good at when you started the list?

Wrap-up: Often athletes associate their self-worth with how they are performing athletically. When their athletic performance is poor, their self-worth becomes poor. Unfortunately, that can lead to mental health problems. Although it is not the scope of this book to deal with mental problems, realizing that you are good at many things, including things that are not athletic related, will help you to realize you are a well-rounded person. Athletics is only one of the things that you are good at. As you have learned throughout the chapter, it is important to talk to yourself in a positive manner. Activity 4.16 is a sample script that can be used for track and field athletes. I encourage you to use the self-talk script as guide and develop your own personal, meaningful script.

Activity 4.17
Positive Self-Talk Script for a Track and Field Athlete

I like to learn. I like to learn about things I will use the rest of my life, for my family, and for my career. Going to school with a positive learning attitude gives me the opportunity to learn the skills I can use for my lifetime. With all the learning experiences I am receiving, I am confident I will be successful. Although every day is not perfect, I have people to help me. These friends and family care about me and help me to succeed. I enjoy spending time with my friends, but I also enjoy my time alone. This time allows me to relax and think positive. I like who I am and I don't feel the need that I have to impress others.

I like track and field because the challenge makes me feel good. I know the challenges of running, jumping, or throwing will make me better. They will make me stronger and help me become a better track and field athlete. I like to work hard. It makes me successful and I enjoy stepping up and meeting the challenges. I like the satisfaction of knowing that I have given it my all. I enjoy being a role model in practice and leading BY example. I am confident that my hard work and effort also helps my teammates become better. The harder I work, the better I get and the better my teammates get. Although I am busy, I have time to get everything done because I effectively manage my time. I like being busy and accomplishing many things because it makes me a better person.

In this chapter you have analyzed how you talk to yourself. You have learned the guidelines for enhancing self-talk and how to develop powerful affirmations and cue words. You have learned how to re-frame negative thoughts into positive thoughts. To further your mental skills in self-talk you are now able to use mental drills such as the confidence card, the power picture, and positive self-talk script. With an understanding of the power of being positive and the importance of self-talk, you can help improve not only athletic performance but also carry it over to help performance in other areas of your life. And perhaps the best thing about being positive, it is much more enjoyable than being negative!

Remember your attitude determines your altitude. Think positive and fly high!

Chapter 5

Imagery

Imagery is recognized as one of the most useful mental skills in improving athletic performance. It is used by many of the top athletes in the world. However, it is a mental training tool that has not been used to its fullest capacity. In this chapter, you will be introduced to imagery and be provided with evidence that it works! We will discuss how to use imagery effectively and give ideas on how you can implement imagery training.

What is Imagery?

Imagery involves using the senses to re-create or create an experience in one's mind. In a physical skill, athletes experience the action with their bodies. In imagery, athletes experience the action only in their minds. Track and field athletes using imagery do not actually see the track, feel the implement in their hand, the sensation of sprinting, or hear the sound of the starter's gun. However, they do experience all these sensory cues in their mind. Imagery can be used to help you gain "experiences" when you haven't actually "been there before."

In this chapter, we will focus on two types of imagery, mental recall, and mental rehearsal.

Activity 5.1 **Eating a Lemon**
In your mind, see a lemon. Notice the bright yellow color of the lemon; see how smooth and shiny it is. Pick up the lemon and feel it in your hands…slide your fingers over the smooth skin of the lemon…feel the texture of the lemon. Lift the lemon to your face and breathe in that lemon smell. Now slice the lemon open, see the bright yellow flesh exposed and see the juice run out. Smell the lemony citrus aroma filing the room. You cut a slice and put it into your mouth…bite down on it…and feel the juice run over your tongue and your mouth fills with sour lemon juice.
For Thought: Were you able to clearly visualize the experience of a lemon in your mind?
Wrap-up: Recalling eating the lemon recalls your distinctive reaction to your past experiences with a lemon and your body responds with a conditioned reflex. The Eating a Lemon visualization exercise demonstrates that words have a profound physical effect on the body.

Mental Recall

Mental recall is a stage where you recall one of your best performances ever. It involves visualizing in as much detail as you can a day when everything worked perfectly and you were in the flow! Mental recall puts you in a strong, positive frame of mind.

Mental Rehearsal

Mental rehearsal previews the upcoming performance. You visualize the upcoming performance in as much detail as possible. You are in control as you guide the mind. Use a positive frame of mind and see yourself being successful. Visualize different situations. When you visualize performance, you are laying down a neuromuscular blueprint. For example, if you were visualizing an 800-meter track and field race, you might see yourself arriving at the track, feel your nerves, hear the crowd, see the opponents, and see yourself warming up. Visualize in as much detail as you can (always being positive.) See yourself getting off to a good start, maintaining pace, keeping contact, surging, pushing through the comfort zone, and your kick. See yourself after the race receiving congratulations from fellow athletes, coaches, and parents. Feel that intrinsic feeling of a job well done.

We will cover both mental recall and mental rehearsal in more detail in the chapter, but first, more information on imagery.

Imagery is creating or recreating an experience in the mind. Imagery is similar to a real sensory experience (seeing, feeling, hearing), with the entire experience occurring in the mind. Our minds can imagine events that have not yet occurred. Imagery should involve as many senses as possible. The kinesthetic, auditory, tactile and olfactory senses are all potentially important. The kinesthetic sense is particularly important to athletes because it involves the feeling of body position and movement that arise from the stimulation of sensory nerve endings in muscles, joints, and tendons. By using more than one sense, you can create more vivid images. Learning to use cue words to attach various emotional states or moods to our imagined experiences is also important. Creating positive thoughts through imagery can help with the key mental skills of confidence and focus.

Before we get further into the development of your imagery skills, let's assess where you are now.

Activity 5.2 **Sensory Checklist**
This is an exercise designed to help you integrate your senses into your imagery. Rate your ability to create each of the following images in your mind on a scale of 1-10.
Scale: 0 = No image   5 = Some image   10 = Very clear image
1. The place you are currently in   ____   2. Tasting a juicy lemon   ____   3. The clothes you will wear in practice   ____   4. The last track you competed at   ____   5. The feeling at the end of an exhausting workout   ____   6. Practicing or competing on a very cold, windy day   ____   7. The applause of spectators   ____   8. The anticipation and anxiety before your event   ____   9. Tasting your favorite food   ____   10. Performing a drill related to your event   ____

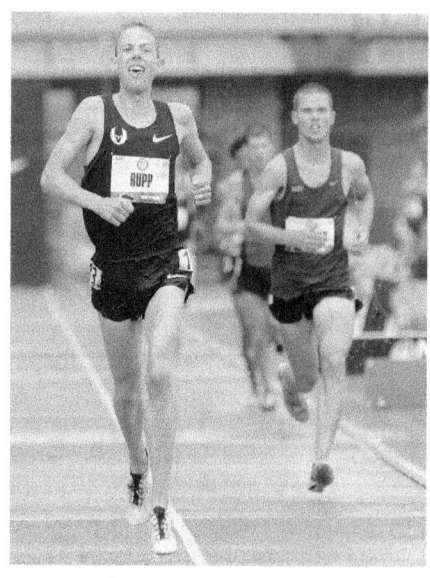

Does it Work?

Scientific research has supported the value of imagery in learning and performing motor skills. (Feltz and Landers 1983, Murphy 1994, Murphy and Martin 2002). In 1990, 90% of Olympic Athletes used some form of imagery, with 97% stating that it helped their performance. 94% of the athletes used imagery during their training sessions with 20% using it every practice session. Orlick and Partington (1988) reported that 99% of Canadian Olympians used imagery. Woolfork, Parrish and Murphy (1985) have shown that positive imagery is associated with significantly better performance than negative imagery.

Imagery is often viewed as mysterious or magical. How can something that takes place only in the mind and 'between your ears,' make a difference? Every imagery experience has personal meaning to the individual that no one else can fully understand.

Even our simplest experiences such as hearing a song on the radio often recalls memories and feelings because our experiences are stored in a web of interrelated memories (such as where we were when we first heard the song or the feelings we experience with listening to the song). An important feature of imagery is that it tends to have more associations than other cognitive processes. For example, psychologists have shown that people's memory for a list of unfamiliar words is much greater if they are asked to create an image of each word than if they are asked to speak the word aloud. The image creates more association for learning the word than saying the word. A cognitive template for a movement pattern is likely to be better remembered during competition if it is imagery-based rather than offered as a set of verbal instructions. The many associations of imagery are a benefit when used to improve performance, but they also make imagery more complex and difficult to understand.

Activity 5.3 **Imagery Association**		
In column one there is an experience that you have associated memories with. For each experience list some associated memories in column two and in column three list why it is a strong memory.		
	Associated Memories	**Why a strong memory?**
Least Favorite Foods		
Mom		
Favorite Song		

Every athlete has a personal history, experience, fears and beliefs that color the interpretation of the image so that no two people will have the same experience, even if a script is exactly the same.

Imagery and physical practice

Researchers have suggested that imagining a sport skill immediately prior to performance helps by "priming" the movement, that is, the cognitive template is readied and is immediately available for activation. This pre-performance rehearsal is likely to benefit the athlete by increasing confidence and concentration. Imagery is not only a useful approach for learning new athletic skills but is also necessary for maintaining skilled performance. Once we gain a cognitive template for the skill, activating that template regularly helps maintain the skill.

Imagery can be used to develop and plan a strategy that will help make quick effective decisions. The great advantage of imagery for planning tactics and strategies is that it allows the athlete to try several approaches to the same problem to sense and feel which one feels right. Imagery can combat the negative effects of competitive anxiety on performance. Anxiety can be reduced by imaging a calm, peaceful, scenario and reducing the sympathetic nervous system arousal.

Imagery can help you set goals and fuel the motivation to achieve them. Imagery is closely related to goal setting because it aids in the selection of both direction and intensity of effort. Images of far-off goals bring them close and positive images may also serve as secondary reinforcers of effort and persistence. Repeated imagery may help bridge the gap between long-range and short-range goals, bringing the desired goal closer and motivating you to work hard in order to achieve it. Process-oriented athletes imagine themselves making constant progress, setting personal bests, and mastering difficult challenges. They want to see that image of a better, improved athlete becoming a reality, which serves as motivation to work hard, seek feedback and make necessary adjustments. Although successful performance is the greatest influence on confidence, vicarious experience-imagining success or watching someone else achieve success is also a consistent source of confidence.

A mentally skilled person who is good at imagery uses all of the senses to create an effective image. These senses would be visual, kinesthetic, hearing, and smell. The most commonly used are visual and kinesthetic.

Imagery can also be divided into internal or external imagery. Internal imagery refers to imagery of the execution of a skill from your own vantage point. It's as if you had a camera on your head, you are seeing it just the way you would see it through your own eyes as if you performed the skill. There is a large emphasis on the kinesthetic feel. For example, if you are a shot putter, you might feel the fingers gripping the shot.

In external imagery, you view yourself from the perspective of an outsider. It's like you are watching yourself in a movie. There is little emphasis on the kinesthetic feel because you are just watching yourself perform.

Which is better, internal or external imagery? Well, the research is indecisive. Most Olympic athletes indicate they use both internal and external imagery. The imagery may be task specific. Internal imagery may be better for performance of skills that depend heavily on perception and anticipation for successful execution. External imagery may be superior on activities that depend on form.

The nature of the task and the skill level of the performer affect the extent to which imagery will enhance performance. Novice and highly skilled performers who use imagery on cognitive tasks show the most positive effects. Imagery is a skill, and therefore, the vividness and controllability of your imagery can be improved with practice

Uses of Imagery

Imagery can be successfully used for a variety of situations. In this book, we have covered several mental skills that are essential to being a mentally skilled athlete. Seeing yourself in the proper arousal zone can be done through the use of imagery, as well as helping with further development of proper use of positive self-talk and cue words. In the next chapter, we will talk about how to achieve, maintain, and improve focus.

Athletes who are high in confidence use more mastery imagery and arousal imagery and have better ability with kinesthetic and visual imagery than athletes with low confidence. Perhaps the best known use of mental imagery is to acquire and practice sports skills. Athletes can practice many skills in their minds as well as acquiring and practice strategy through imagery. Mental imagery has shown to be a valuable tool in coping with pain and injury. It can speed up recovery of the injured area and keep skills from deteriorating, as you can image doing practice drills and performing the activity. Mental practice may also be a valuable tool in helping to prevent overuse injuries. By using a combination of physical and mental practice, physical overuse of the body can be reduced. I think we would all agree that injuries are no fun.

We often think of injuries from the physical standpoint. However, they can also be very challenging mentally. As an active, healthy athlete playing at the top of your game, you are self-confident. Your coaches, teammates, and friends support you daily in practice and games. Now imagine becoming injured. Suddenly your regular physical activity is taken away. You feel like you can no longer contribute to the team. You may feel alone and separated from the team. When you need the most support for your confidence, you may get it the least from the team. How ironic that when you needed less support for your confidence when you were at the top of your game, you received it the most.

Imagery Guidelines

1. Use all senses. See in vivid color, hear the sounds, smell the smells, feel the equipment as you touch it or the track underneath you. Develop control of your imagery skills and visualize positive outcomes. Good imagers use all of their senses to make their images as vivid and detailed as possible. It is important to recreate or create as closely as possible the actual experience in your mind. Things to focus on might include: environment, layout of facilities, surface, spectators, and closeness. Try to feel the anxiety, concentration, frustration, exhilaration or anger associated with your performance.
Hint: If you have trouble getting clear, vivid images, first try to imagine things that are familiar to you such as the furniture in the room. Then use your practice facilities.

2. You will want to master control of your imagery skills. For example, high jumpers may have difficulty visualizing a perfect jump by seeing themselves missing a jump. Or they see positive imagery in practice, but more negative imagery in competition. Research studies have shown that positive imagery is associated with significantly better performance than negative imagery. Telling yourself not to imagine something that you don't want to do will in fact make it more likely that you will imagine it, resulting in a decrement in performance (remember the *Do Not Think of Pizza* activity in Chapter 1). Work toward visualizing exactly what you want to perform every time.

3. Use both internal and external imagery. Both types are effective, and you will have to determine which part works best for you.

4. Practice imagery regularly. Practice makes permanent. Make it a part of your practice routine so it is as natural as physical activity. Using imagery consistently will allow it to work for you.

5. Practice imagery in a relaxed state when you are initially learning the skill of imagery.
Relaxation can clear your mind of distractions so you can concentrate on your imagery skills. Highly skilled people can perform imagery anywhere. However, for beginners it's best to practice in a situation with no distractions. You could practice before going to sleep, during a break, or in the locker room. As your imaging skills improve, you will be able to use imagery amid distractions and in competition. When you are in a relaxed state of mind, your mind accepts things more readily. A good analogy of this would be if we were both in a room and suddenly I started yelling, "Fire! Fire!" and ran out of the room. Would you follow me? Chances are you would listen for the fire alarm, and look and smell for smoke. In a conscious, rational mind, and seeing no signs of a fire, you probably would think I am crazy. However, if I frantically knocked on your door at 3:00 a.m. yelling, "Fire! Fire!" while you were in a very relaxed state of mind (subconscious), you would sprint out of your house in your pajamas. Why? Because in a rational mind, your mind likes the status quo. It doesn't like change. In the relaxed subconscious mind, our mind accepts things as if they were true. So in a relaxed state, when we use our affirmations

or visualize things that we have not accomplished yet, our minds do not know the difference between the real and the imagined.

6. Develop coping strategies through imagery. Visualize an unexpected event and how to cope with it. More on this later in the chapter.

7. Use cues or triggers to help your imagery rehearsal. Cues can help athletes focus on imagery strategies. For instance, on the vault, a cue might be 'power' or 'push.' You can experiment with words that make your imagery more powerful.

8. Practice kinesthetic imagery to make your imagery more effective. Practice actually feeling the sensations in your body as you perform on each event. Feel your muscles, feel your hands sweat, feel your movement of the skill. Many world-class high jumpers close their eyes and visualize the jump. You may even see their slight body movements as they go through their mental rehearsal as they mentally practice what they are feeling.

Activity 5.4 You are in Control
1. Imagine working on a specific skill that has given you trouble in the past.
2. Notice what you are doing wrong.
3. Now see and feel yourself performing that skill perfectly.
4. Think about a troublesome competitive situation in the past. See yourself being positive and performing in the clutch.

Use imagery logs to help track how you will use imagery. When you learn new skills, you can monitor your progress by having a written record. Determine how you will use imagery and keep tabs on what you do, how much you do, and when you do it. You can look back and see your progress.

Activity 5.5 Imagery Log				
Date	Time	Describe Imagery	Practice Time	Success
3/25	1:30 pm	Practiced 10 high jumps	5 min	A little trouble seeing clearances

Most people can see images but the rest of the senses can be more difficult to experience. Use *Activity 5.6 Sensory Imagery* to help improve using all your senses. An example using the shot put is provided. More specific examples are presented in the event-by-event chapters.

Activity 5.6
Sensory Imagery

Directions: Close your eyes and imagine in as much detail as possible.
Vividness: Imagine a shot put. Notice the dull gray color. Notice it may have some dirt or chalk on it. Notice how round it is.
Auditory: What sounds do you hear while you are getting ready to throw?
Tactile: Imagine holding a shot put. What does it feel like? Notice its shape and roundness. Feel how heavy the shot feels as you rotate the ball in your hand. Note how hard the shot feels as you squeeze it.
Kinesthetic: Imagine throwing the shot during warm-ups. Feel what your body is doing during the throwing. Feel the muscles in your leg moving as you move into the power position, feel the muscles in your shoulder and arms as you bring the ball forward. Note the tempo and rhythm of the throwing motion. Do a couple of power position throws with or without holding the shot, but do not actually throw the shot.
Smell: Smell the shot, the field, the grass, the dust from the landing sector. Smell the sweat after a hard practice.
Taste: Taste the salt from the sweat on your lips. Imagine taking a drink of water during a hot day of practice.
Emotion: Experience the confidence you feel when you step into the ring. Experience the satisfaction of throwing far. Experience the pride you feel in achieving a PR. Experience the excitement of being on a successful team.
Vividness Evaluation What were the strongest images and sensations? What senses do you need to improve?
Follow-up: Certain senses may produce clearer attention than others. Use this exercise to provide direction for extra attention and practices.

The ability to visualize includes the ability to dream of accomplishing goals. Use *Activity 5.7 Sports Headline* to write your own story.

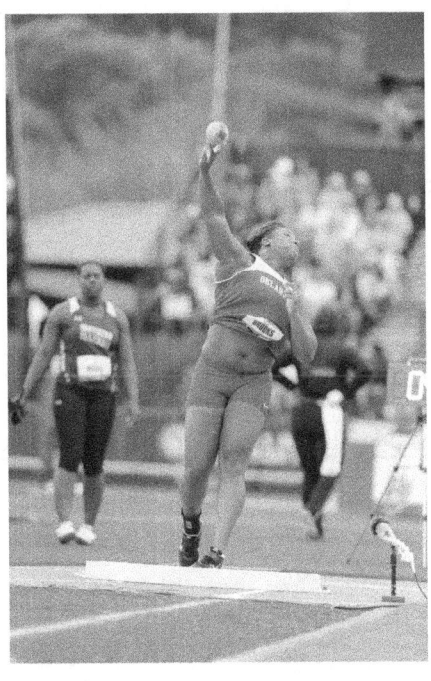

Activity 5.7
Sports Headline
Imagine the local newspaper reporter is at the next track meet. You have a great meet and as soon as you are done competing the reporter rushes up to you to interview you about your outstanding performance. Create the sports headline and write the story of what will run on the front page of the sports section. Headline:_____ _____ Story:_____ _____ _____ _____
Variations: (1) Type the report up, (2) add a picture to the story, (3) add an action picture if possible

Making vivid images that you control are extremely important as a performance enhancement tool. You control the image and see what you want to see happen. Use *Activity 5.8 Control the Outcome* and *Activity 5.9 Imaging Track and Field Skills* to gain control of your vision.

Activity 5.8
Control the Outcome
1. Approach a track and field competition arena where you have competed and have vivid memories. Imagine how you want to be feeling: What I want to be saying to myself:
2. Imagine yourself at varying times before competition. How I want to be feeling: What I want to be saying to myself:
3. Imagine yourself during competition How I want to be feeling: What I want to be saying to myself:
4. Imagine yourself after competition: How I want to be feeling: What I want to be saying to myself:
Controlling the imagery at times may become difficult. You may see images of what typically happens rather than what you want to happen. As it is counterproductive to image scenes you cannot control and which will lead to undesirable outcomes, stop the imagery. Rewind or repeat the imagery and start over.

Activity 5.9
Imaging Track and Field Skills

As you refine your ability to image with all of your senses, it is important to use imagery to see yourself performing your track and field event. Work through the progression at your own pace. If you can't image yourself performing sports skills right now, keep working on your practice situation and movement imagery until they are vivid and controllable.

1. Imagine you are at the venue where you usually practice.

Use your imaging skills to see your practice environment. Look around the area and imagine in as much detail as possible:

- Feel the track or your event area under your feet
- Imagine yourself in your practice gear
- Imagine yourself holding and using the implements

What are some other things you can incorporate into this image form where you practice?
- a.
- b.

2. Movement Imagery

Feel yourself:
- Walk around the track
- Run around the track
- Do some warm-up stretches
- Take warm-up throws, or jumps, or runs

See other skill movements in your events (i.e., start, finish)

Follow-up:
- What was easy to image?
- What was hard to image?
- Did you have a hard time using one sense or another?
- Could you see some things and not others?

Homework for Later: Practice the images that were harder to create.

Creating imagery and associating with the actual experience is a vital link that can be accomplished with practice. Use *Activity 5.10 Act Like* to help complete that link

Activity 5.10
Act Like
Creating a specific image (object, animal, person) can aid in your creation of images. In the following space pick a skill you are working on in practice and choose an image to pair with that skill. **Examples:** **Skill:** Running relaxed and fast **Image:** Gazelle **Affirmation:** I run like a gazelle. **Skill:** Throwing **Image:** Dynamite **Affirmation:** I explode like dynamite.
Skill: **Image:** **Affirmation**: How will this image help?
Skill: **Image:** **Affirmation:** How will this image help?
Skill: **Image:** **Affirmation** How will this image help?

Instant replay gives us the ability to see an event over and over. *Activity 5.11 Rewind It* asks you to see an image over and over to get a clearer picture of it.

Activity 5.11
Rewind It
Imagine yourself performing your event for 30 seconds. It can be helpful when you're having difficulty controlling your imagery to slow it down, in which you see and feel yourself performing in slow motion, frame by frame. As you gain imagery control in slow motion, you can progressively increase the speed of your imagery until you are able to perform at real speed. When you see a mistake or think negative thoughts, rewind your image and play that part over. Watch yourself performing on an actual video then immediately close your eyes and reproduce the video images. As the visual image of how you perform becomes clearer, put away the video for a while and repeat the accurate visual images of your performances. If the image starts to fade, return to the video until you're able to see yourself perform consistently. This exercise will help you ingrain an accurate image of how you perform.

In Chapter 2, the focus was on achieving your proper arousal by using relaxation techniques. Imagery can be a valuable tool for achieving relaxation or energization to achieve the proper arousal level. Try *Activity 5.12 Using Imagery for Relaxation* to achieve a relaxed state of mind.

Activity 5.12
Using Imagery for Relaxation
You can effectively calm yourself down by using your imagination to mentally take yourself to a calm, safe place. Sit quietly, close your eyes, and imagine yourself going to a totally relaxing place like a favorite beach, mountainside, woods, or vacation spot. Experience yourself comfortably enjoying this place in as much detail as possible, seeing, hearing, and feeling everything that you would as if you were actually there. Allow yourself to stay in this calming place for 5 – 10 minutes at a time until you feel calm, relaxed and in control.
Regular "visits" to this mental "relaxation room" will make it available to you under pressure, right before that big competition and right before your event. However, if you never consistently practice this exercise at home when you're completely relaxed, then you'll find that it won't be "open" and available for you when you need it the most.

Activity 5.13 Mentally Recalling a Great Performance is an example of a mental recall. It involves recalling an event when you were at your best. Since you have already achieved what you are about to visualize, you do not need to be in a relaxed state.

Activity 5.13
Mentally Recalling a Great Performance

Think of one of your best performances ever. It may be in track and field or it could be in something else, such as singing or giving a speech. Recall a time when you felt so good and everything came together perfectly. Recall it in as much detail as possible.

Performance #1
Where were you at?
_____
_____

What were you doing?
_____
_____

How did you feel?
_____
_____

Why do you think you performed so well that day?
_____
_____

Performance #2
Where were you at?
_____
_____

What were you doing?
_____
_____

How did you feel?
_____
_____

Why do you think you performed so well that day?
_____
_____

The above activity should have been fun as you recalled when you performed at your best. One of the major focuses of this book is to get you into the "zone" or "flow" of what you just recalled. With mental imagery skills, your odds of getting in the "zone" are greatly increased.

Mental rehearsal previews the upcoming performance in as much detail as possible. Since you want your mind to readily accept something that has not happened, you should do some relaxation exercises to achieve a relaxed state. Remember you are in control as you guide the mind.

Activity 5.14
Goal Achievement Visualization

Begin to think of a time in our life when you were "right on" and performed perfectly. See yourself at that time... notice what you look like, what you are wearing, who is with you, what sounds are around you. Feel the environment and the energy. Begin to see yourself doing whatever it was you did when you knew you were right on... when everything worked perfectly... when you were in complete control and at your peak... Feel that feeling as you watch yourself and connect with all the feelings you experienced as you achieved at your highest level... perfectly...competently... exactly the way you wanted to. What did it feel like... sound like... look like...Let it all come back to you... let it in... know it again... the joy... the power... the pride and confidence ... the completeness... the rush of knowing you were perfection... let it become part of you...part of your spirit...part of your being. Fully connect with it.

Now give yourself a word or short phrase that brings all these feelings, pictures and sounds into focus, a word or phrase that completely connects you with that time and those feelings when you knew you were perfect and right on...say the word or words to yourself several times... slowly allow yourself to experience your sense of power ... feel it in your whole body.

Think of your goal... what you want to achieve now... the importance it has for you... Remember how it felt to write it down and see it on paper. Begin to see yourself preparing to accomplish this goal. Where are you? What do you look like? Are there other people there to assist you? How will they assist you? Begin to go for your goal... feel yourself starting... moving toward your goal... toward your personal fulfillment. Give yourself permission to have it just the way you want it to be.... See it perfectly as you move closer and closer to your goal... feel that excitement and rush that comes with doing something well...flawlessly and with control...Connect with your excellence as you reach and attain this important goal... let yourself have it...feel it...see it...know it completely... Say your special word or phrase... know those feelings... that power ... see your peak performance... exactly the way you want it to be.

Each event chapter will contain a rehearsal script specific to your event. However, I encourage you to make your own personalized rehearsal script. *Activity 5.15 Personalized Rehearsal* gives ideas on how you can write your own script.

Activity 5.15
Personalized Rehearsal

Objective:
To write a personalized guided mental script.

In your own words, write a mental rehearsal of an upcoming performance. This visualization will let you see, hear, and feel yourself performing your sport.

Directions:
Write a personalized guided visualization script. Be as specific as possible. Include as many senses you can. Write it down as full and complete as you can. Remember to use positive statements and include your affirmations. Use the worksheet to formulate your ideas. Then, write out your guided visualization in an essay format. After writing the visualization, I would encourage you to record the script. Find a quiet time to play some relaxation music and then play your recorded script. As you talk to yourself, see the visualization coming to life!

Worksheet for your guided visualization

Preparation Period
    See yourself in the preparation phase leading up to the event
    What have you done well?
    Think of some of your best workouts
    Focusing on your goal and the outcome you wish to achieve

Day of the Event
    See yourself getting up in the morning with confidence
    What will you have to eat?
    See yourself dressing for the competition, putting on your clothing

Arriving at the Site
    See yourself arriving at the site
    See the competition
    See the environment, weather, temperature
    Focus on your goal and the outcome you wish to achieve

The Warm-up
    See yourself doing your general warm-up
    See yourself stretching, drills
    See yourself doing your final preparations
    See yourself putting on your competition shoes

First part
    See yourself at the beginning of your event
    Hear the start of the event
    See yourself performing well, just the way you want to

The Middle
    See yourself right where you want to be
    See yourself in perfect position
    Feel yourself under control and on top of your game
    Feel yourself competing

The Finish
    Although fatigued, you feel confident
    Think of all the workouts that have prepared you for this
    Focus on your form and affirmations
    See yourself finishing strong

> Post Event
>   Feel the satisfaction of a job well done
>   See teammates, coaches, family and friends congratulating you
>   As you cool down, you feel good about your performance
>
> As you go through your rehearsal keep these guidelines in mind.
>
> 1. Take your time to enjoy, to learn to experience each movement and moment.
> 2. As you arrive at the event go through your normal preparatory routine and the few minutes before you perform.
> 3. Go into vivid detail about the event and your experience of it, including sounds, colors, smells, the crowd, the weather, the positive feelings in your body and your mental state.
> 4. Imagine yourself being totally relaxed, confident, powerful and in complete control of your body and mind.
> 5. Include your affirmation and key words that will help you during your real performance.
> 6. Go through your whole event thinking of each significant point. Feel yourself moving smoothly and perform with strength and endurance.
> 7. Write your rehearsal in script form, reread it and edit it. Then dictate it to yourself or have someone else dictate to your recorder.
> 8. Listen to the recorded rehearsal for flaws and make changes to the script.
> 9. Dictate a progressive relaxation section that you feel will relax you effectively before the visualization.
> 10. Listen to the finished audio frequently.

You should practice imagery in many different places and positions. You will want to spend time developing your imagery skills in quiet, less distracting settings, but once you become proficient at imagery, you should engage in it in many different settings. You should be able to engage in imagery in the locker room, at the track and field area, during practice, during competition, or any type of setting. I encourage you to mentally practice your event skill by walking through and moving your body in ways that match the different segments of your images. You may want to hold implements in your hand to facilitate your images. Repeat your imagery triggers to yourself to cue into the perfect response.

Once you have developed basic imagery skills, your goals are to build imagery into your daily routine. Incorporate it into practice and then competition. If you execute a skill well, take a moment to form an image of the execution and etch it into your mind. Use your imagery before practice to see yourself accomplishing the goals for the practice session. Imagery practice must be systematic. Imagery is most effective when practiced on a continual basis, not just the day before and the day of the competition. Initially, you will use imagery to focus on physical skills and strategies. Eventually, you should be able to use imagery to develop your mental skills such as focus, positive self-talk, and achieving the proper arousal zone.

Imagery is ideal to use in track and field because athletes can use it between events and between attempts to create optimal arousal levels. I encourage you to keep an imagery log to assess your improvement, with the goal of increasing your vividness and your ability to control the image.

Now that you know what imagery is and have become more aware of how it can improve performance, it should be viewed as an integral part of your training experience.

Chapter 6

Focus

How many times have you been told to "just focus?" Doesn't that sound easy? You get your game face on, stare intently, and try even harder to focus. But the harder you try, the more elusive an effective state of focus becomes. Focus skills are extremely important for achieving athletic excellence. However, it is just like the rest of the mental skills we have discussed thus far; it must be practiced through drills to develop the skills. Just check the post-game interviews of coaches and you will often hear the comments, "we weren't focused" or "we weren't mentally strong." Whose fault is it if the athlete is not focused? Has the athlete had the opportunity to practice focus and thereby improve the skill of focus? In this chapter, we will take a look at how important focus is, how to obtain focus and sustain focus over time.

Let's start off by doing *Activity 6.1 Catching Markers* to illustrate the important of knowing what to focus on.

Activity 6.1
Catching Markers

You will need 10 different colored magic markers to try the following "focus test." Your task is to throw all 10 markers up at the same time above your head and try to catch as many as possible. It is important that when you attempt to catch them, you only use your hands and your hands must be away from your body (no trapping the markers against your body). Now, throw all 10 up at the same time.

How many did you catch?

If you do this correctly without cheating, then like most people, you probably only caught 1 or 2 at most. Does that mean your ability to focus is very low? Absolutely not! This is an impossible task because there are too many things to focus on all at once. The fact of the matter is: YOU CAN ONLY CONCENTRATE ON ONE THING WELL AT A TIME. While you can focus on many things at once, when it comes down to peak performance, you can only focus on one thing well at a time. You better make sure that the one thing you are focusing on is WHAT'S IMPORTANT!

Now, pick one special marker in your group of 10 to focus on. For example, let's say the red one. Take that marker, stick it in the middle of the other 9 and throw all 10 up once again at the same time. Remember, you are focusing on catching only the one red marker.

What happened?

If you didn't catch the red marker the first time, try it again. If you have relatively decent hand-eye coordination, then you'll be able to catch that red marker.

As demonstrated in the above activity, our senses are continually bombarded with stimuli. We continuously have internal stimuli such as being hungry, tired, or our numerous thoughts. We often have external stimuli such as people talking or a radio or television playing in the background. It is impossible to become aware of all the sensory information coming into the central nervous system. Once you notice certain sensory information, you must decide what action to take and that process requires focus.

The ability to block out distractors is called focus. Focus involves perceiving sensory information and using it to make decisions and choose responses. The key to focus is to focus on task-relevant stimuli and ignore all others. Imagine how difficult it is to block out all distraction under normal conditions. Now imagine how much harder it is with a stadium full of fans yelling. To compound the problem of focus, the cues an athlete needs to focus on can often change very quickly. Thus athletes must be able to switch focus depending on the demands of the task.

Success in track and field requires the ability to focus your attention on the task. Unfortunately, you can't force focus. The harder you try to focus, the more frustrated you become. To focus, you need to relax and feel confident. Then you need to acquire the ability to block out distraction and become absorbed in the moment of what you are doing. How do you develop focus? Through much practice it becomes permanent. Different events require different types of attention. Robert Nideffer explains the Attentional Dimensions Theory as occurring along two dimensions: width (broad or narrow) and direction (internal or external).

Attentional width refers to how many stimuli athletes need to attend to at any given moment. Attentional direction refers to the athlete focusing inward on thought or outward on events happening around him or her. A broad attentional focus is needed when the runner analyzes the situation to decide when to begin the kick to the finish. A narrow focus is needed when a high jumper begins the approach. An internal attentional focus is important for analyzing what is happening in the event, planning strategy, and reading one's body. An external focus is needed in order to assess a situation and execute sport skills and strategies. Attentional width can be broad or narrow. A broad attention focus involves being sensitive to many things that are going on around you. A narrow attentional focus involves focusing directly in front of you and knocking out your peripheral vision. Attentional direction can be internal or external. An internal attentional focus involves focusing on your own feelings or thoughts. An external attentional cue involves focusing outwardly to other things and people around you.

Consider a runner in an 800-meter race. At the starting line, the runner needs an internal focus to mentally rehearse as he/she walks to the line. Once the gun goes off, the runner must shift to a broad external focus to gauge their speed compared to other runners to be able to place themselves where they want at the cut-in. To pass someone, the focus shifts to the person that will be passed. Another example of shifting focus would be the 300/400 hurdler who uses a broad internal to focus on stride lengths, wind, track conditions, and pace. The hurdler uses a broad external to assess other competitors and a narrow internal for personal race judgment and effort distribution.

A skilled athlete is able to shift on demand among these different attentional styles. Most track and field athletes cannot shift attentional focus this easy and will benefit dramatically from practicing concentration skills.

Some examples of attentional dimension are provided in Table 6.1 to help understand how dimensional attention works.

		Table 6.1 Attentional Dimensions Example		
	Broad		**Broad**	
Internal	You decide to pass when the pace slows		Realize situation for final attempt	**External**
Internal	Check arousal level and use cue words		See the shot flying through the air	**External**
	Narrow		**Narrow**	

Activity 6.2
Concentration Exercise

Practice these exercises on a daily basis for a couple of weeks. Do at least 10 minutes of the previous exercise everyday as your sport psychology homework. How else will you get better if you don't practice?

1. Listen to outside sounds (Broad External): Lie down with eyes closed and just concentrate on the sounds in the environment. (3 minutes)
2. Broad Internal: Monitor sounds of your body: Lie on your back with your eyes closed and fingers in your ears. Focus on all the sounds of the body- growling of stomach, breathing, heartbeat, etc. (2 minutes)
3. Narrow Internal: Flowing thoughts. Lie down and pay particular attention to thoughts that your mind brings to the surface. Perform this with a passive attitude. Recognize the thoughts and allow them to come into and leave the mind at your own pace. (2 minutes)
4. Narrow External: Study an object. Take a small object that can be manipulated in the hand (such as a coin, paper clip, ring) and focus internally on this object. If the mind begins to wander, refocus on the object. Each time you perform this exercise, change the object. (5 minutes)
5. Pick a problem (Narrow Internal): Pick an issue and ask your mind to give you as many solutions as it can. As the mind presents each solution, place it into a bubble and allow it to slowly flow away. Quietly wait on the next solution to appear. (5 minutes)
6. Narrow Internal: Listen to your own heartbeat. Close eyes while in a comfortable position and listen to your heartbeat. Attempt to hear nothing but your own heart beating. (3 minutes)

Activity 6.3
Learn to Focus

1. Take some time and focus on your breathing. See how long you can be aware of your inhalations and exhalations and the movement of your chest without allowing your mind to wander.
2. Pay attention to sounds around you. Notice any voices or noises in your environment. Focus on the noise you hear.
3. Focus on how your body feels. Feel your arms, head, neck, shoulders, stomach, and legs. Notice the feeling of the chair you are sitting in or the pressure of the floor you are standing on.
4. Now attend to your emotions and thoughts. Again, see how long you can maintain focus without your mind wandering.
5. Now choose an object in your environment and look at it. Focus on this object. Now shift your focus to what is happening around you. Shift back to the object. Can you easily shift focus?

In the early stages of learning a skill, you use controlled processing. This requires conscious focus to a full awareness of the actions involved in the skill. This focus is slow, deliberate, and attention demanding, as you are inexperienced at this activity. However, after numerous hours of practice, you develop the ability to perform basic skills automatically, without a lot of conscious thought. This automatic processing is called skill automaticity. This is the focus that occurs during a "flow state" experience. Because automatic processing is not attention demanding, it allows performers to focus on other tasks while executing basic skills and to do several tasks at the same time. Not only do you perform basic skills without conscious thoughts, you will also be able to make smart decisions automatically.

The challenge becomes in recognizing when the attentional system is overloaded (i.e. you have too many markers in the air—Activity 6.1). Here are three tips to help prevent attentional overload.

Simplify the skill when first learning a skill. Use appropriate developmental skill progressions or divide complex skills into meaningful components. For example, in the high jump, a beginning athlete may be thinking of many things, including hitting the bar. Sometimes the bar hurts or it is embarrassing to miss. By jumping without the bar or using a bungee cord, the athlete has reduced the attentional requirements of that event.

Simplify the strategy. For example, if a thrower is having a hard time getting into the proper power position, consider eliminating part of the approach to start in the power position.

Overlearn and automate fundamental skills. As you overlearn skills, rather than thinking about how to execute the skill, you can become more aware of what is around you.

Activities 6.4, 6.5, and 6.6 will illustrate the importance of your thoughts and begin to get you thinking about how you will direct your thoughts to improve your focus.

Activity 6.4   **Quiet Your Mind**
For the next minute, think about nothing. Empty your mind of all thoughts.   **For thought:** How did this work?   **Wrap-up:** It is impossible to completely empty the mind. However, we do have some control over the thoughts that enter our mind and we can direct those thoughts into positive thoughts by using such mental skills as triggers and releases.

Activity 6.5   **Focus On What You Can Do**
Picture your home track and field venue in your mind. See the familiar place you practice or have meets at. Now, the challenge is for you to tell yourself to NOT think about a wild lion standing in the middle of the track infield. Again, do not see the wild lion that escaped from the zoo and is standing in the infield.   **For Thought:** What did you think about? Chances are you thought about the lion in the infield and what in the world it was doing there!   **Wrap-up:** What typically happens when you tell yourself not do something like, "do not slow down" or "do not focus on your competition." You think about what you are not supposed to do and often do those things. A more effective strategy is to direct your self-talk so you are telling yourself what to do instead of what not to do.

Activity 6.6
Control the Controllables
Exercise: In column one is a list of some typical uncontrollables. Add five more uncontrollables to the list. In column two, list things you can control.

Uncontrollables	Controllables
your opponent	attitude
the officiating	effort
temperature (hot-cold)	_____
wind	_____
rain	_____
snow	_____
the schedule	_____
_____	_____
_____	_____
_____	_____
_____	_____

For Thought: Has focusing on uncontrollables gotten you into trouble before?

Wrap-up: Our focus should be on things we can control. However, it is perfectly natural to periodically think about the uncontrollable. Briefly thinking about an uncontrollable is ok, but you should recognize what you are focusing on is an uncontrollable. Use a release technique to forget about the uncontrollable and use cues to immediately return to focus on something you can control at that moment. One thing that you can learn to control is how you choose to react to the uncontrollable. The ability to shift your focus and stay calm under distractors is an important mental skill that needs to be consistently practiced to become automatic.

When you become distracted by thoughts, other events, and emotions, you do not focus on the proper cues. Physically, your muscles tighten, heart rate goes up, breathing rate goes up, and your mouth becomes dry. Instead of focusing externally on the relevant cues in your environment, your attention becomes narrow and internal as you focus on your own worries and fears of losing and failing. You lose your ability to change focus as the situation dictates. This affects timing, coordination, fatigue, muscle tension, and poor judgment. Your focus will often bring inappropriate cues.

As *Activity 6.1 Catching Markers* illustrated, we can only focus on a limited number of stimuli at one time. Therefore, you must learn which information is critical to performance and direct attention to that. In most cases, learning to focus on the right thing at the right time may be by trial and error and many hours of making mistakes in practice and competition. This process can be improved and made more effective and efficient by learning what cues to focus on. For example, if you are a high jumper and the speed of your approach is vital to your jumping success, by focusing on a cue word such as "attack," you are developing your selective focus skills.

It is very important to learn what cues to focus on and then develop a mind-set to be alert for those cues. In running events on the track, your focus may be on cues to read your opponents and being prepared to implement your race strategy. In field events, a more a narrow focus is needed such as focusing on rhythm, acceleration, or exploding.

The development of focusing on important cues should occur in practice. You will find it useful to develop task-relevant, performance-related cue words to help focus on the right information. Two examples of performance related cues are listed in Table 6.2.

Table 6.2
Performance Related Cues Example

100 meters	Long Jump	800 meters
Explode	Push	Control, Even pace
Tear up track	Attack	Stay strong, Keep contact
Drive	Explode	Hot track, Quick hands

Use the examples in Table 6.2 and develop cue words for your event in Activity 6.7 based upon different time phases. Place performance related cue words in your events.

Activity 6.7
Develop Cues for your Event

Time in Event	Event 1	Event 2
Early phase		
Middle phase		
End phase		

In track and field, having a performance focus plan should be an important part of your routine. Before pilots get ready to fly their airplane, they have to go through a checklist. This checklist ensures that they are ready. Athletes should develop their own checklist. Focus plans for track and field events should specify the focus of attention during the event's different time segments. A well-developed focus plan that is overlearned will prompt the right focus automatically, leading to more opportunities to be in the "flow."

Expect the Unexpected

Congratulations for stepping up to the challenge to make the commitment to improve your mental skills that will lead to a better performance. However, when you develop the mental skill focus and you know what cues to focus on, it can still be very difficult because of the unexpected events that occur. Any unexpected stimulus is likely to capture your focus. The natural tendency to attend to this type of stimulus is called the orienting response. This orientation response may alert us to focus more on our task. For example, a runner may notice that two people have collided and they must dodge the fallen runners. Athletes must block out these irrelevant distractors and focus on the task at hand. With repeated exposure to the unexpected distraction, athletes can rely on an automatic response. The most effective way to prevent the unwanted orienting response is to make the unexpected expected. Astronauts often train by using flight simulations that purposely have flight and equipment failures that force the astronauts to respond to distractors. A common example of this would be in American football where teams practice their offense with a recording of loud crowd noise to become accustomed to the crowd. Wouldn't it be nice if excessive crowd noise was a factor in track and field? Although excessive crowd noise is usually not a problem in track and field, there are plenty of other unexpected events that arise that can cause you to lose focus.

In *Activity 6.8 Distractors*, you are asked to list some possible distractors. Use the distractor examples in column 1 and continue to add to the list in column 2 with additional distractors.

We will cover recovery plans in Chapter 7 and in the event-by-event chapters and talk about how to effectively handle distractions that may cause us to lose focus.

Activity 6.8 **Distractors**	
Distractors	**Additional Distractors**
Wind	
Rain	
Cold	
Heat	
Fall down	
Blocks slip	
Miss first two attempts	
Foul first two attempts	

Once you achieve focus, how do you sustain it? Although the terms focus and concentration are often used synonymously, they should not be. Concentration is the ability to sustain focus on selected stimuli over time. Helping athletes sustain their concentration skills is a key component of focus training.

Intense concentration is difficult to sustain because it is energy demanding. To maintain focus for a long period of time is draining. Seldom does trying to concentrate yield positive results. Concentration occurs when your mind becomes absorbed in the task, rather than trying to make you focus. When you allow yourself to become completely involved in what you are doing, sustained concentration comes naturally.

In the field events, the multi-events, and in running races with prelims and finals, you need to learn when and how to turn concentration on and off. In situations where you perform, wait, then perform again, concentration must be managed effectively. If you fail at concentration, you will fail to select the correct cues, be prone to being distracted and make poor decisions.

With practice, you will be able to concentrate for longer and longer periods of time. You should spend time in practice sustaining concentration in exactly the same way you must sustain it when competing. Simple activities such as stretching can be turned into a focus activity by focusing closely on what each stretch feels like. If your mind wanders, redirect your attention back to stretching. With practice, you will get better at concentrating. The ability to concentrate requires quieting the mind, focusing on the present, and becoming absorbed in the activity.

There are many roadblocks that you need to overcome if you are to become effective in maintaining your focus. It can be difficult to focus on the present because your mind may wander to the past or think of the future. Your past could be holding onto mistakes you have made and your future might be thinking of the negative things that might occur if you have a bad performance. Or maybe you have already chalked up your victory in your mind and you are focused on how you will celebrate your victory. People have difficulty letting go of a bad mistake. Looking backwards prevents you from focusing on the present. Your mind may be occupied by "what if" questions. What if questions might include: "What if I foul?" "What if I slow down?" "What if I miss?" or "What if I get tired?"

With all the "what if" questions, you mind can become cluttered with excessive thinking. Remember the Walk the Plank activity in Chapter 1? Your lack of trust on the high plank caused your mind to wander and think consciously of keeping your balance and not falling and these negative thoughts interfered with performance, compared to a free mind when walking the plank on the ground. The free mind responds automatically and trusts your training and skills.

Fatigue makes it difficult to sustain focus on the task. When you are tired, your mind is preoccupied with fatigue. Fatigue can make cowards of us all, if we let it. If your focus skills are well developed you will greatly increase your odds of blocking out the feelings of fatigue.

Now that you know more about focus and the roadblocks that get in your way of achieving sustained focus, let's turn our attention to improving your ability to overcome focus roadblocks.

Triggers

Focus can be improved through the use of triggers. A trigger is an action or words that remind you to focus. Triggers are reminders to focus your attention back to the task at hand. Triggers are used to program the proper image. *Activity 6.9 Triggers* lists some triggers that can be used in implementing your mental plan.

Activity 6.9 Triggers	
Some examples of triggers are given in column one. Can you add more triggers to the list in column two that may help you initiate your own mental plan?	
Example Triggers	**Additional Triggers**
Look at the implement	
See the long jump board	
Touch your muscles and think of them as coiled springs	
Clap your hands twice quickly	

Releases

A release is a technique that allows you to let go of negative thoughts and feelings that prevent you from concentrating on the present. Releases can also be used to free the mind to focus. An example may be when you enter the locker room, you place your hand on the bench and imagine any problems you have flowing from your mind to the bench. After practice, you can touch the bench and your concerns will flow back into your mind. Similar to the locker room release is the concept of parking thoughts. You can eliminate negative thoughts by parking them in a safe place until after your performance. Identify unwanted thoughts in your mind, write them on paper and place the paper in another location. You will not be concerned about the thoughts you have left on the paper. After your performance is over, go back and un-park the paper by looking at it. At that time, you can address your concerns. Another version of the parking method would be to imagine your problems or concerns parked in the trunk of your car in the parking lot. During the performance, they are safe in the car as you forget about them. After your performance, you can un-park your concerns from your car trunk and deal with them.

Other release examples may be a thrower picking up the shot and imagining the mistake moving into that object, placing the shot on the ground, stepping on the shot, and seeing the mistake going into the ground. Ken Ravizza, a very successful sports psychologist who has done considerable work with baseball takes a small plastic toilet into the baseball dugout and has players flush their bad plays away to put their problems behind them. Although you probably won't take your toilet to the track, you can make a hand signal as though you were flushing a toilet and achieve the same effect. In fact, you may even buy a small toilet that goes on your key chain to remind you to flush your mistakes.

Another quick technique that you can use to help let go of mistakes could be a garbage dump somewhere in the track venue. The garbage dump is where you put your mistakes and frustration during the meet or practice so they don't distract you. Pick one or more spots or objects around the track before practice or the meet starts. Your spot should be easy to see from the track or competition area. Maybe you choose somewhere in the stands, a landing pit, a flagpole, or maybe even an actual wastebasket. If you make a mistake, deposit it in the garbage dump by taking a quick look at the spot and symbolically leaving the mistake there. Your garbage dump could also be an extra bag you bring along with you.

Use *Activity 6.10 Using Releases* to add to the example of releases you could use.

Activity 6.10 Using Releases	
Some examples of releases are given in column one. Can you add more releases to the list in column two that may help you initiate your own mental plan?	
Release Examples	**More Release Techniques**
Parking-Imagine trouble in your trunk of car	
Step on shot and grind mistake into ground	
Wipe hand across shirt to wipe mistake away	
Pick up a blade of grass and throw it in the air	
Use flushing toilet movement with your hand	

All athletes will lose focus at some point no matter how good their focus skills. However, what separates great athletes from average athletes is the ability to quickly regain focus after losing it. Mentally strong athletes have a recovery plan to react to the distracting situation. The keys to the recovery plan are called the 3 R's: recognize, relax, refocus.

Table 6.3 The 3 R's	
Recognize	Recognize you have lost focus and need to regain it.
Relax	Use self-talk and breathing to relax and get back in your proper arousal zone.
Refocus	Re-focus attention on task by using triggers, releases, and cue words.

Activity 6.11 Myself After a Mistake
Think about the last time you made a mistake such as false started, fouled or missed three times in a row, threw out-of-bounds, or dropped the baton. When did you recognize you lost focus? Were you able to relax and get back into the flow of things? How successful were you in refocusing? Now that you know about the signs of being in your proper arousal zone, the components of relaxation, and how to re-focus using cue words, how would you respond in a more positive productive manner? How would you: Recognize: _____ Relax: _____ Refocus: _____

Where you put your focus is called a focal point. Focal points can be something you feel, see, or hear. Developing a focal point allows you to place your concentration in a pre-determined place and will help distract you from anything negative that will adversely affect performance

Activity 6.12
Focal Points

Exercise: Use the examples in column one and then list 4 focal points that you can use in column two in a pre-meet/event situation.

Comment: Because the athletic performance happens quickly, it is difficult to be totally aware of the feeling during the actual flow of performance. Feeling focal points are most often useful before the event, in the pre-performance plan as a tool to stay calm and focused.

Feeling Focal Points Examples:	**Feeling Focal points**
Feel the stretch of your muscles	1.
Feel your breathing-the air in and out	2.
Feel your feet on the track or the runway	3.
Feel the throwing implement in your hands	4.

Visual Focal Points: Visual focal points are points that you only look at before and during competition to keep in your proper arousal zone. Use the examples in column one and then list 4 visual focal points that you can use in column two in a pre-meet/event situation, then 4 you can use during the event.

Examples	**Visual focal points Pre-event**	**Visual Focal Points During Event**
1. Looking at the finish line before your race	1.	1.
2. Focus on the track	2.	2.
3. See yourself doing your event	3.	3.
4. See yourself stretching	4.	4.

Hearing Focal Points:
Listen to only those things that get you in the proper arousal zone and make you feel calm and confident. Use the examples in column one and then list 4 hearing focal points that you can use in column two in a pre-meet/event situation, then 4 you can use during the event.

Examples	**Hearing focal points Pre-event**	**Hearing Focal Points During Event**
1. Negative Sounds	1.	1.
2. Others talking about being scared they are or how big the meet is	2.	2.
3.	3	3.
4.	4.	4.

By developing familiar focal targets, you can consistently increase your focus both before and during your performances. Although we developed several focal points during the activity, I recommend selecting one or two that work for you and develop them.

Use the following activities to help develop your focus skills.

Activity 6.13
Focus Cue Development

Phase 1:
Runners, jumpers, hurdlers should use their shoes or spikes for this exercise. Throwers may use their throwing implement.

Take your shoes/spikes or throwing implement and place them five feet away from you. Pick a specific spot on the object to focus your eyes on. Your eyes should stay focused on this spot during the entire exercise.

Place your focus on your breathing. As you inhale feel the energy coming into your body. Feel your stomach rising. As you exhale, feel the stomach loosen and the tension flow out of your body. When you exhale, repeat a cue word to yourself. This word is your concentration cue and keeps you focused.

Common words that may be used are "strong," "focus," "relax," etc. Whenever you feel your focus start to drift from your visual target, use your breathing and cue word to return your focus on the object.
Continue to focus on the object until you can focus for three minutes without distractions, then move on to phase 2.

Phase 2:
Turn on music but with very low volume at first. Try to stay focused on your spot for the next minute and a half without getting distracted by the music. Whenever you feel your focus start to drift from your visual target, use your breathing and cue word to return your focus on the object.

Continue to focus on the object until you can focus for two minutes without distractions. When you can focus for two-minutes, increase the volume of the music. When you can focus for one minute without losing focus you are ready for phase 3.

Phase 3:
Place your object directly in front of a TV set. Sit far enough back so that in order for you to still see your object you also see the entire screen. Turn the TV on but with very low volume at first. Try to stay focused on your spot for the next minute and a half without getting distracted by the images on the TV screen. Whenever you feel your focus start to drift from your visual target, use your breathing and cue words to return your focus to the object.

Activity 6.14
Concentration Breathing

Silently say one word related to your event as you inhale and two words related to your event as you exhale. See how many breathing cycles you can go through without letting thoughts wander to something else. Set concentration goals.

What caused you to lose concentration?

Activity 6.15
Stick with my Number

Phase 1: Sit quietly with your eyes closed and your feet flat on the floor. Concentrate on your breathing. When you inhale, feel the energy coming into your body and focus on the feeling in your stomach of the air coming in. When you exhale, feel the air going out, and focus on the number one. See the number one in your mind's eye. Repeat "one" in your head, or you can do a combination. Inhale, feel the breath. Exhale, focus on the number one. This is really quite boring, so you'll find your mind wandering. When your mind wonders, recognize that you've lost the proper focus. Return your concentration to your breathing and the feeling of the air coming in. As you exhale, now focus on the number two. See the number two in your mind's eye, repeat the sound "two" in your head, or do a combination. Each time you lose your focus and drift, add a number. Do this exercise for 2 minutes and see what number you are up to.

Phase 2: Turn on some music and try the same exercise for two minutes.

Activity 6.16
Learn to Maintain Focus

Find a quiet place and choose a track and field object such as the shot, discus, javelin, pole, shoes, etc. Hold the object in your hands. Get a good sense of how it feels, its texture, color, etc. Put the object down and focus your attention on it. If thoughts wander, bring attention back to the object. Record how long you can maintain your focus on the object. Once you are able to focus for 5 minutes, practice with distractions present. Chart how long you can maintain your attention under these conditions.

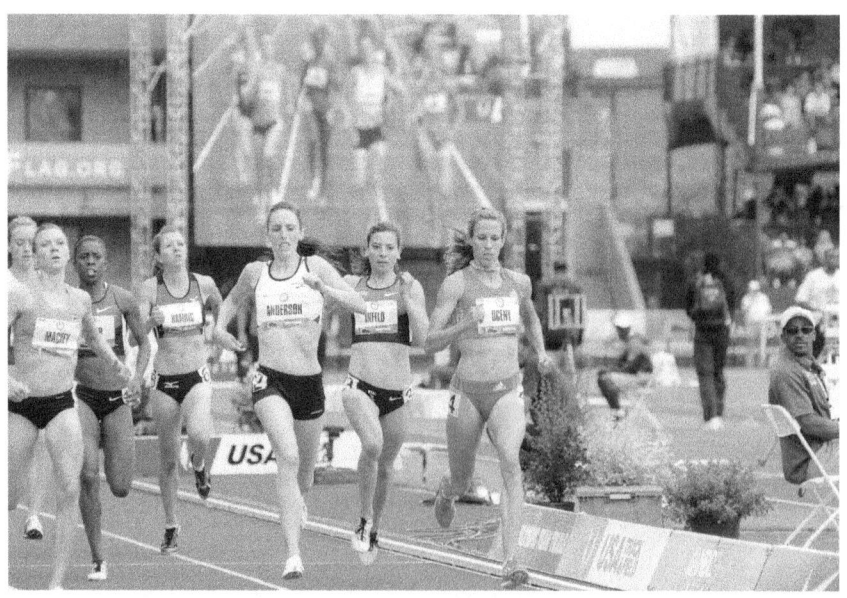

Activity 6.17
Concentration Grid Exercise

This exercise helps increase focus and is a fun activity that athletes enjoy participating in.

1. You will need a pencil and a timer. The concentration grid has numbers from 1 to 99 spread out randomly in the grid.
2. Go for one minute and see how many numbers you can cross off, starting at 1 and going up in number.
3. As a means of comparison, people who are able to concentrate effectively and scan well, score in the upper 20's and 30's.
4. Now for the fun part, have somebody distract you. Start at 99 and work down. The person distracting you can use distracting methods other than hitting you.

10	99	43	71	9	76	61	23	96	90
93	21	97	37	86	17	56	4	66	85
89	8	58	80	49	52	29	42	72	19
15	28	54	38	77	95	34	84	13	26
50	92	70	1	24	30	87	59	100	44
64	45	82	63	91	2	12	68	53	33
75	67	39	27	88	14	83	47	98	62
36	3	31	18	60	35	5	78	11	25
81	57	40	73	48	51	65	41	20	94
46	22	7	79	16	32	6	69	74	55

Table 6.4
Checkpoint Cue Words

Divide your event into different phases. For each phase, list two to three things that you will focus on during that phase. Then, list one cue word that will bring everything in that phase into focus. Once you have developed your cue words, draw a diagram of your event and place your cue words in the appropriate place. An example is given for the 400-meter hurdles.

Phase		Main points to focus on	Cue Word(s)
Phase 1	Start to 1st Hurdle	Get to first hurdle without stutter Set rhythm of race Get out of blocks strong Attack first hurdle	BOOM
Phase 2	Clearing Hurdles	Lead leg attacks hurdle Trail leg drives forward	Rhythm
Phase 3	¾ way through race (6th or 7th hurdle)	Fatigue beginning to set in. Look forward to the challenge	Love it!
Phase 4	After last hurdle	Where the race is made Power through final yards	Relax and use power

In your event-by-event chapters later in the book, you will be asked to break your event down into phases, list the main points to focus on, and come up with one cue word for each phase

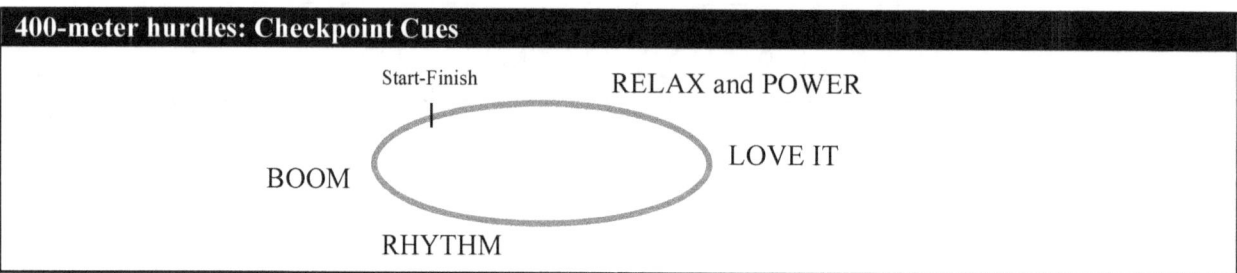

400-meter hurdles: Checkpoint Cues

Many sport psychologists and coaches believe that the ability to focus is the most important skill an athlete can possess. This important mental skill of the ability to focus is not a natural ability and can be improved by mental drills. We started the chapter with the Catching Markers activity that illustrated how important it is to know what to focus on. We covered the different types of attentional focus and you developed cues to keep you focused on your event. The important skills of using triggers and releases appropriately will allow you to relax and re-focus on achieving the proper arousal level. Finally, you engaged in several mental drills that will help you to achieve and sustain focus.

Successful, mentally strong athletes maintain a positive focus no matter what is going on around them. They stay focused on the next action steps they need to take to get them closer to the fulfillment of their goals rather than all the other distractions that are going on. You are making a commitment to be a mentally strong athlete. Stay focused, go after your dreams, and keep moving toward your goals.

Chapter 7

Introduction to Mental Plans

Knowing about mental training is one thing, but integrating mental training techniques into sport and developing mental tough athletes is a completely different challenge. Finding ways to implement mental skills training programs is critical to helping you deal with problems and adversity in competition. The mental skills you have learned in previous chapters must be integrated to promote optimal performance in practice and in challenging competitive situations. Mental plans are your answer to integrating the mental skills and becoming mentally tough.

Many coaches and athletes leave mental toughness to chance, resulting in inconsistent performance and preventing athletes from fully developing their talents. Great athletes use systematic mental and physical preparation to consistently create and maintain a flow mindset in practice and competition.

Mental plans involve a series of systematic, individualized strategies designed to build mental skills into your game. Athletes move deliberately through the steps, which include goal setting, self-talk, imagery, energization and any other mental training tool or skill, in an order that helps them personally create a flow mindset. Mental plans are designed for use during practice and competition but they are also needed to help you get back on track when things go wrong in practice or competition.

Mental plans should become routines that you follow to combine mental and physical skills in order to enhance performance. Mental plans are not superstitious rituals such as putting on the jersey before the shorts or putting your left shoe on first. You are in control of your mental plan and it is designed to help you promote, retain and regain a flow mindset.

What do mental plans do?

1. Create a flow mindset: The flow mindset stimulates optimal performance, and if you can achieve it, maintain it, and regain it, you will be mentally strong. Mental plans will help you to obtain your goal of being mentally strong. Although every practice will not be a flow experience, you should strive to attain the flow mindset, of being confident, optimistic, and in control when you practice or compete. A good mental plan will help you focus on needed improvement.
2. Enhance Performance Quality: A mental plan will provide you with a needed tool for practicing and performing with composure. When you experience flow, you are able to concentrate on performance related cues, are physically and mentally relaxed yet energized, experience optimal arousal and feel positive. The combination of these mental skills will allow you to focus on executing automatically.
3. Increase Consistency: Champion athletes use a consistent mental preparation routine regardless of opponents, circumstances, or what's at stake. Less successful athletes often have no plan and widely vary their approach.
4. Dealing with adversity: What separates champions from others is the willingness to admit that competition seldom follows a script. A good mental plan includes recovery plans that will help you handle problems.

Types of Mental Plans

There are three types of mental plans that we will focus on. 1. Mental preparation 2. Mental performance and 3. Mental recovery

Mental Preparation Plans

A mental preparation plan is a pre-performance routine that is pre-planned. It is a systematic sequence of thoughts and behaviors that you engage in prior to performing a specific skill. You should keep your routines simple and flexible, so that they are easily repeatable yet open to some change if competitive conditions dictate this. These routines will help you lock in to an automatic pilot, which is where the best performances occur. The key is to develop a routine, then practice it through imagery in physical training sessions and use it consistently in competition so it becomes natural.

Mental preparation plans will help you warm-up mentally by using a structured routine to promote a flow mind-set that will enable you to practice and play at your best. By integrating the mental warm-up into the physical one, you can ready your mind and body together. Preparation plans include a basic plan for ideal conditions and a backup plan for use when the warm-up is constrained by time or circumstance. Just like a pilot has a pre-flight checklist that is reviewed step-by-step, this pre-competition checklist will prepare you to fly high!

Mental Performance Plan

Mental performance plans are used during practice and competition to help you perform at your best by maintaining and using your flow mindset. These plans include a standard mental performance plan for use when things go well and backup mental recovery plans to cover several common contingencies when problems occur or when your first plan proves ineffective. Your mental performance plan will focus on your goals for practice or competition and your action plans for attaining them. For track races, your mental performance plan will focus on developing specific strategies to maintain a flow mindset during each major part of the race. The field events are self-paced tasks that are repetitive and you should construct and automate pre-performance and between performance routines that will maximize the quality and consistency of your performance.

Mental Recovery Plans

Mental recovery plans emphasize overcoming specific problems that regularly arise or adjusting to get the most out of practice or competition in the face of trouble. Back-up mental plans help athletes recover from the unexpected. When the unexpected arises, you often lose focus, which takes you out of your game. Mental recovery plans will help you make the best of difficult situations and performance as well as circumstances allow. A mental recovery plan is a simple routine designed for the wide range of unexpected practice and competitive situations that cause you to lose composure. Mental recovery plans are designed to provide a routine that can be used regardless of the problem that caused the lack of composure.

For mental plans to be effective, they must be practiced until they are automatic. You will need the ability to use rapid techniques to focus attention and initiate action without prompting excessive analysis. This need is filled by triggers, releases, and cue words. Triggers and releases also provide a way for coaches to see if athletes are following their routines.

We covered triggers and releases earlier in the book, but a brief review will help remind us of their usefulness.

Triggers: Cue words or actions that remind you to concentrate. You may use the word "focus " as a reminder to direct your attention back to the task at hand after losing focus. Especially in the field events, athletes tend to lose focus while waiting to compete again. It is too much to expect concentration the entire time of the event, while your competitors are also competing. Using a trigger such as touching your uniform, patting the implement, or stepping into the ring will bring your attention back to the task at hand.

Releases: Releases are specific behaviors used to shed the effects of mistakes that create negative thoughts. You can learn to use releases to let go of negative thoughts and feelings that prevent you from concentrating on the present. An effective release sets the stage for you to use cue words to help re-focus.

Designing Your Mental Preparation Plan

Mental preparation plans provide a blueprint for mental warm-up to maximize creating a flow mindset. Preparation plans should be individualized to meet your specific needs, but should include two basics steps.

1. Using mental training tools to develop mental preparation skills and strategies.
2. Combining physical and mental warm-ups.

Table 7.1 is an example of how a mental preparation plan could be incorporated into a week. The example of a distance runner is provided as an example to stimulate thinking. Because of the great individualization between athletes and because coaches may have differing training, programs, terminology, plans, etc., use this as a guide. Adapt and adjust as necessary to fit your individual needs and situations.

You will notice in Table 7.1 under mental practice, a section called "outside of practice." Yes, this is homework. Although mentally skilled athletes incorporate mental skills into actual physical practice, highly mentally skilled athletes go beyond regular practice to further develop their mental skills on their own. I highly encourage you to do your homework. The extra effort will pay off in your ability to use your mental skills automatically when needed.

Table 7.1 is an example of what a mental preparation plan would look like prior to a competition. A specific Mental Preparation Plan is provided in the event-by-event chapters. A blank form is provided in Chapter 19 to allow you to complete your own plan.

Table 7.1
Sample Mental Preparation Plan for a Distance Runner

Day	Physical Practice	Mental Practice
Monday	1 mile warm-up Dynamic warm-up 4 mile tempo run Static stretch 1 mile jog cool down	Incorporate into practice **Outside of practice:** Review weekly goals Positive self-talk Relaxation Imagery of achieving weekly goals
Tuesday	1 mile warm-up Work on relays	Incorporate into practice **Outside of practice:** Mental recall Affirmations:
Wednesday	1 mile warm-up Dynamic warm-up 6 x 100 meter strides 8 x 400 meters with 3 minute rest 1 mile jog cool down	Incorporate into practice **Outside of practice:** Develop competition plan Visualize competition plan
Thursday	1 mile warm-up 20 minutes fartlek Team games Character Building Mental Training	Incorporate into practice **Outside of practice:** Relaxation Visualize competition plan Visualize mental recovery plans
Friday	Competition	See Table 7.3 for example of meet day mental preparation plan
Saturday	Easy recovery jog Stretch	Complete post-competition evaluation Use mental recall to see highlights Use mental recall to see lowlights-rewind to make it a highlight Review previous week goal progress Set new goals with emphasis on process and effort goals
Sunday	Recovery- Walk Bike Swim Stretch	Relaxation Mental rehearsal of next week's goals Positive Self-talk Read about a motivating athlete

The ultimate use of mental skills is incorporating them into a practice or competition to improve performance. Table 7.2 lists ways you could incorporate mental training into practice. Specific ideas to incorporate mental skills into workouts are provided in the event-by-event chapters. A blank form is provided in Chapter 19 to allow you to complete your own plan.

Table 7.2 Ideas to Incorporate Mental Skills Into a Workout		
Physical Activity	When to use	Mental Activity
Interval Training	During recovery period	Visualize parts of the upcoming race
Starting block practice	Standing behind blocks	Rapid energization to achieve proper arousal
Running 2-3 hurdles	Before and during	Use cue words before and during Focus on rhythm
High Jumping	Before jump	Rapid relaxation or energization Visualize jump
Long jump full approach and jump	Before and during jump	Focus on Acceleration Cue words
Pole Vault simulation jumping with two misses	Before and during jump	Rapid relaxation Positive self-talk Focus on process cues
Throwing discus, javelin, or shot putting	Simulate time between throws in competition	Positive self-talk Relaxation- focus on breathing
Throwing	After throw	Mental recall to review throw Mental rehearsal to see corrections

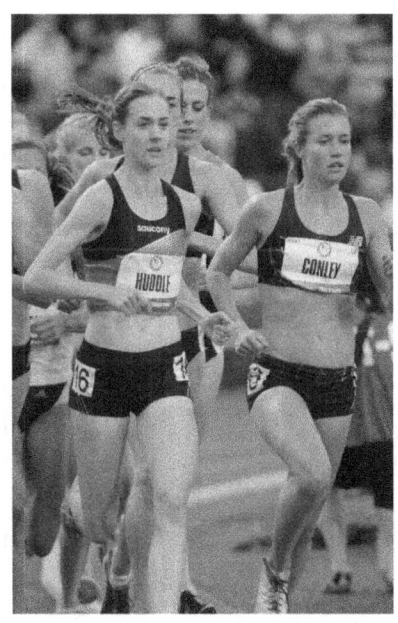

Once you get to the track and field meet, you should have a prepared mental performance plan. Table 7.3 demonstrates an example mental performance plan covering from 80 minutes before competition to competition. A specific Pre-Competition Mental Preparation Plan is provided in the event-by-event chapters. A blank form is provided in Chapter 19 to allow you to complete your own plan.

Table 7.3 Pre-Competition Mental Preparation Plan		
Time Prior to Start	**Physical WU**	**Mental WU**
75-80 min	Initial check-in Pick-up number Check heat, lane assignments, flight	Relaxation and Cue Words
65-75 min	Easy jog to get blood flowing	Go over mental performance plan Imagery involving running with perfect form Confidence card or self-talk script Review back-up plans
50-65 min	Stretching	Focus on breathing, relaxation Positive self-talk Quick imagery of portions of event
40-50 min	Dynamic Warm-up Good form	Cue Words Energization techniques
30-40 min	Drills Proper technique Relax body while doing drills	Positive self-talk Relaxed while doing drills
20-30 min	Strides Specific warm-up to event	Cue words- event specific Increase arousal if needed to get in proper arousal zone Positive mental attitude high Focus on personal goals and the processes to make it happen
15-20 min	Bathroom Break	Rapid relaxation to deal with pre-race nervousness
10-15 min	Isolation Check final meet gear equipment	Quick review of overall race plan Vividly see running and hitting goal time and splits Use rapid relaxation or energization techniques to get in your proper zone Positive self-talk
10 min	Check-in at event Do final event prep such as starts, strides, final jumps or throws Remove warm-ups React automatically	Maintain proper arousal zone Rapid relaxation Positive self-talk Cue words

Mental performance plans focus on your goals for practice or competition and are an action plan for achieving them. The focus is on developing specific strategies to maintain a flow mindset during each major phase of your event. Table 7.4 is an example of a mental performance plan for a hurdler. A specific Mental Performance Plan is provided in the event-by-event chapters. A blank form is provided in Chapter 19 to allow you to complete your own plan.

Table 7.4
Mental Performance Plan for a Hurdler

Competition Phase	Physical	Mental	Cue Words
Start to 1st Hurdle	Get to first hurdle without stutter Set rhythm of race Get out of blocks strong Attack first hurdle	Energization out of blocks Focus on power	BOOM Explode Attack
Clearing Hurdles	Lead leg attacks hurdle Trail leg drives forward	Focus on hurdle	Rhythm Smooth
¾ way through race	Fatigue beginning to set in. Look forward to the challenge	Use of cue words Positive self-talk	Love it! Strong Compete

You have seen examples of mental preparation plans for a week, ideas on how to integrate mental skills into physical practice, and a general example of a mental performance plan. In the event-by-event chapters, you will see more examples of mental preparation plans and mental performance plans that are specific to your event. You will also be given the opportunity to develop your own mental plans for your event.

Table 7.5 provides some general guidelines to think about as you develop your mental plans. You can develop your own mental preparation plan in Activity 19.1 and develop your mental performance plan in Activity 19.2. Remember you will get a chance to further develop these for your event in the event chapters.

Table 7.5
Guidelines to Develop Mental Plans

1. How will you achieve the proper arousal zone for practice or competition?
    a. How will you use your relaxation and energization skills to create optimal arousal?
    b. What are you goals for practice or competition?
    c. What do you want to focus on?
    d. Do you have cue words ready?
    e. What imagery will you use?
2. How will you develop positive self-talk for practice or competition?
    a. How will you use your positive affirmations and cue words?
    b. How will you use your positive self-talk script?
    c. How will your goals fit into your self-talk?
    d. Will you use imagery to help?
3. How will you combine your mental warm-up with your physical warm-up?

Mental Recovery Plans

Mental recovery plans provide a coping strategy to help you recover from unanticipated problems. A mental recovery plan is a set procedure for getting back on track. Sometimes mental recovery plans allow you to completely return to form, usually they just provide a means of damage control and help you take away something positive. How complete a recovery you make depends on how quick the need to use a mental plan is identified and then how effectively it is implemented.

All athletes lose focus at some point. It is inevitable. But what separates great athletes is the ability to quickly regain focus after losing it. Instead of reacting to the situation that distracts you mentally, you will have a recovery plan for regaining focus.

Here are some tips for implementing your recovery plan.

1. Develop a physical trigger to start the recovery plan.
2. Use a release to forget about the damage.
3. Relax to get back into the proper arousal zone.
4. Re-focus on the process not the outcome.
5. Use positive self-talk.

A technique used by many leading sports psychologists involves imagining a stoplight. A green light indicates that you are in the flow mindset. A yellow light indicates potential problems and a red light indicates the need to use a recovery plan. If you can foresee a problem coming and recognize it will affect your proper arousal level, you are able to get back to the proper level. Using the traffic light analogy, if you see it turning yellow, you should use your mental skills to get it back into the green. Failing to recognize it is turning yellow (potential problems with focus) will lead to a red light, which is much more difficult to recover from.

Tables 7.6 and 7.7 provides examples of mental recovery plans. You should always expect the unexpected. By practicing the unexpected, your automatic response will be a response that will allow you to get your focus back on track. The event-by-event chapters will give more examples of each event. Use the information in Table 7.6 as a guide to develop a list of your own mental recovery plans. A blank form is provided in Chapter 19 to allow you to complete your own Mental Recovery Plan.

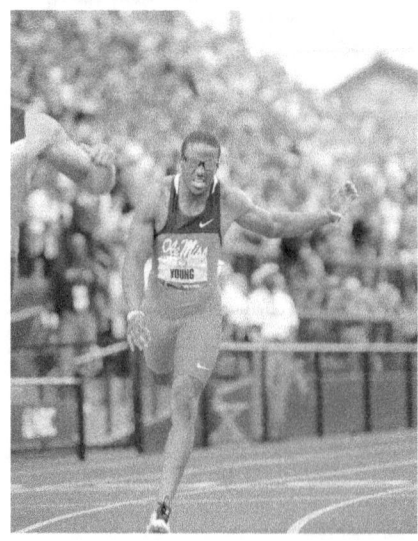

Table 7.6
Mental Recovery Plan for Field Events

Distractors-Field Events	Release	Re-focus	How to prepare for
Windy day	Exhale air out, blow the wind away	Focus on process goals not outcome Focus on process cues	Practice with a cross wind or occasionally into the wind
Rain	Wipe forehead	Positive self-talk Arousal techniques such as energization	Practice on some rainy days
Cold	Rub sweats or clothing	Positive self-talk Imagery of goal achievement	Practice in cold
Weather delays	Relaxation breathing	Relaxation Positive self-talk	Start practice and delay it for several minutes to simulate a delay
Miss first two attempts	Park mistake in an object	Cue words that focus on process	Simulation

Table 7.7
Mental Recovery Plans for Track Events

Distractors-Track Events	Release	Re-focus	How to prepare for
Fall down during race	Getting up	Focus on gradually catching up Measure your energy over the remaining distance	In practice, kneeling down and let your teammates get ahead of you and gradually catching up
False start	Flush Toilet	Relaxation Positive self-talk Imagery of next event	False start in practice and work on regaining composure
Drop the baton	See baton	Focus on securing baton Focus on runners ahead Measure your energy	Practice having to pick-up baton in crowed situations- simulate in practice
Boxed in	Take a mental snapshot of race ahead of you	Relaxation Focus on vision looking for gap Cue words to accelerate through gap	Simulate boxed in positions in practice
Hit hurdle that knocks you off rhythm	Look at next hurdle	Focus on rhythm Process cue words	Use padded hurdle to simulate hitting hurdle

Being a mentally skilled athlete means performing your best under any circumstances. The key to performing your best is to create mental plans to obtain a flow mindset. Mental plans are very time-intensive to develop and implement. It can be overwhelming to try to do everything at once, so start by developing just one plan at a time. Once you have mastered one plan, add another. I suggest you identify the mental plan that would be most valuable to you and work on that first. The actual implementation of your mental plan may be somewhat of a trial and error process. Try out your plan and then evaluate how effective it is. Keep modifying it until you like it. Use imagery to try your plan out. Try your mental plans out in practice. I encourage you to keep a mental training log and note what plans work best to prepare you mentally. The more experienced and comfortable you get with mental plans, the better your plans will work to create both the physical and mental positive mindset that will take your performance to an optimal level!

Chapter 8

Sprints

Activity 8.1
Sprints Power Picture
Directions: Find a good picture of when you are competing. Make sure the picture shows you in good form and looking strong. Put the picture on a page (preferably cardboard stock). Place your cue words around the picture.

L I G H T N I N G

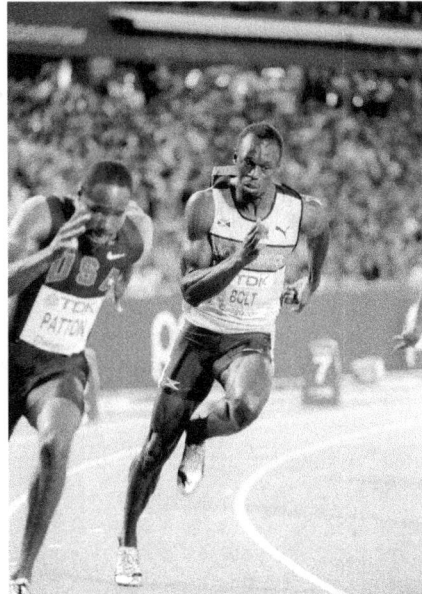

E X P L O D E

SPEED

Activity 8.2
Sprint Affirmations

- I am fast.
- I am committed to a sprinter's lifestyle.
- I have the skills to be a great sprinter.
- Each day I become a better sprinter.
- I love to run fast.
- My form is fluid, smooth, controlled and relaxed.
- My body feels light and runs fast.
- I run comfortable and relaxed.
- My strides are rhythmic and powerful.
- I explode from the starting blocks.
- I drive strong with my arms and legs out of the blocks.
- I have a quick, smooth acceleration.
- My eyes are focused ahead.
- I am running in a straight line.
- My sprinting form is fluid.
- My sprinting form is fluid.
- I run the curve under control.
- I maintain my form when fatigue sets in.
- My legs are quick and strong.
- I have speed and endurance.
- I run in a tall sprinting position.
- I sprint relaxed, even when behind.
- My shoulders and hands are relaxed.
- Running fast makes me feel good.
- I stay strong.
- My legs are powerful.
- I am running fast.
- I relax and let it happen.
- I am proud to be a sprinter.
- I am a great sprinter.

Activity 8.3
Sprint Mental Recall

Begin to think of a time in your life when you had an outstanding performance... one of your best runs ever, when you were right on and performed perfectly. See yourself at that time... notice what you look like, what you are wearing, who is with you... what sounds are around you, where are you? ... Feel the environment and the energy. Begin to see yourself sprinting when you knew you were right on... when everything worked perfectly... when you were in complete control and at your peak. Watch yourself and feel that feeling...connect with all of the feelings you experienced as you achieved at your highest level. Perfectly...competently... exactly the way you wanted to...what did it feel like? ...sound like? ...look like?

Remember your thoughts before you ran that day. Remember how comfortable and relaxed you felt. Feel the rhythm of that run come back. How you exploded out of the starting blocks with one of your best starts ever. How smooth, fluid and powerful it felt, as you built up your speed and power... and came up with a PR. Let it all come back to you... let it in... know it again... the joy... the power... the pride and confidence...the rush of knowing you were perfection... let it become part of you ... part of your spirit... part of your being ... Fully connect with it.

Feel the movements that you perfectly executed. How good the start felt as you exploded from the starting blocks. Feel the power being unleashed. Remember how you accelerated powerfully out of the blocks. Remember how relaxed the shoulders and arms felt, in perfect balance and control, driving strongly. Remember the strong powerful drive of the legs. Remember the quick turnover of the legs as they moved quickly... the ground was flying by. You felt strong all the way through the race. Your fitness level was very high, you were fit, physically and mentally. All the forces came together perfectly as you exploded with a personal best run. See the speed... feel the speed... as you ran perfectly.

Remember the finish as you sprinted to the line. Although there was fatigue, you ran through it...staying strong...and under control. It felt so good to run so fast.

While completely involved with this feeling, give yourself a cue word or affirmation that brings all these feelings and pictures into focus...a cue word or affirmation that completely connects you with that time and those feelings when you knew that you were perfect and right on...say the words or words to yourself several times... allow yourself to experience your sense of power and control...feel it in your whole body.

See and feel yourself sprinting that day. How you ran so effortlessly. Faster than you had ever ran before and it felt so easy. It felt so good to run so fast. Everything worked perfectly, just the way you wanted it to.

Activity 8.4
Sprint Mental Rehearsal

See yourself arriving at the track meet... you're wearing your favorite competition clothes... your thoughts are focused on your race... you feel good today... you are looking forward to running fast... you have some really good feelings about your performance.

Picture the weather... the sun...the clouds... the wind... the temperature. This is a great day for a P.R... you are excited and ready to sprint.

You notice some runners you will be running against. You remain calm, confident, and relaxed...you feel ready to run... you have a deep, calm yet somewhat nervous feeling inside... your heart is pounding and the adrenaline is flowing... you say your cue words or affirmations to yourself... what a day this is going to be for you!

You feel good because you know that you have been working hard, training well, and have made many sacrifices to be the best you can be...think of all the time you have spent running, sprinting, stretching, working on drills...technique...weight training...sit-ups...mental training. All this work is going to pay off today! You are physically and mentally ready to run very fast.

See yourself going through your normal warm-up routine... light running... the muscles begin to limber up... the stretching... the sprinting... your breathing hard indicates the muscles are getting oxygen and will be ready to perform when called upon. You prepare mentally as you think about your race. You loosen up... feel the sweat on your body and your heart pumping... as your body gets warmer and warmer... preparing itself for competition. See yourself going through some sprints and starts, using good form. Your body feels so light and strong today. You are tuned and in control. Your warm-up went well... you feel ready... you feel fast...just the way you want to be. You relax while waiting for the competition to start. While waiting, repeat your cue words, say your affirmations to yourself... take a deep breath... inhale...exhale...inhale...exhale... Your warm-up and strides felt strong and powerful... your workouts have been going well... you are ready to run faster than you have all year.

You check in with the clerk of the course. You notice your competitors... see the colors of their uniforms... you acknowledge them but remain focused on yourself... You will run your race... you know what heat you are in... you feel the tinge of anticipation as the official wishes everyone "good luck."

You stay loose and confident while you are waiting for your heat. Hear the official call your heat and lane assignment. You set your starting blocks. Feel yourself getting in the starting blocks and practicing your start. You feel strong and powerful as you drive out of the blocks. You are ready! You return to the starting line. You take a deep breath and gather your thoughts. You exhale and relax saying your cue words or affirmations. Your body and mind responds positively. You have been looking forward to this.

You line up behind your starting blocks. The starter commands "On Your Marks." See and feel yourself backing into the starting blocks, flexing and stretching your legs like a cat ready to leap. You feel comfortable and confident when the starter says, "SET," and you rise to the set position. You feel your hips slightly higher than your shoulders, feel your body weight on your fingers... your gaze is low. You are concentrating on your first movement, totally focused and relaxed... ready to explode at the sound of the gun. Hear the gun and see and feel the powerful drive of the legs and arms as you explode out of the starting blocks. Feel the powerful force you apply to the starting blocks. You drive hard the first few steps, tearing up the track behind you. Staying low... leaning from the ankles... the eyes focused down the track. Feel the acceleration as you build up the speed...each stride getting longer and longer as you build up speed. Feel the arms driving vigorously as you remain under control of your power. Feel the power as your drive off the track, driving the knee towards the chest. Feel the range of motion of the legs as you run faster and faster. You feel good... in control... and powerful. You got a great start, just the way you wanted, and it has put you in excellent race position. Feel yourself running tall, light and quick on your feet. You are running very relaxed and fast. Feel the relaxation of floppy cheeks in your face... the shoulders relax, the hands loose and relaxed. You are in perfect running form. If running the curve, see yourself coming out of the blocks... running as close as possible to the inside lane. When running the curve, see yourself driving the right arm across the midline of the body, a slight lean to the inside with the left shoulder slightly forward. Feel the smoothness and speed which you negotiate the turn. Fluid, smooth, powerful. As you come off the bend into the straightway, you focus on staying on the inside of the lane. On the straightaway, you see the finish line, you are running fast...relaxed...fluid...smooth...and under control. Feel the turnover of the legs as the finish line gets closer and closer. Feel the arms synchronize as you stay relaxed. Your head remains lined up with your trunk... your focus is past the finish line. You maintain your relaxation as you drive through the line. You feel great... you have that inner feeling that you've given it your all and have done your best.

You stop, bend down, and put your hands on your knees to catch your breath. You are breathing hard. The adrenaline of success is rushing through your body... You hear friends congratulating you... as you walk off the track, people pat you on the back and shake your hand. Feel the exhilaration of accomplishment... the joy of success. As you walk back to put on your sweats, you feel a tremendous sense of accomplishment as you responded to the challenge. You know that you have run one of the best races of your life... you know that you were psychologically and physically prepared. All your training, both physical and mental, has paid off. After you accept congratulations from your coach and friends, take time to thank your body... your legs, your lungs and your entire body... You have achieved your goal!

Now begin to let go of this image and this feeling.... feel your body... move your toes.... move your fingers... begin to notice your breathing...inhale...exhale...inhale...exhale... You feel relaxed and filled with a new quiet energy.

To help further develop all of your senses in imagery use Activity 8.5. Certain senses may produce clearer attention than others. Use this exercise to provide direction for extra attention and practices.

Activity 8.5
Sensory Imagery for Sprints

Vividness: Imagine the track. Notice how round it is. Notice the oval that you will run. Notice how big it is. Follow it all the way from the start to the finish.

Auditory: What sounds do you hear while you are getting ready to run? Can you hear your own footsteps as you run?

Tactile: Image the feel of your feet on the track. What does it feel like? Notice how soft or hard it feels to land on it. Feel your feet pressed against the starting blocks.

Kinesthetic: Imagine running during warm-ups. Feel what your body is doing during the warm-ups. Feel the muscles in your legs as you run. Note the power in your legs as you do your warm-ups. Feel the sensation of your body sprinting on the track.

Smell: Smell the track, your shoes, and the grass. Smell the sweat after a hard practice.

Taste: Taste the salt from the sweat on your lips. Imagine taking a drink of water during a hot day of practice.

Emotion: Experience the confidence you feel when you step up to run. Experience the satisfaction of running fast. Experience the pride you feel in achieving a PR. Experience the excitement of being on a successful team.

Vividness Evaluation
What were your strongest images and sensations?
What senses do you need to improve?

The Sprint Self-Evaluation can be used periodically to evaluate practice or competition. A general Team Post-Meet Evaluation form can be found in Activity 19.4.

Activity 8.6
Sprint Self-Evaluation

Rate yourself on a scale of 1-10 (with 10 being high)

1. Overall Performance	_____	11. Ability to push yourself	_____
2. Warm-ups	_____	12. Contribution to team	_____
3. Performance in meets	_____	13. Progress towards your goal	_____
4. Encouragement of others	_____	14. Start	_____
5. My positive attitude	_____	15. First few steps	_____
6. Use of mental training	_____	16. Middle of race	_____
7. Mental training on own	_____	17. Last 1/3 of race	_____
8. Proper sleep	_____	18. Finish	_____
9. Proper nutrition	_____	19. Visualization of run	_____
10. Good hydration practices	_____	20. Focus	_____

Activity 8.7
Personalized Guided Visualization

Objective:
To write a personalized guided visualization script. In your own words write a visualization of an upcoming performance. This visualization will let you see, hear, and feel yourself performing your sport.

Directions: Write a personalized guided visualization script. Be as specific as possible. Include as many senses you can. Write it down as full and complete as you can. Remember to use positive statements and include your affirmations. Use the worksheet to formulate your ideas. Then write out your guided visualization in an essay format. After writing the visualization, I would encourage you to record the script. Find a quiet time to play some relaxation music and then play your recorded script. As you talk to yourself, see the visualization coming to life!

Worksheet for your guided visualization

Preparation Period
- See yourself in the preparation phase leading up to the event.
- What have you done well?
- Think of some of your best workouts.

Day of the Event
- See yourself getting up in the morning with confidence.
- What will you have to eat?
- See yourself dressing for the competition, putting on your clothing.

Arriving at the Site
- See yourself arriving at the site
- See the competition
- See the environment, weather, temperature
- Focus on your goal and the outcome you wish to achieve

The Warm-up
- See yourself doing your general warm-up
- See yourself stretching, drills, strides
- See yourself doing your final preparations
- See yourself putting on your competition shoes
- See yourself taking a practice start

The Start
- See yourself in the blocks
- Hear and feel your first few steps
- See yourself getting out to a good powerful start

Driving out of blocks
- See and feel your arms and legs driving powerfully
- Drive out of the blocks
- Feel yourself running under control but fast

Middle of the Race
- See and feel yourself running tall
- Feel the control and rhythm of the race
- Feel relaxed and strong
- Feel yourself slicing through the wind

To the Finish Line
- Hear your cue words that keep you relaxed and controlled
- Focus on running through the finish line.
- Feel the satisfaction of running an outstanding race

A sample week for a Sprinter Mental Preparation Plan is provided in Table 8.1. Use the example to help complete the blank form in Activity 19.1 to develop your Mental Preparation plan.

Table 8.1
Sample Weekly Sprinter Mental Preparation Plan

Day	Physical Practice	Mental Practice
Monday	½ mile warm-up Dynamic warm-up 6 x 200 meters Static stretch ½ mile jog cool down	Incorporate into practice (See Table 8.2) **Outside of practice:** Review weekly goals Positive self-talk Relaxation Imagery of achieving weekly goals
Tuesday	½ mile warm-up Dynamic warm-up Work on relays	Incorporate into practice (Table 8.2) **Outside of practice:** Mental recall Affirmations
Wednesday	½ mile warm-up Dynamic warm-up 6 x 100 meter strides 4x 400 meters with 5 minute rest 1 mile jog cool down	Incorporate into practice (Table 8.2) **Outside of practice:** Develop competition plan Visualize competition plan
Thursday	½ mile warm-up 20 minutes fartlek Team games Character Building Mental Training	Incorporate into practice **Outside of practice:** Relaxation Visualize competition plan Visualize mental recovery plans
Friday	Competition	See Tables 8.3 and 8.4
Saturday	Easy recovery jog Stretch	Complete post-competition evaluation Use mental recall to see highlights Use mental recall to see lowlights-rewind to make it a highlight Review previous week goal progress New goals to emphasize process and effort
Sunday	Recovery-Walk Bike Swim Stretch	Relaxation Mental rehearsal of next week's goals Positive Self-talk Read about a motivating athlete

Table 8.2 provides ideas to incorporate mental skills into your regular practice. A blank form is provided in Activity 19.6 to help you develop your plan to incorporate mental skills into your workouts.

Table 8.2
Ideas to Incorporate Mental and Physical Plan into Workouts

Physical Activity	When to use	Mental Activity
Interval Training	During recovery period	Visualize parts of the upcoming race
Starting block practice	Standing behind blocks	Rapid energization to achieve proper arousal
Speed work	Sprinting full speed	Cue words Relaxing breathing

Use Table 8.3 for ideas on how to develop a Mental Performance Pre-Competition Plan. In Activity 19.2, a blank form is provided to help you develop your plan to incorporate mental skills into your pre-competition warm-up.

	Table 8.3 Example Sprinter Mental Performance Pre-Competition Plan	
Time Prior to Start	**Physical WU**	**Mental WU**
75-80 min	Initial Race check-in Pick-up number Check heat, lane assignments	Relaxation and Cue Words
65-75 min	Easy jog to get blood flowing	Go over race plan from assigned lane Imagery involving running with perfect form Confidence card or self-talk script Review back-up plans
50-65 min	Stretching	Focus on breathing, relaxation Positive self-talk Quick imagery of portions of event
40-50 min	Dynamic Warm-up	Focus on energization
30-40 min	Drills Proper technique	Positive self-talk Relaxed while doing drills
20-30 min	Strides Focus on pushing while staying low	Cue words- to stay fast Increase arousal if needed to get in proper arousal zone Positive mental attitude high Focus on personal goals and the processes to make it happen
15-20 min	Bathroom Break	Rapid relaxation to deal with pre-race nervousness
10-15 min	Isolation Check final meet gear equipment	Quick review of overall race plan Vividly see running and hitting goal time and splits Use rapid relaxation or energization techniques to get in your proper zone Positive self-talk
10 min	Check-in at line Set up blocks and do three starts Remove warm-ups Think of gun and react	Maintain proper arousal zone Rapid relaxation Positive self-talk Cue words

In Table 8.4, a Mental Performance Competition Plan is provided. The plan is divided into different phases of the competition. To help incorporate your mental skills into your performance, complete Activity 19.3 and develop your Mental Performance Plan.

Table 8.4
Example Sprinter Mental Performance Competition Plan

Competition Phase	Physical	Mental	Cue Words
Start	Drive hard and low Push with legs	Energization Control breathing in blocks Focus on explosive movement	Relax, Explode, Drive, React, Go, Boom
First 10 strides	Stay low Drive	Focus on driving	Low, Power, Accelerate
Middle	Good form Rhythm	Breathing Relaxed	Cruise, Smooth
Finish	Maintain form to finish Run through line	Positive Self-talk Focus in lane and on finish line Focus on process not outcome	Finish, Form, Strong

Table 8.5 provides examples of Mental Recovery Plans for Track Events. See Activity 19.5 for a blank form to complete that will help you develop your Mental Recovery Plan.

Table 8.5
Mental Recovery Plans for Track Events

Distractors-Track Events	Release	Re-focus	How to prepare for
Fall down during race	Getting up	Focus on gradually catching up Measure your energy over the remaining distance	In practice, kneeling down and let your teammates get ahead of you
False start	Flush Toilet	Relaxation Positive self-talk Imagery of next event	False start in practice and work on regaining focus
Drop the baton	See baton	Focus on securing baton Focus on runners ahead Measure your energy	Practice having to pick-up baton in crowed situations-simulate in practice
Boxed in	Take a mental snapshot of race ahead of you	Relaxation Focus on vision looking for gap Cue words to accelerate through gap	Simulate boxed in positions in practice
Hit hurdle that knocks you off rhythm	Look at next hurdle	Focus on rhythm Process cue words	Use padded hurdle to simulate hitting hurdle

Chapter 9

Hurdles

Activity 9.1
Power Picture
Directions: Find a good picture of when you are competing. Make sure the picture shows you in good form and looking strong. Put the picture on a page (preferably cardboard stock). Place your cue words around the picture.

S P R I N T　　　　　　　C O N T R O L

SPEED

Activity 9.2
Hurdle Affirmations

- I am fast.
- I am a hurdler.
- Each day I become a better hurdler.
- I love to hurdle.
- I am committed to a hurdler's lifestyle.
- I have the skills to be a great hurdler.
- My body feels light and runs fast.
- I run comfortable and relaxed.
- I sprint over the barriers.
- I explode from the starting blocks.
- I have speed and endurance.
- My coordination and balance help me to perform.
- I run in a tall sprinting position.
- I lead powerfully with the knee.
- My hips and shoulders remain square.
- I accelerate powerfully to the first hurdle.
- My trail leg is tight and active.
- I run off the hurdle.
- My getaway stride is aggressive.
- I attack the finish line in proper sprint form.
- I am flexible.
- I sprint relaxed even if behind.
- I am in control.
- I am a great hurdler.
- I am proud to be a hurdler.

Activity 9.3
Hurdle Mental Recall

Begin to think of a time in your life when you had an outstanding performance... one of your best runs ever, when you were right on and performed perfectly. See yourself at that time... notice what you look like, what you are wearing, who is with you?...What sounds are around you?...Where are you? ... Feel the environment and the energy. Begin to see yourself hurdling when you knew you were right on... when everything worked perfectly... when you were in complete control and at your peak. Watch yourself and feel that feeling...connect with all of the feelings you experienced as you achieved at your highest level.... perfectly...competently... exactly the way you wanted to...what did it feel like?...sound like?...look like?

Remember your thoughts before you ran that day. Remember how comfortable and relaxed you felt. Feel the rhythm of that hurdle run come back. How you exploded out of the starting blocks with one of your best starts ever. How smooth, fluid and powerful it felt, as you built up your speed and power. Let it all come back to you... let it in... know it again... the joy... the power... the pride and confidence...the rush of knowing you were perfection. Let it all come back to you...become part of you ... part of your spirit.. part of your being ... Fully connect with it.

Feel the movements that you perfectly executed. How good the start felt as you exploded from the starting blocks. Feel the power being unleashed. Remember how you accelerated powerfully to the first hurdle. Remember how relaxed the shoulders and arms felt, in perfect balance and control. Remember the strong powerful drive of the legs. As you approached each hurdle you drove the knee powerfully...balanced over the hurdle... tight active trail leg clearance...coming off the hurdle and preparing for the upcoming hurdle. Your endurance level was very high, you were fit, physically and mentally. All the forces came together perfectly as you glided over the hurdles. Feel the rhythm.... Feel the speed between hurdles...each hurdle coming up with perfect timing.

Remember the finish as you stormed home after the last hurdle. Although there was fatigue you ran through it, staying strong, and under control. It felt so good to run so fast.

While completely involved with this feeling, give yourself a cue word or affirmation that brings all these feelings and pictures into focus...a cue word or affirmation that completely connects you with that time and those feelings when you knew that you were perfect and right on...say the words or words to yourself several times... slowly allow yourself to experience your sense of power and control...feel it in your whole body. See and feel yourself hurdling that day. How you cleared the hurdles so effortlessly. It felt so good to run so fast. Everything worked perfectly, just the way you wanted it to.

Activity 9.4
Hurdle Mental Rehearsal

See yourself arriving at the track meet... you're wearing your favorite competition clothes...your thoughts are focused on your race... you feel good today... you are looking forward to running fast... you have some really good feelings about your performance. Picture the weather... the sun...the clouds... the wind... the temperature. This is a great day for a PR... you are excited and ready to hurdle.

You notice some hurdlers you will be competing against. You remain calm, confident, and relaxed...you feel ready to run... you have a deep, calm yet somewhat nervous feeling inside... your heart is pounding and the adrenalin is flowing... you say your cue words or affirmations to yourself... what a day this is going to be for you!

You feel good because you know that you have been working hard, training well, and have made many sacrifices to be the best you can be...think of all the time you have spent running, sprinting, stretching, working on drills...technique...weight training...sit-ups...mental training. All this work is going to pay off today! You are physically and mentally ready to hurdle very fast.

See yourself going through your normal warm-up routine... light running... the muscles begin to limber up... the stretching... the sprinting... your breathing hard indicates the muscles are getting oxygen and will be ready to perform when called upon...You prepare mentally as you think about your race. You loosen up...feel the sweat on your body and your heart pumping...as your body gets warmer and warmer...preparing itself for competition. See yourself going through some sprints and over hurdles, using good form.

Your body feels so light and strong today. You are tuned and in control. Your warm-up went well…you feel ready… you feel fast…just the way you want to be... You relax while waiting for the competition to start. While waiting repeat your cue word say your affirmations to yourself…take a deep breath… inhale…exhale…inhale…exhale…Your warm-up and strides felt strong and powerful…your workouts have been going well… you are ready to run faster than you have all year.

You check in with the clerk of the course. You notice your competitors… see the colors of their uniforms…you acknowledge them but remain focused on yourself… You will run your race. You know what heat you are in… you feel the tinge of anticipation as the official wishes everyone "good luck."

You stay loose and confident while you are waiting for your heat. Hear the official call your heat and lane assignment… You set your starting blocks. Feel yourself getting in the starting blocks and practicing your start. You feel strong and powerful as you drive out of the blocks and effortlessly clear the hurdles in your lane. You are ready! You return to the starting line. You take a deep breath and gather your thoughts. You exhale and relax saying your cue words or affirmations. Your body and mind respond positively. You have been looking forward to this.

You line up behind your starting blocks. The starter commands "On Your Marks." See and feel yourself backing into the starting blocks, flexing and stretching your legs like a cat ready to leap. You feel comfortable and confident when the starter says, "SET," and you rise to the set position. You feel your hips slightly higher than your shoulders, feel your body weight on your fingers and your gaze is low. You are concentrating on your first movement, totally focused and relaxed, ready to explode at the sound of the gun. Hear the gun and see and feel the powerful drive of the legs and arms as you explode out of the starting blocks. Feel the powerful force you apply to the starting blocks. You drive hard the first few steps, tearing up the track behind you. Staying low… leaning from the ankles, the eyes focused down the track. You drive strong to the first hurdle. Feel the acceleration as you build up the speed, each stride getting longer and longer as you build up speed. Feel the arms driving vigorously as you remain under control of your power. Feel the power as you drive off the track, driving the knee towards the chest. Feel the range of motion of the legs as you run faster and faster. You feel good, in control, and powerfully. You got a great start, just the way you wanted and it has put you in excellent race position. Feel yourself running tall, light and quick on your feet. You are running very relaxed and fast. Feel the relaxation of floppy cheeks in your face and the shoulders relax, the hands loose and relaxed.

As you approach each hurdle you drive the knee powerfully, balanced over the hurdle, tight active trail leg clearance, coming off the hurdle and preparing for the upcoming hurdle. See yourself fit, physically and mentally. All the forces come together perfectly as you glide over the hurdles. Feel the rhythm…. feel the speed between hurdles…each hurdle coming up with perfect timing.

Remember the finish as you stormed home after the last hurdle. Although there was fatigue you ran through it, staying strong, and under control. It felt so good to run so fast. On the straightaway you see the finish line, you are running fast, relaxed, fluid, smooth and under control. Feel the turnover of the legs as the finish line gets closer and closer... Feel the arms synchronize as you stay relaxed. Your head remains lined up with your trunk… your focus is past the finish line. You maintain your relaxation as you drive through the line. You feel great. You have that inner feeling that you've given it your all and have done your best.

You stop, bend down and put your hands on your knees to catch your breath. You are breathing hard. The adrenaline of success is rushing through your body… You hear friends congratulating you… as you walk off the track, people pat you on the back and shake your hand. Feel the exhilaration of accomplishment…the joy of success. As you walk back to put on your sweats you feel a tremendous sense of accomplishment as you responded to the challenge. You know that you have run one of the best races of your life… you know that you were psychologically and physically prepared. All your training both physical and mental have paid off. After you accept congratulations from your coach and friends, take time to thank your body… your legs, your lungs and your entire body. Now begin to let go of this image and this feeling….feel your body… move your toes…. Move your fingers… begin to notice your breathing…inhale…exhale…inhale…exhale… You feel relaxed and filled with a new quiet energy.

To help further develop all of your imagery senses, use Activity 9.5. Certain senses may produce clearer attention than others. Use this exercise to provide direction for extra attention and practices.

Activity 9.5
Sensory Imagery for Hurdles

Vividness: Imagine the track. Notice the color of the hurdles. Notice the shape of the hurdles. Notice the hurdle and follow the hurdle from the start to the finish.

Auditory: What sounds do you hear while you are getting ready to hurdle? Notice the sound of your feet on the track.

Tactile: Image the feel of your feet on the track. What does it feel like? Notice how soft or hard it feels on the track after each hurdle.

Kinesthetic: Imagine hurdling during warm-ups. Feel what your body is doing during the warm-ups. Feel the muscles in your legs as you run and hurdle. Note the power in your legs as you do your warm-up jumps. Feel yourself rocketing up into the air. Feel the sensation of your body clearing the hurdle.

Smell: Smell the track, your shoes, and the grass. Smell the sweat after a hard practice.

Taste: Taste the salt from the sweat on your lips. Imagine taking a drink of water during a hot day of practice.

Emotion: Experience the confidence you feel when you hurdle. Experience the satisfaction of running fast. Experience the pride you feel in achieving a PR. Experience the excitement of being on a successful team.

Vividness Evaluation
What were your strongest images and sensations?
What senses do you need to improve?

A Hurdle Self-Evaluation can be found in Activity 9.6 and can be used periodically to evaluate practice or competition. A general Team Post-Meet Evaluation form can be found in Activity 19.4.

Activity 9.6
Hurdle Self-Evaluation

Rate yourself on a scale of 1-10 (with 10 being high)

1. Overall Performance _____
2. Warm-ups _____
3. Performance in meets _____
4. Encouragement of others _____
5. My positive attitude _____
6. Use of mental training _____
7. Mental training on own _____
8. Proper sleep _____
9. Proper nutrition _____
10. Good hydration practices _____
11. Contribution to team _____
12. Progress towards your goal _____
13. Start _____
14. To first hurdle _____
15. Hurdle take off _____
16. Hurdle clearance _____
17. Trail leg action _____
18. Lead leg action between hurdles _____
19. Run-in off last hurdle _____
20. Visualization of run _____

Activity 9.7
Personalized Guided Visualization

Objective:
To write a personalized guided visualization script. In your own words write a visualization of an upcoming performance. This visualization will let you see, hear, and feel yourself performing your sport.

Directions:
Write a personalized guided visualization script. Be as specific as possible. Include as many senses you can. Write it down as full and complete as you can. Remember to use positive statements and include your affirmations. Use the worksheet to formulate your ideas. Then write out your guided visualization in an essay format. After writing the visualization, I would encourage you to record the script. Find a quiet time to play some relaxation music and then play your recorded script. As you talk to yourself, see the visualization coming to life!

Worksheet for your guided visualization

Preparation Period
    See yourself in the preparation phase leading up to the event.
    What have you done well?
    Think of some of your best workouts.

Day of the Event
    See yourself getting up in the morning with confidence.
    What will you have to eat?
    See yourself dressing for the competition, putting on your clothing.

Arriving at the Site
    See yourself arriving at the site
    See the competition
    See the environment, weather, temperature
    Focus on your goal and the outcome you wish to achieve

The Warm-up
    See yourself doing your general warm-up
    See yourself stretching, drills, strides
    See yourself doing your final preparations
    See yourself putting on your competition shoes

The Start
    See yourself in the blocks
    Hear and feel your first few steps
    See yourself getting out to a good powerful start

Driving out of blocks
    See and feel your arms and legs driving powerfully
    Drive to the first hurdle
    Feel yourself running under control but fast

Middle of the Race
    See and feel yourself running tall
    Feel the control and rhythm of the race as you clear the hurdles
    Feel relaxed and strong
    Feel yourself slicing through the wind

To the Finish Line
    Hear your cue words that keep you relaxed and controlled
    Focus on running through the finish line as your clear the last hurdle
    Focus and feel yourself keep good form

A sample week for a Hurdler Mental Preparation Plan is provided in Table 9.1. Use the example to help complete the blank form in Chapter 19.1 to develop your Mental Preparation plan.

Table 9.1 **Sample Weekly Mental Preparation Plan for a Hurdler**		
Day	**Physical Practice**	**Mental Practice**
Monday	½ mile warm-up Dynamic warm-up Hurdle drills 6 x 200 meters ½ mile jog cool down	Incorporate into practice (see Table 9.2) **Outside of practice:** Review weekly goals Positive self-talk Relaxation/Imagery of weekly goals
Tuesday	½ mile warm-up Dynamic warm-up Work on relays	Incorporate into practice (Table 9.2) **Outside of practice:** Mental recall/Affirmations
Wednesday	½ mile warm-up Dynamic warm-up 6 x first 2 hurdles, 6 x first 3 hurdles 4x 400 meters with 5 minute rest ½ mile jog cool down	Incorporate into practice (Table 9.2) **Outside of practice:** Develop competition plan Visualize competition plan
Thursday	½ mile warm-up 20 minutes fartlek Team games Character Building Mental Training	Incorporate into practice (Table 9.2) **Outside of practice:** Relaxation Visualize competition plan Visualize mental recovery plans
Friday	Competition	See Table 9.3 and 9.4 for example of meet day mental preparation plan
Saturday	Easy recovery jog Stretch	Complete post-competition evaluation Use mental recall to see highlights Use mental recall to see lowlights-rewind to make it a highlight Review previous week goal progress Set new process and effort goals
Sunday	Recovery- Walk Bike Swim Stretch	Relaxation Mental rehearsal of next week's goals Positive Self-talk Read about a motivating athlete

Use Table 9.2 for ideas to incorporate mental skills into your regular practice. A blank form is provided in Activity 19.6 to help you develop your plan to incorporate mental skills into your workouts.

Table 9.2 **Ideas to incorporate mental and physical plan into a workout**		
Physical Activity	**When to use**	**Mental Activity**
Interval Training	During recovery period	Visualize parts of the upcoming race
Starting block practice	Standing behind blocks	Rapid energization to achieve proper arousal
Running 2-3 hurdles	Before and during	Cue words- focus on rhythm

Use Table 9.3 for ideas on how to develop a Mental Performance Pre-Competition Plan. In Activity 19.2, a blank form is provided to help you develop your plan to incorporate mental skills into your pre-competition warm-up.

	Table 9.3 Example Hurdle Mental Performance Pre-Competition Plan	
Time Prior to Start	**Physical WU**	**Mental WU**
75-80 min	Initial Race check-in Pick-up number Check heat, lane assignments	Relaxation and Cue Words
65-75 min	Easy jog to get blood flowing	Go over race plan from assigned lane Imagery involving running with perfect form Confidence card or self-talk script Review back-up plans
50-65 min	Stretching	Focus on breathing, relaxation Positive self-talk Quick imagery of portions of event
40-50 min	Dynamic Warm-up Good form	Focus on energization Cue words
30-40 min	Drills Proper technique	Positive self-talk Relaxation while doing drills
20-30 min	Strides-over hurdles Focus on pushing while staying low	Cue words- to stay fast Increase arousal if needed to get in proper arousal zone Positive mental attitude high Focus on personal goals and the processes to make it happen
15-20 min	Bathroom Break	Rapid relaxation to deal with pre-race nervousness
10-15 min	Isolation Check final meet gear equipment	Quick review of overall race plan Vividly see running and hitting goal time and splits Use rapid relaxation or energization techniques to get in your proper zone Positive self-talk
10 min	Check-in at line Set up blocks and do three starts Remove warm-ups Think of gun and react	Maintain proper arousal zone Rapid relaxation Positive self-talk Cue words

In Table 9.4, a Mental Performance Competition Plan is provided. The plan is divided into different phases of the competition. To help incorporate your mental skills into your performance, complete Activity 19.3 and develop your Mental Performance Plan.

Table 9.4
Example Hurdler Mental Performance Competition Plan

Competition Phase	Physical	Mental	Cue Words
Start to 1st Hurdle	Get to first hurdle without stutter Set rhythm of race Get out of blocks strong Attack first hurdle	Energization out of blocks Focus on power	BOOM Explode Attack
Clearing Hurdles	Lead leg attacks hurdle Trail leg drives forward	Focus on hurdle	Rhythm Smooth
¾ way through race	Fatigue beginning to set in. Look forward to the challenge	Use of cue words Positive self-talk	Love it! Strong Compete
To Finish Line	Drive off last hurdle Maintain form	Positive self-talk Focus on hurdle and lane Focus on process not outcome	Focus Form Finish

Table 9.5 provides examples of Mental Recovery Plans for Track Events. See Activity 19.5 for a blank form to complete that will help you develop your Mental Recovery Plan.

Table 9.5
Mental Recovery Plans for Track Events

Distractors-Track Events	Release	Re-focus	How to prepare for
Fall down during race	Getting up	Focus on gradually catching up Measure your energy over the remaining distance	In practice, kneeling down and let your teammates get ahead of you
False start	Flush Toilet	Relaxation Positive self-talk Imagery of next event	False start in practice and work on regaining focus
Drop the baton	See baton	Focus on securing baton Focus on runners ahead Measure your energy	Practice having to pick-up baton in crowed situations- simulate in practice
Boxed in	Take a mental snapshot of race ahead of you	Relaxation Focus on vision looking for gap Cue words to accelerate through gap	Simulate boxed in positions in practice
Hit hurdle that knocks you off rhythm	Look at next hurdle	Focus on rhythm Process cue words	Use padded hurdle to simulate hitting hurdle

Chapter 10

Middle Distance/Distance

Activity 10.1
Distance Power Picture

Directions: Find a good picture of when you are competing. Make sure the picture shows you in good form and looking strong. Put the picture on a page (preferably cardboard stock). Place your cue words around the picture.

S T R O N G

R E L A X E D

ENDURANCE

Activity 10.2
Middle Distance/Distance Affirmations

- I am a distance runner.
- I am committed to a runner's lifestyle.
- I am physically tough and mentally tough.
- I train harder and smarter than my opponents.
- I have the courage to be a great distance runner.
- Each day I become a better runner.
- I love to run.
- When fatigue sets in, I am mentally tough.
- My form is fluid, smooth, controlled and relaxed.
- My body feels light and runs fast.
- I relax and let it happen.
- I am proud to be a distance runner.
- I run comfortable and relaxed.
- My strides are rhythmic and powerful.
- I am in control.
- My shoulders and hands are relaxed.
- My legs are powerful.
- I feel full of energy.
- I am running fast.
- I have great endurance.
- I respond to pick up the pace at the end of my race.
- I am a great runner.

Activity 10.3
Middle Distance/Distance Mental Recall

Begin to think of a time in your life when you had an outstanding performance and one of your best runs ever. See yourself at that time. What did you look like? What were you wearing? Who is with you? What sounds are around you? Where were you running at? Feel the environment and the energy… See yourself running when you knew you were right on… when everything worked just as you wished… when you were in complete control and at your peak… watch yourself and feel that feeling. Let those feeling come back in and connect with all of the feelings you experienced as you achieved at your highest level… perfectly… competently… exactly the way you wanted to… what did it feel like? Sound like? Look like? Remember your thoughts before you ran that day. Remember how you felt. Feel the rhythm of that run come back. How smooth, fluid, and powerful it felt, as you built up your speed and power. Feel the energy as these feelings come back… let them in… know the performance again… the joy… the power… the pride and confidence… the rush of adrenaline of knowing you were perfection… let it become part of our again… part of your spirit… part of your being. Completely connect with these feelings.

Feel the movement that you perfectly executed… how good the start felt as you were under control and established good position. Feel the power that was stored up and then unleashed. Remember how you passed people effortlessly. How relaxed the shoulders and arms felt. Remember the strong powerful drive of the legs. Your endurance level was very high, your speed was sharp, and you were fit, physically and mentally. All the forces came together perfectly as you exploded with a personal best run.

Remember the finish as you stormed home with an outstanding kick. Although there was fatigue, you ran through it, staying strong, and under control, it felt so good to run so fast. While completely involved with this feeling, give yourself a cue word or affirmation that brings all these feelings, pictures, and sounds sharply into focus… a cue word or affirmation that completely connects you with that time and those feelings when you knew… that you were perfect and performing at your best. Exhale and relax and as you exhale say the word or words to yourself several times… slowly… and allow yourself to experience your sense of power and control… feel it in your whole body.

See and feel yourself running that day. How you sliced the air so effortlessly. Faster than you had ever ran before and it felt so easy. It felt so good to run fast. Everything worked perfectly just the way you wanted it to

Activity 10.4
Middle Distance/Distance Mental Rehearsal

See yourself at the track where you will be competing…wearing your competition clothes…your mind is on your race. Notice the weather… the clouds… the wind… the sun… the temperature…whatever it is that you can picture and feel in your mind. Notice your competition…visually check out the other competitors…you are calm, confident, and relaxed and feeling really good. You are looking forward to running your race and you have a feeling of being well-prepared for your race… you are feeling good both mentally and physical. Your hard work and sacrifices are paying off! See yourself doing your normal warm-up and stretching routines… also see the strides and whatever else you do to get ready for competition.

After you have completed the warm-up… see yourself taking off your sweats… doing your final stretches… and whatever you need for final preparation. See yourself lining up at the starting line for your race… hear the starter giving the final instructions… notice the other runners… feel the relaxation in your body and racing of the heart and pumping of the adrenaline throughout the body. You are nervous with anticipation…take a couple of deep breaths and say your affirmations. You are confident… you know you are ready to compete.

Now, see yourself at the starting line… the familiar pounding of your heart and the familiar dry mouth feeling… the excitement and anticipation that flows through your body… the energy that will soon be turned into a great performance. Hear the starter give the commands and hear the gun. You bolt off the starting line quickly… measuring your start… gauging where you want to position yourself. The start feels good …you are under control and establish good position. Feel the power that was stored up and now is unleashed… you are moving effortlessly… your shoulders and arms are relaxed as you are in the position you want to be. The strong powerful drive of the legs is carrying you down the track… your endurance level is very high…your speed is sharp. It is all coming together perfectly as you run!

You hear your splits… right where you want to be. You are saying your affirmations to yourself… you feel some slight fatigue…but your body is rising to the challenge. Feel your body step up to the challenge and respond. You are running to the key point in your race… you are right on your goal pace. You are on PR pace!

You have set yourself up in perfect position… you come into the final portion of your race. This is the point at which your hard training and confidence in yourself are paying off. You focus on your form… staying tall… loose hands… quick feet… you are a competitor and you compete all the way. See and feel the final drive to the finish line. In the last 40 meters, visualize exactly what you expect to be happening… running alone or side by side with a competitor… you dig down for that last burst of power… you maintain your form… see the finish line and you cross the line.

What a feeling of satisfaction. You just ran that race exactly as you planned… you were strong, confident, and powerful… all your training is paying off…you are strong both mentally and physically. Hear the coach come up to you and tell you your time… it's a P.R.! The feelings you are experiencing right now, you wouldn't trade for anything. You are breathing hard and trying to catch your breath… your teammates and friends congratulate you… listen to the excitement in their voices… see the smile on your face… hear what they are saying to you.

Now, begin to see yourself start your cool-down… savor your run… this special moment that no one can take from you. You have done your best and you are satisfied…take time to thank your heart, your legs, and your lungs.

Begin to let go of this image and this feeling….slowly re-enter your present space… feel your body… move your toes… move your fingers… begin to notice your breathing…inhale…exhale…inhale…exhale. You feel relaxed and filled with a new quiet energy.

To help further develop all of your imagery senses use Activity 10.5. Certain senses may produce clearer attention than others. Use this exercise to provide direction for extra attention and practices.

Activity 10.5
Sensory Imagery for Mid-Distance/Distance
Vividness: Imagine the track. Notice the color of the track. Notice how flat it is. Notice the oval that you will run on. Follow the track all the way from the start to the finish line.
Auditory: What sounds do you hear while you are getting ready to run? Can you hear your footsteps?
Tactile: Image the feel of your feet on the track. What does it feel like? Notice how soft or hard it feels to land on it.
Kinesthetic: Imagine running during warm-ups. Feel what your body is doing during the warm-ups. Feel the muscles in your legs as you run. Note the power in your legs as you do your warm-ups. Feel the sensation of your body running on the track.
Smell: Smell the track, your shoes, and the grass. Smell the sweat after a hard practice.
Taste: Taste the salt from the sweat on your lips. Imagine taking a drink of water during a hot day of practice.
Emotion: Experience the confidence you feel when you step up to run. Experience the satisfaction of running fast. Experience the pride you feel in achieving a PR. Experience the excitement of being on a successful team.
Vividness Evaluation   What were your strongest images and sensations?   What senses do you need to improve?

The Mid-Distance/Distance Self-Evaluation can be found in Activity 10.6 and can be used periodically to evaluate practice or competition. A general Team Post-Meet Evaluation form can be found in Activity 19.4.

Activity 10.6	
Middle Distance/Distance Self-Evaluation	
Rate yourself on a scale of 1-10 (with 10 being high)	
1. Overall Performance _____	11. Ability to push yourself _____
2. Warm-ups _____	12. Contribution to team _____
3. Performance in meets _____	13. Progress towards your goal _____
4. Encouragement of others _____	14. Race Plan _____
5. My positive attitude _____	15. Start _____
6. Use of mental training _____	16. First ¼ of race _____
7. Mental training on own _____	17. Second ¼ of race _____
8. Proper sleep _____	18. Third ¼ of race _____
9. Proper nutrition _____	19. Last ¼ of race _____
10. Good hydration practices _____	20. Visualization of race _____

Activity 10.7
Personalized Guided Visualization

Objective:
To write a personalized guided visualization script. In your own words write a visualization of an upcoming performance. This visualization will let you see, hear, and feel yourself performing your sport.

Directions:
Write a personalized guided visualization script. Be as specific as possible. Include as many senses you can. Write it down as full and complete as you can. Remember to use positive statements and include your affirmations. Use the worksheet to formulate your ideas. Then write out your guided visualization in an essay format. After writing the visualization, I would encourage you to record the script. Find a quiet time to play some relaxation music and then play your recorded script. As you talk to yourself, see the visualization coming to life!

Worksheet for your guided visualization

Preparation Period
- See yourself in the preparation phase leading up to the event.
- What have you done well?
- Think of some of your best workouts.

Day of the Event
- See yourself getting up in the morning with confidence.
- What will you have to eat?
- See yourself dressing for the competition, putting on your clothing.

Arriving at the Site
- See yourself arriving at the site
- See the competition
- See the environment, weather, temperature
- Focus on your goal and the outcome you wish to achieve

The Warm-up
- See yourself doing your general warm-up
- See yourself stretching, drills, strides
- See yourself doing your final preparations
- See yourself putting on your competition shoes

The Start
- See yourself lined up on the starting line
- Hear and feel your first few steps
- See yourself getting out to a good powerful start
- See and feel your arms and legs driving powerfully
- Feel yourself running under control, establishing good position

Middle of the Race
- See and feel yourself running tall
- Feel the control and rhythm of the race as you run fluidly and smoothyl
- Feel relaxed and strong
- Feel yourself slicing through the wind

To the Finish Line
- Hear your cue words that keep you relaxed and controlled
- Focus on running through the finish line.
- Feel the satisfaction of meeting the challenge.

A sample week for a Mid-Distance/Distance Mental Preparation Plan is provided in Table 10.1. Use the example to help complete the blank form in Activity 19.1 to develop your Mental Preparation plan.

Table 10.1
Sample Mental Preparation Plan for a Mid-Distance/Distance Runner

Day	Physical Practice	Mental Practice
Monday	1 mile warm-up Dynamic warm-up 4 mile tempo run Static stretch 1 mile jog cool down	Incorporate into practice (See Table 10.2) **Outside of practice:** Review weekly goals Positive self-talk Relaxation Imagery of achieving weekly goals
Tuesday	1 mile warm-up Work on relays	Incorporate into practice (Table 10.2) **Outside of practice:** Mental recall Affirmations
Wednesday	1 mile warm-up Dynamic warm-up 6 x 100 meter strides 8 x 400 meters with 3 minute rest 1 mile jog cool down	Incorporate into practice (Table 10.2) **Outside of practice:** Develop competition plan Visualize competition plan
Thursday	1 mile warm-up 20 minutes fartlek Team games Character Building Mental Training	Incorporate into practice (Table 10.2) **Outside of practice:** Relaxation Visualize competition plan Visualize mental recovery plans
Friday	Competition	See Table 10.3 and 10.4 for example of meet day mental preparation plan Outside of practice:
Saturday	Easy recovery jog Stretch	Complete post-competition evaluation Use mental recall to see highlights Use mental recall to see lowlights-rewind to make it a highlight Review previous week goal progress Set new goals with emphasis on process and effort goals
Sunday	Recovery- Walk Bike Swim Stretch	Relaxation Mental rehearsal of next week's goals Positive Self-talk Read about a motivating athlete

Use Table 10.2 for ideas to incorporate mental skills into your regular practice. A blank form is provided in Activity 19.6 to help you develop your plan to incorporate mental skills into your workouts.

Table 10.2
Ideas to incorporate mental and physical plan into a workout

Physical Activity	When to use	Mental Activity
Interval Training	During recovery period	Visualize parts of the upcoming race
Distance Runs	Before and during run	Use cue words to focus
Fartlek Runs	Before each surge	Rapid energization to achieve proper arousal

Use Table 10.3 for ideas on how to develop a Mental Performance Pre-Competition Plan. In Activity 19.2, a blank form is provided to help you develop your plan to incorporate mental skills into your pre-competition warm-up.

Table 10.3
Example Middle-Distance/Distance Performance Pre-Competition Plan

Time Prior to Start	Physical WU	Mental WU
75-80 min	Initial check-in Pick-up number Check heat, lane assignment	Relaxation and cue words
65-75 min	Easy jog to get blood flowing	Go over mental performance plan Imagery involving running with perfect form Confidence card or self-talk script Review back-up plans
50-65 min	Stretching	Focus on breathing, relaxation Positive self-talk Quick imagery of portions of event
40-50 min	Dynamic Warm-up Good form	Cue Words Energization techniques
30-40 min	Drills Proper technique Relax body while doing drills	Positive self-talk Relaxed while doing drills
20-30 min	Strides Specific warm-up to event	Cue words- event specific Increase arousal if needed to get in proper arousal zone Positive mental attitude high Focus on personal goals and the processes to make it happen
15-20 min	Bathroom Break	Rapid relaxation to deal with pre-race nervousness
10-15 min	Isolation Check final meet gear equipment	Quick review of overall race plan Vividly see running and hitting goal time and splits Use rapid relaxation or energization techniques to get in your proper zone Positive self-talk
10 min	Check-in at event Do final event prep such as starts, strides Remove warm-ups React automatically	Maintain proper arousal zone Rapid relaxation Positive self-talk Cue words

In Table 10.4, a Mental Performance Plan is provided. The plan is divided into different phases of the competition. To help incorporate your mental skills into your performance, complete Activity 19.3 and develop your Mental Performance Plan.

Table 10.4 Example Mid-Distance/Distance Mental Performance Competition Plan			
Competition Phase	**Physical**	**Mental**	**Cue Words**
Start	Push with legs	Energization Control breathing at line Focus on explosion	Relax, Drive, React, Go
First 10 strides	Pass quickly Drive strong	Focus on driving	Power, Accelerate
Middle of race	Good form Rhythm	Breathing Relaxed	Cruise, Smooth
Last ¼ of race	Maintain form to finish Run through line	Positive Self-talk Focus on finish line Focus on process not outcome	Form, Strong, Finish

Table 10.5 provides examples of Mental Recovery Plans for Track Events. See Activity 19.5 for a blank form to complete that will help you develop your Mental Recovery Plan.

Table 10.5 Sample Mental Recovery Plans for Track Events			
Distractors-	**Release**	**Re-focus**	**How to prepare for**
Fall down during race	Getting up	Focus on gradually catching up Measure your energy over the remaining distance	In practice, kneeling down and let your teammates get ahead of you
False start	Flush Toilet	Relaxation Positive self-talk Imagery of next event	Practice false start and regaining composure
Drop the baton	See baton	Focus on securing baton Focus on runners ahead Measure your energy	Practice having to pick-up baton in crowded situations- simulate in practice
Boxed in	Take a mental snapshot of race ahead of you	Relaxation Focus on vision looking for gap Cue words to accelerate through gap	Simulate boxed in positions in practice
Feeling sick in race	Rub stomach	Focus on breathing Positive cue words Slow down if needed	Practice slowing down, and gradually catching back up

Chapter 11

Relays

Activity 11.1
Relay Power Picture
Directions: Find a good picture of when you are competing. Make sure the picture shows you in good form and looking strong. Put the picture on a page (preferably cardboard stock). Place your cue words around the picture.

S   Q
P   U
E   I
E   C
D   K

FAST

Activity 11.2
Relay Affirmations

- I am fast.
- I am committed to a sprinter's lifestyle.
- I have the skills to be a great sprinter.
- Each day I become a better sprinter.
- I love to run fast.
- My form is fluid, smooth, controlled and relaxed.
- My relay team is confident.
- Our exchanges have perfect timing.
- My strides are rhythmic and powerful.
- I explode from the starting blocks.
- I drive strong with my arms and legs out of the blocks.
- I accelerate through the exchange zone.
- I accelerate quickly to start my relay leg.
- I have a quick, smooth acceleration.
- My eyes are focused ahead.
- I run the curve under control.
- I maintain my form even when fatigue sets in.
- My legs are quick and strong.
- I have speed and endurance.
- I run in a tall sprinting position.
- I sprint relaxed, even when behind.
- My shoulders and hands are relaxed.
- There is perfect spacing on my handoff.
- I maintain the speed on my handoff.
- My legs are powerful.
- I am running fast.
- I relax and let it happen.
- I enjoy running relays.
- Our relay is very competitive.
- My sprinting form is fluid.

Activity 11.3
Relay Mental Recall

Begin to think of a time in your life when you had an outstanding performance… one of your best runs ever, when you were right on and performed perfectly. See yourself at that time… notice what you look like, what you are wearing, who is with you… what sounds are around you, where are you? … Feel the environment and the energy. Begin to see yourself running a relay on a day when you knew you were right on… when everything worked perfectly… when you were in complete control and at your peak. Watch yourself and feel that feeling…connect with all of the feelings you experienced as you achieved at your highest level…. Perfectly…competently… exactly the way you wanted to…what did it feel like?...sound like?…look like?

Remember your thoughts before you ran that day. Remember how comfortable and relaxed you felt. Feel the rhythm of that run come back. How your baton exchanges were some of your best ever. How smooth, fluid and powerful it felt, as you built up your speed and power… Let it all come back to you… let it in… know it again… the joy… the power… the pride and confidence…the rush of knowing you were perfection… let it become part of you … part of your spirit… part of your being … Fully connect with it.

Feel the movements that you perfectly executed. How good the start felt as you quickly accelerated. Feel the power being unleashed. Remember how you accelerated powerfully. Remember how relaxed the shoulders and arms felt, in perfect balance and control, driving strongly. Remember the strong powerful drive of the legs. Remember the quick turnover of the legs as they moved quickly… the ground was flying by. You felt strong all the way through the race. Your endurance level was very high; you were fit, physically and mentally. All the forces came together perfectly as you exploded with a personal best run. Feel the speed as you ran down the straightaway… see the speed as you ran perfectly.

Remember your hand-offs…feel the speed that you entered the zone with and maintained all the way through. Remember how smooth the exchange was… just like clockwork. Remember how the baton kept moving at a top speed all the way through the exchange. It felt so good to run so fast.

While completely involved with this feeling, give yourself a cue word or affirmation that brings all these feelings and pictures into focus…a cue word or affirmation that completely connects you with that time and those feelings when you knew that you were perfect and right on…say the word or words to yourself several times… slowly and allow yourself to experience your sense of power and control…feel it in your whole body.

See and feel yourself running the relay that day. How you ran so effortlessly. Faster than you had ever ran before and it felt so easy. It felt so good to run so fast. Everything worked perfectly, just the way you wanted it to.

Activity 11.4
Relay Mental Rehearsal

See yourself arriving at the track meet… you're wearing your favorite competition clothes… your thoughts are focused on your race… you feel good today… you are looking forward to running fast… you have some really good feelings about your performance. Picture the weather… the sun…the clouds… the wind… the temperature. This is a great day for a P.R… you are excited and ready to sprint. You notice the other relay teams you will be running against. You remain calm, confident, and relaxed…you feel ready to run… you have a deep, calm yet somewhat nervous feeling inside… your heart is pounding and the adrenaline is flowing… you say your cue words or affirmations to yourself… what a day this is going to be for you!

You feel good because you know that you have been working hard, training well, and have made many sacrifices to be the best you can be…think of all the time you have spent running, sprinting, stretching, working on drills…technique…weight training…sit-ups…mental training. Think of all the time your relay team has spent perfecting hand-offs. All this work is going to pay off today! You are physically and mentally ready to run very fast. See yourself going through your normal warm-up routine… light running… the muscles begin to limber up… the stretching… the sprinting… your breathing hard indicates the muscles are getting oxygen and will be ready to perform when called upon. You prepare mentally as you think about your race. You loosen up… feel the sweat on your body and your heart pumping… as your body gets warmer and warmer… preparing itself for competition. See yourself going through some sprints and starts, using good form.

Your body feels so light and strong today. You are tuned and in control. Your warm-up went well... you feel ready... you feel fast...just the way you want. You relax while waiting for the competition to start. While waiting, repeat your cue words, say your affirmations to yourself... take a deep breath... inhale...exhale...inhale...exhale... Your warm-up and strides felt strong and powerful... your workouts have been going well... you are ready to run faster than you have all year.

You check in with the clerk of the course. See your teammates with you. You notice your competitors... see the colors of their uniforms... you acknowledge them but remain focused on yourself. You will run your race... you know what heat you are in... you feel the tinge of anticipation as the official wishes everyone "good luck."

You stay loose and confident while you are waiting for your heat. Hear the official call your heat and lane assignment. See yourself lining up for your start. You feel strong and powerful. You are ready! You return to the starting line. You take a deep breath and gather your thoughts. You exhale and relax saying your cue words or affirmations. Your body and mind responds positively. You have been looking forward to this.

Feel yourself lined up to start, flexing and stretching your legs like a cat ready to leap. You feel comfortable and confident. You are concentrating on your first movement, totally focused and relaxed, ready to explode. As you start, feel the powerful drive of the legs and arms as you explode into running. Feel the powerful force you apply to the ground. You drive hard the first few steps, tearing up the track behind you. Staying low... leaning from the ankles, the eyes focused down the track. Feel the acceleration as you build up the speed, each stride getting longer and longer as you build up speed. Feel the arms driving vigorously as you remain under control of your power. Feel the power as you drive off the track, driving the knee towards the chest. Feel the range of motion of the legs as you run faster and faster. You feel good, in control, and powerful. You got a great start, just the way you wanted, and it has put yourself in excellent race position. Feel yourself running tall, light and quick on your feet. You are running very relaxed and fast. Feel the relaxation of floppy cheeks in your face and the shoulders relax, the hands loose and relaxed. You are in perfect running form. If running the curve, see yourself running as close as possible to the inside lane. When running the curve, see yourself driving the right arm across the midline of the body, a slight lean to the inside with the left shoulder slightly forward. Feel the smoothness and speed which you negotiate the turn. Fluid... smooth... powerful.

See yourself taking off before you receive the hand-off. Notice how smooth, controlled and relaxed you are as you confidently take the hand-off. The baton is sticking in your hand like glue as you take control of it and continue to accelerate. See yourself running into the exchange zone. You maintain your speed all the way into the exchange. Your timing on your outgoing teammate is perfect. Your body positioning in the lane is right on. You extend the baton to your teammate, perfect extension, perfect spacing. Your relay is really flying and everyone is doing their part.

You run fast, relaxed, fluid, smooth, and under control. Feel the turnover of the legs. Feel the arms synchronize as you stay relaxed. Your head remains lined up with your trunk... your focus is on keeping form. You maintain your relaxation as you drive through your finish. You feel great... you have that inner feeling that you've given it your all and have done your best.

You stop, bend down, and put your hands on your knees to catch your breath. You are breathing hard. The adrenaline of success is rushing through your body... You hear your teammates congratulating you as you walk off the track, people pat you on the back and shake your hand. Feel the exhilaration of accomplishment... the joy of success. As you walk back to put on your sweats and visit with your team, you feel a tremendous sense of accomplishment as you responded to the challenge. You know that you have run one of the best races of your life... you know that you were psychologically and physically prepared. All your training, both physical and mental, has paid off. After you accept congratulations from your coach and friends, take time to thank your body... your legs, your lungs and your entire body... You have achieved your goal!

Now begin to let go of this image and this feeling. Feel your body... move your toes.... Move your fingers... begin to notice your breathing...inhale...exhale...inhale...exhale. You feel relaxed and filled with a new quiet energy.

To help further develop all of your imagery senses, use Activity 11.5. Certain senses may produce clearer attention than others. Use this exercise to provide direction for extra attention and practices.

Activity 11.5
Sensory Imagery for Relays

Vividness: Imagine the baton. Notice the color of the baton. Notice how round it is. Notice the exchange zone and follow it all the way around the track.

Auditory: What sounds do you hear while you are running the relay?

Tactile: Image the feel of the baton in your hand. What does it feel like? Image the feel of your feet on the track. What does it feel like? Notice how soft or hard it feels to land on it

Kinesthetic: Imagine running during the relay. Feel what your body is doing during the warm-ups. Feel the muscles in your legs as you run. Note the power in your legs as you do your warm-up. Feel yourself taking the baton and handing it off. Feel the sensation of your body sprinting on the track.

Smell: Smell the track, your shoes, and the grass. Smell the sweat after a hard practice.

Taste: Taste the salt from the sweat on your lips. Imagine taking a drink of water during a hot day of practice.

Emotion: Experience the confidence you feel when you run a great relay. Experience the satisfaction of running fast with your teammates. Experience the pride you feel in achieving a PR. Experience the excitement of being on a successful team.

Vividness Evaluation
What were your strongest images and sensations?
What senses do you need to improve?

A Relay Self-Evaluation can be found in Activity 11.6 and can be used periodically to evaluate practice or competition. A general Team Post-Meet Evaluation form can be found in Activity 19.4.

Activity 11.6
Relay Self-Evaluation

Rate yourself on a scale of 1-10 (with 10 being high)

1. Overall Performance _____
2. Warm-ups _____
3. Performance in meets _____
4. Encouragement of others _____
5. My positive attitude _____
6. Use of mental training _____
7. Mental training on own _____
8. Proper sleep _____
9. Proper nutrition _____
10. Good hydration practices _____
11. Ability to push yourself _____
12. Contribution to team _____
13. Progress towards your goal _____
14. Start _____
15. 1st handoff _____
16. Middle of race _____
17. 2nd handoff _____
18. Lane Positions _____
19. Visualization of relay _____
20. Speed at handoff _____

Activity 11.7
Personalized Guided Visualization

Objective:
To write a personalized guided visualization script. In your own words write a visualization of an upcoming performance. This visualization will let you see, hear, and feel yourself performing your sport.

Directions:
Write a personalized guided visualization script. Be as specific as possible. Include as many senses you can. Write it down as full and complete as you can. Remember to use positive statements and include your affirmations. Use the worksheet to formulate your ideas. Then write out your guided visualization in an essay format. After writing the visualization, I would encourage you to record the script. Find a quiet time to play some relaxation music and then play your recorded script. As you talk to yourself, see the visualization coming to life!

Worksheet for your guided visualization

Day of the Event
    See yourself getting up in the morning with confidence.
    What will you have to eat?
    See yourself dressing for the competition, putting on your clothing.

Arriving at the Site
    See yourself arriving at the site
    See the competition
    See the environment, weather, temperature
    Focus on your goal and the outcome you wish to achieve

The Warm-up
    See yourself doing your general warm-up
    See yourself stretching, drills, strides
    See yourself doing your final preparations with your teammates
    See yourself putting on your competition shoes

The Start
    See yourself in your starting position
    Hear and feel your first few steps
    See yourself getting out to a good powerful start

Exchange
    See and feel the acceleration into the exchange zone.
    See the perfect hand-off
    See and feel the acceleration out of the exchange zone.

Running
    See and feel yourself running tall
    Feel the control and rhythm of the race
    Feel relaxed and strong
    Feel yourself slicing through the wind

Post-Race
    Feel the satisfaction of running well with your relay
    See the teammates, coaches, family and friends congratulating you
    When the event is over, you feel great about your running

A sample week for a Relay Mental Preparation Plan is provided in Table 11.1. Use the example to help complete the blank form in Activity 19.1 to develop your Mental Preparation plan.

Table 11.1
Sample Weekly Mental Preparation Plan for Relays

Day	Physical Practice	Mental Practice
Monday	½ mile warm-up Dynamic warm-up 6 x 200 meters Static stretch ½ mile jog cool down	Incorporate into practice (See Table 11.2) **Outside of practice:** Review weekly goals Positive self-talk Relaxation-Imagery of weekly goals
Tuesday	½ mile warm-up Dynamic warm-up Work on relays	Incorporate into practice (Table 11.2) **Outside of practice:** Mental recall Affirmations:
Wednesday	½ mile warm-up Dynamic warm-up 6 x 100 meter strides 4x 400 meters with 5 minute rest 1 mile jog cool down	Incorporate into practice (Table 11.2) **Outside of practice:** Develop competition plan Visualize competition plan
Thursday	½ mile warm-up Work on relay exchanges Team games Character Building Mental Training	Incorporate into practice (Table 11.2) **Outside of practice:** Relaxation Visualize competition plan Visualize mental recovery plans
Friday	Competition	See Table 11.3 and 11.4 for example of meet day mental preparation plan Outside of practice:
Saturday	Easy recovery jog Stretch	Complete post-competition evaluation Use mental recall to see highlights Use mental recall lowlights/highlights Review previous week goal progress Set new process and effort goals
Sunday	Recovery- Walk Bike Swim Stretch	Relaxation Mental rehearsal of next week's goals Positive Self-talk Read about a motivating athlete

Table 11.2 provides ideas to incorporate mental skills into your regular practice. A blank form is provided in Activity 19.6 to help you develop your plan to incorporate mental skills into your workouts.

Table 11.2
Ideas to Incorporate Mental and Physical Plan into Workouts

Physical Activity	When to use	Mental Activity
Relay handoffs	Relay exchanges	Visualize a perfect exchange
Starting block practice	Standing behind blocks	Rapid energization to achieve proper arousal
Speed work	Sprinting full speed	Cue words Relaxing breathing

Use Table 11.3 for ideas on how to develop a Mental Performance Pre-Competition Plan. In Activity 19.2 a blank form is provided to help you develop your plan to incorporate mental skills into your pre-competition warm-up.

\multicolumn{3}{c}{**Table 11.3**}		
\multicolumn{3}{c}{**Example Relay Performance Pre-Competition Plan**}		
Time Prior to Start	**Physical WU**	**Mental WU**
75-80 min	Initial Race check-in Pick-up number Check heat, lane assignments	Relaxation and Cue Words
65-75 min	Easy jog to get blood flowing	Go over race plan from assigned lane Imagery involving running with perfect form Confidence card or self-talk script Review back-up plans
50-65 min	Stretching	Focus on breathing, relaxation Positive self-talk Quick imagery of portions of event
40-50 min	Dynamic Warm-up Good form	Focus on energization
30-40 min	Drills Proper technique Relax body while doing drills	Positive self-talk Relaxed while doing drills
20-30 min	Strides Relay work with teammates Focus on pushing while staying low	Cue words- to stay fast Increase arousal if needed to get in proper arousal zone Positive mental attitude high Focus on personal goals and the processes to make it happen
15-20 min	Bathroom Break	Rapid relaxation to deal with pre-race nervousness
10-15 min	Isolation Check final meet gear equipment	Quick review of overall race plane Vividly see running and hitting goal time and splits Use rapid relaxation or energization techniques to get in your proper zone Positive self-talk
10 min	Check-in at line Set up blocks and do three starts Remove warm-ups	Maintain proper arousal zone Rapid relaxation Positive self-talk Cue words

In Table 11.4, a Mental Performance Plan is provided. The plan is divided into different phases of the competition. To help incorporate your mental skills into your performance, complete Activity 19.3 and develop your Mental Performance Plan.

Table 11.4
Example Relay Mental Performance Competition Plan

Competition Phase	Physical	Mental	Cue Words
Start	Drive hard and low Push with legs	Energization Control breathing Focus on explosive movement	Relax, Explode, Drive, React, Go, Boom
Exchange zone	Accelerate in Maintain lane position Accelerate out Timing	Focus on driving Positive self-talk	Low, Power, Accelerate, Stick, Smooth
Middle	Good form Rhythm Maintain form to finish	Breathing Relaxed Positive Self-talk Focus in lane Focus on process	Cruise, Smooth

Table 11.5 provides examples of Mental Recovery Plans for Track Events. See Activity 19.3 for a blank form to complete that will help you develop your Mental Recovery Plan.

Table 11.5
Mental Recovery Plans for Track Events

Distractors-Track Events	Release	Re-focus	How to prepare for
Fall down during race	Getting up	Focus on gradually catching up Measure your energy over the remaining distance	In practice, kneeling down and let your teammates get ahead of you
False start	Flush Toilet	Relaxation Positive self-talk Imagery of next event	Practice composing yourself after false starts
Drop the baton	See baton	Focus on securing baton Focus on runners ahead Measure your energy	Practice having to pick-up baton in crowded situations-simulate in practice
Boxed in	Take a mental snapshot of race ahead of you	Relaxation Focus on vision looking for gap Cue words to accelerate	Practice being boxed in
Hit hurdle that knocks you off rhythm	Look at next hurdle	Focus on rhythm Process cue words	Use padded hurdle to simulate hitting hurdle

Chapter 12

High Jump

Activity 12.1
High Jump Power Picture
Directions: Find a good picture of when you are competing. Make sure the picture shows you in good form and looking strong. Put the picture on a page (preferably cardboard stock). Place your cue words around the picture.

E   A
X   T
P   T
L   A
O   C
D   K
E

VERTICAL

Activity 12.2
High Jump Affirmations

- I love to jump.
- I am a high jumper.
- I have the courage to be a great high jumper
- I am strong and explosive.
- My approach is rhythmic and consistent.
- My strides are rhythmic and powerful.
- I run tall and under control on the approach.
- My first steps are consistent and right on.
- My approach is fluid and smooth.
- I am centered and focused.
- I accelerate on my approach.
- I plant my take-off foot with a quick stride.
- I drive up to a vertical take-off position.
- I aggressively drive the knee.
- I keep my hips elevated all the way over the bar.
- I lift my head and legs after my hips clear the bar.
- My jumping motion is fluid, smooth, and under control.
- I want to jump higher and higher.
- I relax and let it happen.
- I enjoy the exhilaration of a good jump.
- I am proud to be a high jumper.
- I am a great high jumper.
- Each day I become a better high jumper.

Activity 12.3
High Jump Mental Recall

Begin to think of a time in your life when you knew that you were right on and performed perfectly. See yourself at that time... notice what you look like... what you are wearing... who is with you... what sounds are around you, where you are. Feel the environment and the energy. Begin to see yourself high jumping when you knew you were right on... when everything worked perfectly... when you were in complete control and at your peak. Watch yourself and feel that feeling... connect with all of the feelings you experienced as you achieved at your highest level.... Perfectly...competently... exactly the way you wanted to...what did it feel like?... sound like?...look like?

Remember your thoughts before you jumped that day. Remember how comfortable and relaxed you felt. Feel the rhythm of that jump come back. How smooth, fluid and powerful it felt, as you built up controlled speed... ran a smooth curve... performed a powerful vertical take-off... achieved an efficient clearance... and came up with a PR. Let it all come back to you... let it in... know it again... the joy... the power... the pride and confidence... the rush of knowing you were perfection... let it become part of you... part of your spirit... part of your being. Fully connect with it.

Feel the movements that you perfectly executed. How good the start of your run-up felt. The first few steps were right where you wanted them to be... consistent... feel the rhythm... starting slow and building up speed. Feel the power that was stored up and then unleashed as you accelerated on your approach. See yourself on that day when you were running tall, erect body position. See the first half of your approach as you ran in a straight line... controlling your speed... running the curve... smoothly... fluidly... powerful. Feel the lean toward the center of the curve and away from the bar. Remember the acceleration over the final three strides, your head up, and eyes focused on the bar. Remember how the hips were ahead of the upper body... in a laid back position, the last two strides landing flat-flat. Feel the powerful plant of the take-off foot. Remember how quick and active it was, in front of the center of gravity...everything flowed together perfectly... just the way you wanted it. Feel the explosiveness as you ran off the ground straight up in the air. Remember the powerful action of the arm and the free leg swing as they occurred synchronized and tight to the body. Feel the power drive of the knee... aggressive... strong...parallel to the bar. Feel the powerful block you achieved that day. Remember the feeling of soaring straight up in the air... higher and higher, up, up, up... straight up. Your chin was lowered as you looked down the bar, you just knew you were going to clear the bar... your hips stayed elevated over the bar, your heels were tucked apart. After you cleared the bar you lifted your head and legs. A tremendous feeling of satisfaction came over you as you knew you had set a personal best. You landed on the broad surface of your back. You cleared! A tremendous rush of adrenaline flowed through you. What a satisfying feeling. It felt so good to jump so high!

While completely involves with this feeling, give yourself a cue word or affirmation that brings all these feelings and pictures into focus...a cue word or affirmation that completely connects you with that time and those feelings when you knew that you were perfect and right on...say the words or words to yourself several times... slowly and allow yourself to experience your sense of power and control...feel it in your whole body. See and feel yourself high jumping that day. How you cleared the heights so effortlessly. Higher than you had ever jumped before and it felt so easy. It felt so good to clear a high height. Everything worked perfectly, just the way you wanted it to.

Activity 12.4
High Jump Mental Rehearsal

See yourself at the track where you will be competing...wearing your competition clothes...your thoughts are focused on jumping high. Notice the weather... the clouds... the wind... the sun... the temperature...whatever it is that you can picture and feel in your mind. Notice your competition...visually check out the other competitors...you are calm, confident, and relaxed and feeling really good. You are looking forward to jumping high and you have a feeling of being well-prepared for your event. You are feeling good both mentally and physical. Your hard work and sacrifices are paying off! See yourself doing your normal warm-up routine...you feel good in the jumping warm-ups, you are ready to jump high. You notice some jumpers you will be jumping against...you remain calm, confident, and relaxed...you feel good and are ready to jump...you have a deep, calm, yet somewhat nervous feeling inside. Your heart is pounding and the adrenaline is flowing....you say your cue words or affirmations to yourself... what a day this is going to be for you!

You feel good because you know that you have been working hard, training well and have made many sacrifices to be the best you can be…think of all the time you have spent jumping, sprinting, stretching, working on drills…technique…weight training…mental training. All this work is going to pay off today! You are physically and mentally ready to jump very high.

See yourself going through your normal warm-up…running… the muscles begin to limber up… the stretching… the sprinting… your breathing hard indicates the muscles are getting oxygen and will be ready to perform when called upon…You prepare mentally as you think about high jumping. You loosen up…feel the sweat on your body and your heart pumping…as your body gets warmer and warmer…preparing itself for competition… You've measured your marks out. See yourself going through some run throughs, your steps are right on and feeling good. Your warm-up jumps feel easy. You are ready to jump high.

Your body feels so powerful and explosive today. You are focused and in control. Your warm-up went well… you feel ready…you feel ready for a personal record…just the way you want. You relax while waiting for the competition to start. While waiting repeat your cue words say your affirmations to yourself…take a deep breath… inhale…exhale…inhale…exhale. Your warm-up and run throughs felt strong and powerful…your workouts have been going well… you are ready to jump higher than you have all year. You check in with the head judge. You notice your competitors… see the colors of their uniforms…you acknowledge them but remain focused on yourself. You will focus on your high jumping… You hear your jumping order… as you hear your name, feel the tinge of anticipation, you hear the official wish everyone "good luck."

You stay loose and confident while you are waiting for your turn to jump. Hear the official call your name and see yourself prepare to jump. As you stand waiting, you are confident. You are ready! You take a deep breath and gather your thoughts. You exhale and relax, saying your cue words or affirmations. Your body and mind responds positively. You have been looking forward to this.

See yourself on the runway, ready to jump. You feel strong and powerful as you start your approach. Your first few steps are right where you want them to be. Feel the speed building up from a controlled start. Your gradual acceleration is smooth, starting slow, gaining speed, under control. Your first few steps are perfect, right where you want them. You are showing excellent form, running tall, erect body position, hips high, shoulders relaxed. You gain speed running a straight line. With a smooth fluid controlled movement you run the curve, leaning toward the center of the curve… feel the push out to stay on the curve… feel the acceleration over the final three strides…your head is up, eyes are focused on the bar…your hips are forward, ahead of the upper body, you can feel the layback as you set up in proper take-off position…your last two strides are flat-flat…quick…quick… you feel the rhythm… you can hear the rhythm….feel the plant… as you plant powerfully with a quick active stride in the front of the center of gravity… feel yourself run up into the air… as your knee drives strongly…feel yourself explode vertically…up… straight up, up, up, up. The take-off feels powerful as you pop off the ground. Feel the arm action and free leg swing… they occur together… synchronized… tight to the body… feel that aggressive knee drive as you bring the knee through quick and fast… as you are in the air you look down the bar… bring your chin toward your chest... The jump feels great. Your hips are over the bar… your hips are elevated as you tuck your glutes… and high over the bar you go… you tuck the heels, keeping the knees apart… you are in control… after the hips clear the bar, you tuck your chin to the chest lifting your heels over the bar. A great jump… a PR… you are filled with a tremendous sense of satisfaction as you fall to the mat on the broad surface of your back in a perfect landing. You feel great… you have that inner feeling that you've given it your all and have done your best.

As you climb off the landing pit, you are catching your breath. The adrenaline of success is rushing through your body. You hear friends congratulating you… as you walk away, people pat you on the back and shake your hand. Feel the exhilaration of accomplishment…the joy of success. As you walk off the high jump approach and put on your sweats, you feel a tremendous sense of accomplishment as you responded to the challenge. You know that you have jumped a personal best height… you know that you were psychologically and physically prepared. All your training, both physical and mental, has paid off. After you accept congratulations from your coach and friends, take time to thank your body… your legs, your lungs and your entire body… You have achieved your goal!

Begin to let go of this image and this feeling. Slowly re-enter your present space… feel your body… move your toes… move your fingers… begin to notice your breathing…inhale…exhale…inhale…exhale. You feel relaxed and filled with a new quiet energy.

To help further develop all of your senses in imagery use Activity 12.5. Certain senses may produce clearer attention than others. Use this exercise to provide direction for extra attention.

Activity 12.5
Sensory Imagery for High Jump

Vividness: Imagine the high jump crossbar. Notice the color of the bar. Notice how round it is. Notice the pit that you will land in. Notice how big it is. Notice the runway and follow it all the way to the pit.

Auditory: What sounds do you hear while you are getting ready to jump? Hear the sound of your approach and hear yourself landing in the pit.

Tactile: Image the feel of your feet on the runway. What does it feel like? Notice the pit and how soft it feels to land on it.

Kinesthetic: Imagine jumping during warm-ups. Feel what your body is doing during the warm-ups. Feel the muscles in your legs as you run and jump. Note the power in your legs as you do your warm-up jumps. Feel yourself rocketing up into the air. Feel the sensation of your body bending over the cross bar. Feel the pressure as you land on your back to complete the jump.

Smell: Smell the pit, your shoes, the grass, and the runway. Smell the sweat after a hard practice.

Taste: Taste the salt from the sweat on your lips. Imagine taking a drink of water during a hot day of practice.

Emotion: Experience the confidence you feel when you step up to jump. Experience the satisfaction of jumping high. Experience the pride you feel in achieving a PR. Experience the excitement of being on a successful team.

Vividness Evaluation
What were your strongest images and sensations?
What senses do you need to improve?

A High Jump Self-Evaluation can be found in Activity 12.6 and can be used periodically to evaluate practice or competition. A general Team Post-Meet Evaluation form can be found in Activity 19.4.

Activity 12.6
High Jump Self-Evaluation

Rate yourself on a scale of 1-10 (with 10 being high)

1. Overall Performance _____	11. Ability to push yourself _____
2. Warm-ups _____	12. Contribution to team _____
3. Performance in meets _____	13. Progress towards your goal _____
4. Encouragement of others _____	14. Approach _____
5. My positive attitude _____	15. Curve _____
6. Use of mental training _____	16. Plant Position _____
7. Mental training on own _____	17. Take-off _____
8. Proper sleep _____	18. Flight _____
9. Proper nutrition _____	19. Visualization of jump _____
10. Good hydration practices _____	20. Focus _____

Activity 12.7
Personalized Guided Visualization

Objective:
To write a personalized guided visualization script. In your own words write a visualization of an upcoming performance. This visualization will let you see, hear, and feel yourself performing your sport.

Directions:
Write a personalized guided visualization script. Be as specific as possible. Include as many senses you can. Write it down as full and complete as you can. Remember to use positive statements and include your affirmations. Use the worksheet to formulate your ideas. Then write out your guided visualization in an essay format. After writing the visualization, I would encourage you to record the script. Find a quiet time to play some relaxation music and then play your recorded script. As you talk to yourself, see the visualization coming to life!

Worksheet for your guided visualization

Day of the Event
- See yourself getting up in the morning with confidence.
- What will you have to eat?
- See yourself dressing for the competition, putting on your clothing.

Arriving at the Site
- See yourself arriving at the site
- See the competition, the environment, weather, temperature
- Focus on your goal and the outcome you wish to achieve

The Warm-up
- See yourself doing your general warm-up, stretching, drills
- See yourself doing your final preparations
- See yourself putting on your competition shoes

The Start
- See yourself on the high jump apron
- Hear and feel your first few steps
- See yourself getting out to a good powerful start

The Approach
- See and feel yourself starting to accelerate
- Feel the inside lean of the shoulder to the curve
- Feel yourself running under control but fast

The Plant
- See and feel the proper take-off position
- Feel you propel yourself straight up into the air
- Feel the strong pop with the knee
- See and feel the arm drive as it lifts you off the ground

On Top of the Bar
- Feel the tight tuck of the hips on top of the bar
- Feel the curve of the back as you fly over the bar
- See and feel yourself dropping your chin after your hips clear
- See and feel the legs clearing the bar

Post Jump
- Feel the satisfaction of clearing the bar
- See the teammates, coaches, family and friends congratulating you
- When the event is over, you feel great about your jumping

A sample week for a High Jump Mental Preparation Plan is provided in Table 12.1. Use the example to help complete the blank form in Activity 19.1 to develop your Mental Preparation plan.

\multicolumn{3}{c}{**Table 12.1 Sample Weekly High Jump Mental Preparation Plan**}
Day	**Physical Practice**	**Mental Practice**
Monday	½ mile warm-up Dynamic warm-up 6 x circle 6 x arch-over 6 x approach no jump 6 x full approach ½ mile jog cool down	Incorporate into practice (see Table 12.2) **Outside of practice:** Review weekly goals Positive self-talk Relaxation Imagery of achieving weekly goals
Tuesday	½ mile warm-up Dynamic warm-up Easy strides	Incorporate into practice (Table 12.2) **Outside of practice:** Mental recall Affirmations:
Wednesday	½ mile warm-up 6 x circle 6 x arch-over 6 x approach no jump 6 x full approach ½ mile jog cool down	Incorporate into practice (Table 12.2) **Outside of practice:** Develop competition plan Visualize competition plan
Thursday	½ mile warm-up 20 minutes fartlek Team games Character Building Mental Training	Incorporate into practice (Table 12.2) **Outside of practice:** Relaxation Visualize competition plan Visualize mental recovery plans
Friday	Competition	See Table 12.3 and 12.4 for example of meet day mental preparation plan Outside of practice:
Saturday	Easy recovery jog Stretch	Complete post-competition evaluation Use mental recall to see highlights Use mental recall to see lowlights-rewind to make it a highlight Review previous week goal progress Set new goals with emphasis on process and effort goals
Sunday	Recovery- Walk Bike Swim Stretch	Relaxation Mental rehearsal of next week's goals Positive Self-talk Read about a motivating athlete

Table 12.2 provides ideas to incorporate mental skills into your regular practice. A blank form is provided in Activity 19.2 to help you develop your plan to incorporate mental skills into your workouts.

Table 12.2 Ideas to Incorporate Mental Plan into Workouts		
Physical Activity	**When to use**	**Mental Activity**
Approach	Before approach	Visualize parts of the approach Cue words
Take-off	Before jump	Rapid energization to achieve proper arousal
Going vertical	During drills	Cue words Visualization

Use Table 12.3 for ideas on how to develop a Mental Performance Pre-Competition Plan. In Activity 19.2, a blank form is provided to help you develop your plan to incorporate mental skills into your pre-competition warm-up.

Table 12.3 Example High Jump Performance Pre-Competition Plan		
Time Prior to Start	**Physical WU**	**Mental WU**
75-80 min	Initial check-in Pick-up number Check flight	Relaxation and cue words
65-75 min	Easy jog to get blood flowing	Go over technical plan Imagery involving jumping with perfect form Confidence card or self-talk script Review back-up plans
50-65 min	Stretching	Focus on breathing, relaxation Positive self-talk Quick imagery of portions of event
40-50 min	Measure in steps Dynamic Warm-up Good form	Cue words Visualization
30-40 min	Drills Proper technique Relax body while doing drills	Positive self-talk Relaxed while doing drills
20-30 min	Jumps	Cue words- to stay fast and explosive Increase arousal if needed to get in proper arousal zone Positive mental attitude high Focus on personal goals and the processes to make it happen
15-20 min	Bathroom Break	Rapid relaxation to deal with pre-race nervousness
10-15 min	Isolation Check-in Check final meet gear equipment	Quick review of overall competition plan Vividly see jumping with good form Use rapid relaxation or energization techniques to get in your proper zone Positive self-talk

In Table 12.4, a Mental Performance Plan is provided. The plan is divided into different phases of the competition. To help incorporate your mental skills into your performance, complete Activity 19.3 and develop your Mental Performance Plan.

Table 12.4
High Jump Mental Performance Plan

Competition Phase	Physical	Mental	Cue Words
The Start	Good powerful start	Positive self-talk Image jump Push off Accelerate	Rhythm Drive
The Approach	Accelerate Inside lean to curve	Fast but under control Focus on curve	Attack Quick
The Plant	Proper position Drive the knee Go up	Stick the plant Focus on cue words	Stick Pop Vertical
Top of the Bar	Tight tuck Drop chin after hips clear	Feel the tuck Focus on finish	Tuck Control
Landing	Land on back	Focus land safely	Made it Great

Table 12.5 provides examples of Mental Recovery Plans for Field Events. See Activity 19.5 for a blank form to complete that will help you develop your Mental Recovery Plan.

Table 12.5
Mental Recovery Plan for Field Events

Distractors-Field Events	Release	Re-focus	How to prepare for
Wind	Exhale air out, blow the wind away	Focus on process goals not outcome Focus on process cues	Practice with a cross wind or occasionally into the wind
Rain	Wipe forehead	Positive self-talk Arousal techniques such as energization	Practice on some rainy days
Cold	Rub sweats or clothing	Positive self-talk Imagery of goal achievement	Practice in cold
Weather delays	Relaxation breathing	Relaxation Positive self-talk	Start practice and delay it for several minutes to simulate a rain delay
Miss first two attempts	Park mistake in an object	Cue words that focus on process	Simulation jumping

Chapter 13

Long Jump

Activity 13.1
Long Jump Power Picture

Directions: Find a good picture of when you are competing. Make sure the picture shows you in good form and looking strong. Put the picture on a page (preferably cardboard stock). Place your cue words around the picture.

P
O
W
E
R

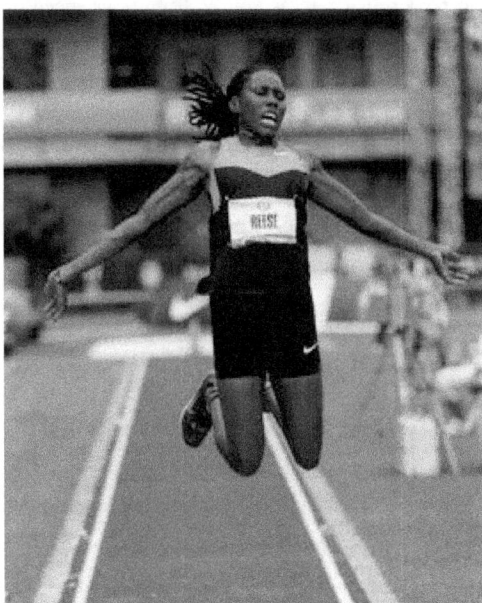

E
X
P
L
O
D
E

FLY

Activity 13.2
Long Jump Affirmations

- I am a long jumper.
- I love to jump.
- I am committed to a long jumper's lifestyle.
- I have the courage to be a great long jumper.
- Each day I become a better jumper.
- My approach is rhythmic and consistent.
- My strides are rhythmic and powerful.
- I run tall and under control on the approach.
- My first steps are consistent and right on.
- My approach is fluid and smooth.
- I want to jump further and further.
- I enjoy the exhilaration of a good jump.
- I accelerate to a fast controllable speed.
- My head is up and eyes on a high focal point.
- I run off the board into the air.
- My free leg drive drives strong on the take-off.
- I stay tall as I run off the board.
- My flight is balanced and prepares me for an efficient landing.
- My jumping motion is fluid, smooth and under control.
- I am proud to be a long jumper.

Activity 13.3
Long Jump Mental Recall

Begin to think of a time in your life when you knew that you were right on and performed perfectly. See yourself at that time... notice what you look like, what you are wearing, who is with you what sounds are around you, where you are... Feel the environment and the energy. Begin to see yourself long jumping when you knew you were right on... when everything worked perfectly... when you were in complete control and at your peak.. Watch yourself and feel that feeling... connect with all of the feelings you experienced as you achieved at your highest level.... Perfectly...competently... exactly the way you wanted to...what did it feel like?... sound like?...look like?

Remember your thoughts before you jumped that day... Remember how comfortable and relaxed you felt. Feel the rhythm of that jump come back.. How smooth, fluid and powerful it felt, as you built up your speed on the runway... ran off the board in a powerful explosive takeoff... maintained balance and control in the flight... had a perfect landing and came up with a PR. Let it all come back to you... let it in... know it again... the joy... the power... the pride and confidence... the rush of knowing you were perfection.. let it become part of you ... part of your spirit... part of your being... Fully connect with it.

Feel the movements that you perfectly executed. How good the start of your run-up felt. The first few steps were right where you wanted them to be... consistent... feel the rhythm... starting slow and building up speed... Feel the power that was stored up and then unleashed as you accelerated on your approach. See yourself on that day when you were running tall, erect body position... knees coming high... head up... arms and shoulders relaxed... running fast. You were a sprinter on the runway that day. Fluid, smooth, under control... powerful... Remember the acceleration over the final few strides. You ran off the board, exploding up and out, sailing through the air... You knew you had popped a great jump. Remember that feeling of power and control as you ran off the board... hips, high, feeling tall... Remember the control and balance of your feet... body balance... just the way you practiced it... arms and legs in perfect control as you started to land... your arms swept down and you just kept sailing through the air, further and further. What a ride... what a feeling... finally the feet touched the sand and your weight collapsed forward over bent legs. You timed the movement of the arms forward perfectly and it helped shift your body forward. Remember the feeling of the sand...a tremendous feeling of satisfaction came over you, as you knew you had set a personal best. What a satisfying feeling.

It felt so good to jump so far. As you walk away from the pit, you receive congratulations from teammates, coaches and friends. What a jump... what a feeling.

While completely involved with this feeling, give yourself a cue word or affirmation that brings all these feelings and pictures into focus...a cue word or affirmation that completely connects you with that time and those feelings when you knew that you were perfect and right on...say the words or words to yourself several times... slowly allow yourself to experience your sense of power and control...feel it in your whole body.

See and feel yourself long jumping that day. How you jumped so effortlessly. Further than you had ever jumped before and it felt so easy. Everything worked perfectly, just the way you wanted it to.

Activity 13.4
Long Jump Mental Rehearsal

See yourself arriving at the track meet. You are wearing your competition clothes... your thoughts are focused on long jumping... you feel good today... you are looking forward to jumping far... you have some really good feelings about your performance. Picture the weather... the sun... the clouds... the wind... the temperature. This is a great day for a P.R. You are excited and ready to jump. You notice some long jumpers you will be jumping against as you warm-up. You remain calm, confident, and relaxed. You feel good and are ready to jump... you have a deep, calm, yet somewhat nervous feeling inside... your heart is pounding and the adrenaline is flowing... you say your cue words or affirmations to yourself... what a day this this is going to be for you. You are looking forward to jumping far and you have a feeling of being well-prepared for your event... you are feeling good both mentally and physical. You feel good because you know that you have been working hard, training well and have made many sacrifices to be the best you can be... think of all the time you have spent jumping, sprinting, stretching, working on drills... technique... weight training... mental training. All this work is going to pay off today! You are physically and mentally ready to jump far. Your hard work and sacrifices are paying off! See yourself doing your normal warm-up routine... you feel good. See yourself going through your normal warm-up... running... the muscles begin to limber up... the stretching... the sprinting... your breathing hard indicates the muscles are getting oxygen and will be ready to perform when called upon... You prepare mentally as you think about long jumping. You loosen up... feel the sweat on your body and your heart pumping... as your body gets warmer and warmer... preparing itself for competition... You've measured your marks out. See yourself going through some run throughs, your steps are right on and feeling good. Your warm-up jumps feel easy. You are ready to jump far today.

Your body feels so powerful and explosive today. You are focused and in control. Your warm-up went well... you feel ready...

you feel ready for a personal record…just the way you want to be… You relax while waiting for the competition to start. While waiting repeat your cue words and say your affirmations to yourself…take a deep breath… inhale…exhale…inhale…exhale…Your warm-up and run throughs felt strong and powerful… your workouts have been going well… you are ready to jump farther than you have all year. You check in with the head judge. You notice your competitors… see the colors of their uniforms… you acknowledge them but remain focused on yourself… You will focus on your long jumping… You hear your jumping order… as you hear your name, feel the anticipation. You stay loose and confident while you are waiting for your turn to jump. Hear the official call your name and see yourself prepare to jump. As you stand on the runway, you are confident. You are ready! You take a deep breath and gather your thoughts. You exhale and relax saying your cue words or affirmations. Your body and mind responds positively. You have been looking forward to this.

See yourself on the runway, ready to jump. You feel strong and powerful as you start your approach. Your first few steps are right where you want them to be. Feel the speed building up from a controlled start. Your gradual acceleration is smooth, starting slow and gaining speed, under control. Your first few steps are perfect, right where you want them. You are showing excellent form, running tall, erect body position, hips high, shoulders relaxed. Your strides are getting longer; your stride tempo is increasing. You feel springy as you run on the balls of your feet… feel the speed… you are under control… your head is up, your eyes are focused beyond the pit. As you approach the take-off board, feel your stride rhythm quicken… you accelerate through the last few strides. Feel the last two foot plants… flat-flat. You run off the board with a fast take-off stride and explosive takeoff. You are running up into the air… forward and upward… what a great takeoff… you know you have a great jump. You drive the knee of your free leg hard… aggressive… you feel tall… your upper body is erect… feel the hips high and forward… perfect… just the what you wanted… feel yourself flying through he air… it feels so good… this is what you enjoy about long jumping… sailing though the air. Feel yourself balanced and in control as you sail through the air… Your arms and legs are synchronized as you begin to achieve an efficient landing position… your arms sweep back and you pull though bent knees… feel your legs staying up and staying up as you continue to ride all you can out of your jump. As the feet touch the sand, feel the legs bend as you collapse your weight forward… see the arms coming forward to help move your entire body forward… you feel your momentum carry you through the sand as you come to a landing. You know it's a great jump… maybe a PR… you are filled with a tremendous sense of satisfaction as you move out of the pit.

You feel great. You have that inner feeling that you've given it your all and have done your best. As you walk away from the landing pit you are catching your breath… The adrenaline of success is rushing through your body… You hear friends congratulating you… as you walk away, people pat you on the back and shake your hand. Feel the exhilaration of accomplishment… the joy of success. As you walk over to put on your sweats, you feel a tremendous sense of accomplishment as you responded to the challenge. You know that you have jumped far… you know that you were psychologically and physically prepared. All your training both physical and mental has paid off. After you accept congratulations from your coach and friends, take time to thank your body… your legs, your lungs and your entire body… You have achieved your goal!

Begin to let go of this image and this feeling… slowly re-enter your present space…feel your body… move your toes… move your fingers… begin to notice your breathing…inhale…exhale…inhale…exhale. You feel relaxed and filled with a new quiet energy.

To help further develop all of your imagery senses, use Activity 13.5. Certain senses may produce clearer attention than others. Use this exercise to provide direction for extra attention.

Activity 13.5
Sensory Imagery for Long Jump

Vividness: Imagine the long jump pit. Notice the color of the sand. See the pit that you will land in. Notice how big it is. Notice the runway and follow it all the way to the pit.

Auditory: What sounds do you hear while you are getting ready to jump? Hear the sound of your feet on the runway and in the pit. Hear the sound as you land in the pit.

Tactile: Image the feel of your feet on the runway. What does it feel like? Notice the pit and how soft it feels to land in it.

Kinesthetic: Imagine jumping during warm-ups. Feel what your body is doing during the warm-ups. Feel the muscles in your legs as you run and jump. Note the power in your legs as you do your warm-up jumps. Feel yourself rocketing up into the air. Feel the sensation of flying through the air. Feel the sand as you land to complete the jump.

Smell: Smell the sand, your shoes, the grass, and the runway. Smell the sweat after a hard practice.

Taste: Taste the salt from the sweat on your lips. Imagine taking a drink of water during a hot day of practice.

Emotion: Experience the confidence you feel when you step onto the runway to jump. Experience the satisfaction of jumping far. Experience the pride you feel in achieving a PR.

Vividness Evaluation
What were your strongest images and sensations?
What senses do you need to improve?

The Long Jump Self-Evaluation can be used periodically to evaluate practice or competition. A general Team Post-Meet Evaluation form can be found in Activity 19.4.

Activity 13.6
Long Jump Self-Evaluation

Rate yourself on a scale of 1-10 (with 10 being high)

1. Overall Performance _____	11. Ability to push yourself _____
2. Warm-ups _____	12. Contribution to team _____
3. Performance in meets _____	13. Progress towards your goal _____
4. Encouragement of others _____	14. Approach _____
5. My positive attitude _____	15. Last few strides _____
6. Use of mental training _____	16. Take off _____
7. Mental training on own _____	17. In air _____
8. Proper sleep _____	18. Landing _____
9. Proper nutrition _____	19. Visualization of jump _____
10. Good hydration practices _____	20. Focus _____

Activity 13.7
Personalized Guided Visualization

Objective:
To write a personalized guided visualization script. In your own words write a visualization of an upcoming performance. This visualization will let you see, hear, and feel yourself performing your sport.

Directions:
Write a personalized guided visualization script. Be as specific as possible. Include as many senses you can. Write it down as full and complete as you can. Remember to use positive statements and include your affirmations. Use the worksheet to formulate your ideas. Then write out your guided visualization in an essay format. After writing the visualization, I would encourage you to record the script. Find a quiet time to play some relaxation music and then play your recorded script. As you talk to yourself, see the visualization coming to life!

Worksheet for your guided visualization

Day of the Event
- See yourself getting up in the morning with confidence.
- What will you have to eat?
- See yourself dressing for the competition, putting on your clothing.

Arriving at the Site
- See yourself arriving at the site
- See the competition
- See the environment, weather, temperature
- Focus on your goal and the outcome you wish to achieve

The Warm-up
- See yourself doing your general warm-up
- See yourself stretching, drills
- See yourself doing your final preparations as you take run throughs and jumps
- See yourself putting on your competition shoes

The Start
- See yourself on the long jump runway
- Hear and feel your first few steps
- See yourself getting out to a good powerful start

The Approach
- See and feel your self starting to accelerate
- Feel the consistency of your steps
- Feel yourself running under control but fast

The Last Two Strides
- See and feel the proper take-off position
- Feel you propel yourself straight up into the air
- Feel the strong pop with the knee
- See and feel the arm drive as it lifts you off the ground

Flight and Landing
- Feel the curve of the back as you fly through the air
- Feel yourself with the leg up as you ride it out
- See and feel yourself pulling the hips through as you land in the sand

Post Jump
- Feel the satisfaction of jumping far
- See the teammates, coaches, family and friends congratulating you
- When the event is over, you feel great about your jumping

A sample week for a Long Jump Mental Preparation Plan is provided in Table 13.1. Use the example to help complete the blank form in Activity 19.1 to develop your Mental Preparation plan.

	Table 13.1 Sample Weekly Mental Preparation Plan	
Day	**Physical Practice**	**Mental Practice**
Monday	½ mile warm-up Dynamic warm-up 6 x 2 steps, 6 x pop-ups 6 x approach no jump/6 x full jump ½ mile jog cool down	Incorporate into practice (see Table 13.2) **Outside of practice:** Review weekly goals Positive self-talk Relaxation/Imagery of weekly goals
Tuesday	½ mile warm-up Dynamic warm-up Easy strides	Incorporate into practice (Table 13.2) **Outside of practice:** Mental recall/Affirmations
Wednesday	½ mile warm-up/Bounding exercises 10 x standing long jump 6 x approach work- run throughs 6 x full approach ½ mile jog cool down	Incorporate into practice (Table 13.2) **Outside of practice:** Develop competition plan Visualize competition plan
Thursday	½ mile warm-up 20 minutes fartlek Team games Character Building Mental Training	Incorporate into practice (Table 13.2) **Outside of practice:** Relaxation Visualize competition plan Visualize mental recovery plans
Friday	Competition	See Tables 13.3 and 13.4 for example of meet day mental preparation plan Confidence Card/ Power Picture
Saturday	Easy recovery jog Stretch	Complete post-competition evaluation Use mental recall to see highlights Use mental recall on low and highlights Review previous week goal progress Set new process and effort goals
Sunday	Recovery- Walk Bike Swim Stretch	Relaxation Mental rehearsal of next week's goals Positive self-talk Read about a motivating athlete

Table 13.2 provides ideas to incorporate mental drills into your regular practice. A blank form is provided in Activity 19.6 to help you develop your plan to incorporate mental drills into your workouts.

	Table 13.2 Ideas to Incorporate Mental Drills into Workouts	
Physical Activity	**When to use**	**Mental Activity**
Approach	Before approach	Cue words
Run off board	Before approach	Rapid energization to achieve proper arousal Cue words
Working on steps	During step work	Cue words Relaxing breathing

Use Table 13.3 to help you develop your plan to incorporate mental skills into your pre-competition warm-up. A blank form is provided in Activity 19.2 for you to write your pre-competition warm-up plan.

	Table 13.3 Example Long Jump Mental Preparation Pre-Competition Plan	
Time Prior to Start	Physical WU	Mental WU
75-80 min	Initial check-in Pick-up number Check flight	Relaxation and Cue Words
65-75 min	Easy jog to get blood flowing	Go over technical plan Imagery involving jumping with perfect form Confidence card or self-talk script Review back-up plans
50-65 min	Stretching	Focus on breathing, relaxation Positive self-talk Quick imagery of portions of event
40-50 min	Measure in steps Dynamic Warm-up Good form	Cue words Focus
30-40 min	Drills Proper technique Relax body while doing drills	Positive self-talk Relaxed while doing drills
20-30 min	Jumps	Cue words- to stay fast and explosive Increase arousal if needed to get in proper arousal zone Positive mental attitude high Focus on personal goals and the processes to make it happen
15-20 min	Bathroom Break	Rapid relaxation to deal with pre-competition nervousness
10-15 min	Isolation Check final meet gear equipment	Quick review of overall competition plan Vividly see jumping with good form Use rapid relaxation or energization techniques to get in your proper zone Positive self-talk

In Table 13.4, a Mental Performance Plan is provided. The plan is divided into different phases of the competition. To help incorporate your mental skills into your performance, complete Activity 19.3 and develop your Mental Performance Plan.

Table 13.4 Example Long Jump Mental Performance Plan			
Competition Phase	**Physical**	**Mental**	**Cue Words**
The Start	Good powerful start	Positive self-talk Image jump Push off Accelerate	Rhythm Drive
The Approach	Accelerate	Fast but under control	Attack Quick
The Take-off	Proper position Drive the knee Run off board	Focus on cue words	Flat, flat Run off Pop
The Flight	Hold position	Focus on slight lean back Feel sensation of flying	Hold Fly
Landing	Pull hips through	Focus on process	Pull

Table 13.5 provides examples of Mental Recovery Plans for Field Events. See Activity 19.5 for a blank form to complete that will help you develop your Mental Recovery Plan.

Table 13.5 Mental Recovery Plan for Field Events			
Distractors-Field Events	**Release**	**Re-focus**	**How to prepare for**
Wind	Exhale air out, blow the wind away	Focus on process goals not outcome Focus on process cues	Practice with a cross wind or occasionally into the wind
Rain	Wipe forehead	Positive self-talk Arousal techniques such as energization	Practice on some rainy days
Cold	Rub sweats or clothing	Positive self-talk Imagery of goal achievement	Practice in cold
Weather delays	Relaxation breathing	Relaxation Positive self-talk	Start practice and delay it for several minutes to simulate a rain delay
Foul first two attempts	Park mistake in an object	Cue words that focus on process	Simulation competing with two fouls in practice.

Chapter 14

Triple Jump

Activity 14.1
Triple Jump Power Picture

Directions: Find a good picture of when you are competing. Make sure the picture shows you in good form and looking strong. Put the picture on a page (preferably cardboard stock). Place your cue words around the picture.

CONTROL

RHYTHM

POWER

Activity 14.2
Triple Jump Affirmations

- I am a triple jumper.
- I love to jump.
- I am committed to a triple jumper's lifestyle.
- I have the courage to be a great triple jumper.
- Each day I become a better triple jumper.
- I have great strength, technique and rhythm.
- My strides are rhythmic and powerful.
- I run tall and under control on the approach.
- My first steps are consistent and right on.
- My approach is fluid and smooth.
- I accelerate to a controllable speed.
- My head is up and eyes on a high focal point.
- I drive off the board into the air.
- I have a flat, fast takeoff.
- My hop phase is under control.
- I am a great triple jumper.

- I land with balance, giving at the hip, knee and ankle joints.
- I have an active landing.
- I drive strong through the step phase.
- My arms and legs work together for smooth, fluid movements.
- I am balanced and under control on the step landing.
- My flight is balanced and prepares me for an efficient landing.
- My jumping motion is fluid, smooth and under control.
- I want to jump further and further.
- I enjoy the exhilaration of a good jump.
- I am proud to be a triple jumper.

Activity 14.3
Triple Jump Mental Recall

Begin to think of a time in your life when you knew that you were right on and performed perfectly. See yourself at that time… notice what you look like, what you are wearing, who is with you what sounds are around you, where you are. Feel the environment and the energy. Begin to see yourself triple jumping when you knew you were right on… when everything worked perfectly… when you were in complete control and at your peak.. Watch yourself and feel that feeling… connect with all of the feelings you experienced as you achieved at your highest level…. Perfectly…competently… exactly the way you wanted to…what did it feel like?... sound like?…look like?

Remember your thoughts before you jumped that day. Remember how comfortable and relaxed you felt. Feel the rhythm of that jump come back. How smooth, fluid and powerful it felt, as you built up your speed on the runway… ran off the board in a powerful explosive takeoff… maintained balance and control during the triple jump… had a perfect landing and came up with a PR. Let it all come back to you… let it in… know it again… the joy… the power… the pride and confidence… the rush of knowing you were perfection.. let it become part of you … part of your spirit... part of your being… Fully connect with it.

Feel the movements that you perfectly executed. How good the start of your run-up felt. The first few steps were right where you wanted them to be… consistent… feel the rhythm… starting slow and building up speed. Feel the power that was stored up and then unleashed as you accelerated on your approach. See yourself on that day when you were running tall, erect body position… knees coming high… head up... Arms and shoulders relaxed… running fast. You were a sprinter on the runway that day. Fluid, smooth, under control… powerful. Remember the acceleration over the final few strides. You ran off the board, exploding up and out, sailing through the air. You knew you had popped a great jump. Remember that feeling of power and control as you ran off the board… hips, high, feeling tall… Remember the control and balance of your feet… body balance… just the way you practiced it… arms and legs in perfect control as you went through the triple jump phases and you just kept sailing through the air, further and further. What a ride… what a feeling… finally the feet touched the sand and your weight collapsed forward over bent legs. You timed the movement of the arms perfectly and it helped shift your body forward.

A tremendous feeling of satisfaction came over you. What a satisfying feeling. It felt so good to triple jump so far. As you walk away from the pit, you receive congratulations from teammates, coaches and friends. What a jump… what a feeling.

While completely involved with this feeling, give yourself a cue word or affirmation that brings all these feelings and pictures into focus…a cue word or affirmation that completely connects you with that time and those feelings when you knew that you were perfect and right on…say the words or words to yourself several times… slowly allow yourself to experience your sense of power and control…feel it in your whole body.

See and feel yourself triple jumping that day. How you jumped so effortlessly. Further than you had ever jumped before and it felt so easy. Everything worked perfectly, just the way you wanted it to.

Activity 14.4
Triple Jump Mental Rehearsal

See yourself arriving at the track meet. You are wearing your competition clothes… your thoughts are focused on triple jumping… you feel good today… you are looking forward to jumping far… you have some really good feelings about your performance.

Picture the weather… the sun… the clouds… the wind… the temperature. This is a great day for a P.R. You are excited and ready to jump.

You notice some triple jumpers you will be jumping against as you warm-up. You remain calm confident and relaxed. You feel good and you are ready to jump… you have a deep, calm, confidence, yet somewhat nervous feeling inside. Your heart is pounding and the adrenaline is flowing… you say your cue words or affirmations to yourself…what a day this this is going to be for you.

You are looking forward to jumping far and you have a feeling of being well-prepared for your event… you are feeling good both mentally and physical. You feel good because you know that you have been working hard, training well and have made many sacrifices to be the best you can be…think of all the time you have spent jumping, sprinting, stretching, working on drills…technique…weight training…mental training. All this work is going to pay off today! You are physically and mentally ready to jump far.

Your hard work and sacrifices are paying off! See yourself going through your normal warm-up… running… the muscles begin to limber up… the stretching… the sprinting… your breathing hard indicates the muscles are getting oxygen and will be ready to perform when called upon…You prepare mentally as you think about triple jumping. You loosen up… feel the sweat on your body and your heart pumping… as your body gets warmer and warmer… preparing itself for competition. See yourself going through your bounds and the rhythm starts to flow… flowing fluidly and smoothly. You've measured your marks out. See yourself going through some run throughs and bounding, your steps are right on, you feel fast and smooth on the approach. You are right on the board. You pop off the board on your warm-ups, you are right on and feeling good. Your warm-up jumps feel easy. You are ready to jump far today.

Your body feels so powerful and explosive today. You are focused and in control. Your warm-up went well…you feel ready… you feel ready for a personal record…just the way you want to be… You relax while waiting for the competition to start. While waiting, repeat your cue words and say your affirmations to yourself…take a deep breath… inhale…exhale…inhale…exhale… Your warm-up and run throughs felt strong and powerful… your workouts have been going well… you are ready to triple jump farther than you have all year.

You check in with the head judge. You notice your competitors… see the colors of their uniforms… you acknowledge them but remain focused on yourself. You will focus on your triple jumping. You hear your jumping order… as you hear your name, feel the tinge of anticipation, you hear the official wish everyone "good luck."

You stay loose and confident while you are waiting for your turn to jump. Hear the official call your name and see yourself prepare to jump. As you stand on the runway, you are confident. You are ready! You take a deep breath and gather your thoughts. You exhale and relax saying your cue words or affirmations. Your body and mind responds positively. You have been looking forward to this.

See yourself on the runway, ready to jump. You feel strong and powerful as you start your approach. Your first few steps are right where you want them to be. Feel the speed building up from a controlled start. Your gradual acceleration is smooth, starting slow gaining speed, under control.

You are showing excellent form, running tall, erect body position, hips high, shoulders relaxed. Your strides are getting longer; your stride tempo is increasing. You feel springy as you run on the balls of your feet… feel the speed… you are under control… your head is up, eyes are focused beyond the pit. As you approach the take-off board, feel your stride rhythm quicken…. you accelerate through the last few strides.

You feel your last two foot plants—flat-flat. You run off the board with a fast takeoff stride and explosive takeoff. You are running up into the air… forward and upward… you know you have a great jump. You drive the knee of your free leg hard… aggressive… feel the hips high and forward… perfect… just what you wanted… feel yourself flying through the air… it feels so good… this is what you enjoy about triple jumping… sailing through the air. Feel yourself balanced and in control as you sail through the air… Your arms and legs are synchronized as you begin to achieve an efficient landing position for the next phase… feel the resiliency of your body as you land off the hop… you hold the body balanced and in control and begin the step phase. Feel the synchronization of the arms, the legs, and the body, all working together in perfect synchronization, driving you further and further. Your arms and legs reach out as you land with a flat foot. When you land you stay balanced…under control… and propel your body for the final phase. Feel the power and drive as you are having one of your best jumps ever. Feel your legs staying up and staying up as you continue to ride all you can out of your jump. As the feet touch the sand feel the legs bend as you collapse your weight forward… see the arms coming forward to help move your entire body forward… you feel your momentum carry you through the sand as you come to a landing. You know it's a great jump… maybe a PR… you are filled with a tremendous sense of satisfaction as you move out of the pit. You feel great… you have that inner feeling that you've given it your all and have done your best.

As you walk away from the landing pit, you are catching your breath. The adrenaline of success is rushing through your body. You hear friends congratulating you… as you walk away, people pat you on the back and shake your hand. Feel the exhilaration of accomplishment…the joy of success. As you walk over to put on your sweats, you feel a tremendous sense of accomplishment as you responded to the challenge. You know that you have triple jumped far… you know that you were psychologically and physically prepared. All your training both physical and mental have paid off. After you accept congratulations from your coach and friends, take time to thank your body… your legs, your lungs and your entire body… You have achieved your goal!

Begin to let go of this image and this feeling… slowly re-enter your present space… feel your body…move your toes…move your fingers…begin to notice your breathing…inhale…exhale…inhale… exhale… You feel relaxed and filled with a new quiet energy.

To help further develop all of your senses in imagery use Activity 14.5. Certain senses may produce clearer attention than others. Use this exercise to provide direction for extra attention.

Activity 14.5
Sensory Imagery for Triple Jump

Vividness: Imagine the triple jump pit. Notice the color of the sand. Notice the pit that you will land in. Notice how big it is. Notice the runway and follow it all the way to the pit.

Auditory: What sounds do you hear while you are getting ready to jump? Hear the sound of your feet on the runway and in the pit.

Tactile: Image the feel of your feet on the runway. What does it feel like? Notice the runway and how soft or hard it feels to land on it. How does it feel to land in the sand?

Kinesthetic: Imagine jumping during warm-ups. Feel what your body is doing during the warm-ups. Feel the muscles in your legs as you run and jump. Note the power in your legs as you do your warm-up jumps. Feel yourself rocketing up into the air. Feel the sensation of your body going through three phases. Feel the sand as you complete the jump.

Smell: Smell the sand, your shoes, the grass, and the runway. Smell the sweat after a hard practice.

Taste: Taste the salt from the sweat on your lips. Imagine taking a drink of water during a hot day of practice.

Emotion: Experience the confidence you feel when you step up to triple jump. Experience the satisfaction of jumping far. Experience the pride you feel in achieving a PR.

Vividness Evaluation
What were your strongest images and sensations?
What senses do you need to improve?

The Triple Jump Self-Evaluation can be found in Activity 14.6 and can be used periodically to evaluate practice or competition. A general Team Post-Meet Evaluation form can be found in Activity 19.4.

Activity 14.6
Triple Jump Self-Evaluation

Rate yourself on a scale of 1-10 (with 10 being high)

1. Overall Performance _____
2. Warm-ups _____
3. Performance in meets _____
4. Encouragement of others _____
5. My positive attitude _____
6. Use of mental training _____
7. Mental training on own _____
8. Proper sleep _____
9. Proper nutrition _____
10. Good hydration practices _____
11. Ability to push yourself _____
12. Contribution to team _____
13. Progress towards your goal _____
14. Approach _____
15. Take-off _____
16. Hop, flight and landing _____
17. Step take-off _____
18. Step, flight and landing _____
19. Jump take-off _____
20. Landing _____

Activity 14.7
Personalized Guided Visualization

Objective:
To write a personalized guided visualization script. In your own words write a visualization of an upcoming performance. This visualization will let you see, hear, and feel yourself performing your sport.

Directions:
Write a personalized guided visualization script. Be as specific as possible. Include as many senses you can. Write it down as full and complete as you can. Remember to use positive statements and include your affirmations. Use the worksheet to formulate your ideas. Then write out your guided visualization in an essay format. After writing the visualization, I would encourage you to record the script. Find a quiet time to play some relaxation music and then play your recorded script. As you talk to yourself, see the visualization coming to life!

Worksheet for your guided visualization

Day of the Event
- See yourself getting up in the morning with confidence.
- What will you have to eat?
- See yourself dressing for the competition, putting on your clothing.

Arriving at the Site
- See yourself arriving at the site
- See the competition
- See the environment, weather, temperature
- Focus on your goal and the outcome you wish to achieve

The Warm-up
- See yourself doing your general warm-up
- See yourself stretching, drills
- See yourself doing your final run throughs and jumps
- See yourself putting on your competition shoes

The Start
- See yourself on the triple jump runway
- Hear and feel your first few steps
- See yourself getting out to a good powerful start

The Approach
- See and feel your self starting to accelerate
- Feel the consistency of your steps
- Feel yourself running under control but fast

The Take-off for Hop
- See and feel the run off the board
- Feel a flat-feet take-off
- Feel yourself drive through the air

Step
- Feel the resiliency as you land
- Feel the synchronization of arms and legs as you go through the step phase.

Jump
- Feel the extension of legs
- Feel the ride as you keep your legs up and eventually hit the sand
- When the event is over, you feel great about your jumping

A sample week for a Triple Jump Mental Preparation Plan is provided in Table 14.1. Use the example to help complete the blank form in Activity 19.1 to develop your Mental Preparation plan.

\multicolumn{3}{c}{**Table 14.1**}
\multicolumn{3}{c}{**Sample Weekly Mental Preparation Plan for a Triple Jumper**}
Day	**Physical Practice**	**Mental Practice**
Monday	½ mile warm-up Dynamic warm-up 6 x 2 steps 6 x pop-ups 6 x approach no jump/6 x full jump ½ mile jog cool down	Incorporate into practice (See Table 14.2) **Outside of practice:** Review weekly goals Positive self-talk Relaxation Imagery of achieving weekly goals
Tuesday	½ mile warm-up Dynamic warm-up Easy strides	Incorporate into practice (Table 14.2) **Outside of practice:** Mental recall/Affirmations
Wednesday	½ mile warm-up Bounding exercises 10 x standing long jump/ Phase work 6 x approach work- run throughs ½ mile jog cool down	Incorporate into practice (Table 14.2) **Outside of practice:** Develop competition plan Visualize competition plan
Thursday	½ mile warm-up 20 minutes fartlek Team games Character Building Mental Training	Incorporate into practice (Table 14.2) **Outside of practice:** Relaxation Visualize competition plan Visualize mental recovery plans
Friday	Competition	See Table 14.3 and 14.4 for example of meet day mental preparation plan Outside of practice:
Saturday	Easy recovery jog Stretch	Complete post-competition evaluation Use mental recall for low and highlights Review previous week goal progress Set new process and effort goals
Sunday	Recovery- Walk Bike Swim Stretch	Relaxation Mental rehearsal of next week's goals Positive Self-talk Read about a motivating athlete

Table 14.2 provides ideas to incorporate mental drills into your regular practice. A blank form is provided in Activity 19.6 to help you develop your plan to incorporate mental drills into your workouts.

\multicolumn{3}{c}{**Table 14.2**}
\multicolumn{3}{c}{**Ideas to Incorporate Mental and Physical Plan into Workouts**}
Physical Activity	**When to use**	**Mental Activity**
Approach	Before approach	Cue words
Run off board	Before approach	Rapid energization for arousal Cue words
Phase work	Before and during phase work	Cue words Relaxing breathing Visualization

Use Table 14.3 to help you develop your plan to incorporate mental skills into your pre-competition warm-up. A blank form is provided in Activity 19.2 for you to write your pre-competition warm-up plan.

	Table 14.3 Mental Preparation Triple Jump Pre-Competition Plan	
Time Prior to Start	Physical WU	Mental WU
75-80 min	Initial check-in Pick-up number Check flight	Relaxation and cue words
65-75 min	Easy jog to get blood flowing	Go over technical plan Imagery involving jumping with perfect form Confidence card or self-talk script Review back-up plans
50-65 min	Stretching	Focus on breathing, relaxation Positive self-talk Quick imagery of portions of event
40-50 min	Measure in steps Dynamic Warm-up Good form	Cue words Focus
30-40 min	Drills Proper technique Relax body while doing drills	Positive self-talk Relaxed while doing drills
20-30 min	Jumps	Cue words to stay fast and explosive Increase arousal if needed to get in proper arousal zone Positive mental attitude high Focus on personal goals and the processes to make it happen
15-20 min	Bathroom Break	Rapid relaxation to deal with pre-race nervousness
10-15 min	Isolation Check final meet gear equipment	Quick review of overall competition plan Vividly see jumping with good form Use rapid relaxation or energization techniques to get in your proper zone Positive self-talk

In Table 14.4, a Mental Performance Plan is provided. The plan is divided into different phases of the competition. To help incorporate your mental skills into your performance, complete Activity 19.3 and develop your Mental Performance Plan.

Table 14.4 Designing Triple Jump Mental Performance Plan			
Competition Phase	Physical	Mental	Cue Words
The Start	Good powerful start	Positive self-talk Image jump Push off Accelerate	Rhythm Drive
The Approach	Accelerate	Fast but under control	Attack Quick
Take-off hop	Proper position Drive the knee Drive Out	Focus on cue words	Run off Pop Drive
Step	Resilient landing Hold position	Focus on landing Feel sensation of flying	Hold High
Step	Arms and legs reach together Flat foot	Focus on process	Balance Drive
Landing	Pull hips through	Focus on profess	Pull

Table 14.5 provides examples of Mental Recovery Plans for Field Events. See Activity 19.5 for a blank form to complete that will help you develop your Mental Recovery Plan.

Table 14.5 Mental Recovery Plan for Field Events			
Distractors-Field Events	**Release**	**Re-focus**	**How to prepare for**
Wind	Exhale air out, blow the wind away	Focus on process goals not outcome Focus on process cues	Practice with a cross wind or occasionally into the wind
Rain	Wipe forehead	Positive self-talk Arousal techniques such as energization	Practice on some rainy days
Cold	Rub sweats or clothing	Positive self-talk Imagery of goal achievement	Practice in cold
Weather delays	Relaxation breathing	Relaxation Positive self-talk	Start practice and delay it for several minutes to simulate a rain delay or between flights and finish
Foul first two attempts	Park mistake in an object	Cue words that focus on process	Simulation jumping

Chapter 15

Pole Vault

Activity 15.1
Pole Vault Power Picture

Directions: Find a good picture of when you are competing. Make sure the picture shows you in good form and looking strong. Put the picture on a page (preferably cardboard stock). Place your cue words around the picture.

P
O
W
E
R

R
I
S
E

VERTICAL

Activity 15.2
Pole Vault Affirmations

- I am a pole vaulter.
- I love to vault.
- I am committed to a pole vaulter's lifestyle.
- I have the courage to be a great pole vaulter.
- Each day I become a better pole vaulter.
- I have great strength, technique and rhythm.
- My strides are rhythmic and powerful.
- I run tall and under control on the approach.
- My approach is consistent and right on.
- My approach is fluid and smooth.
- I plant high, early and aggressive.
- I am proud to be a pole vaulter.
- I relax and let it happen.
- I plant through the box with shoulders square.
- The pole and top hand are high and over the take off foot.
- My swing is a smooth transfer of horizontal speed to vertical speed.
- I am patient with my rock back swing.
- My pull and turn is a quick, powerful movement.
- I want to jump higher and higher.
- I enjoy the exhilaration of a good vault.
- I am a great pole vaulter.

Activity 15.3
Pole Vault Mental Recall

Begin to think of a time in your life when you knew that you were right on and performed perfectly. See yourself at that time… notice what you look like, what you are wearing, who is with you what sounds are around you, where you are. Feel the environment and the energy. Begin to see yourself pole vaulting when you knew you were right on… when everything worked perfectly… when you were in complete control and at your peak.. Watch yourself and feel that feeling… connect with all of the feelings you experienced as you achieved at your highest level. Perfectly…competently… exactly the way you wanted to…what did it feel like?... sound like?… look like?

Remember your thoughts before you jumped that day. Remember how comfortable and relaxed you felt. Feel the rhythm of that jump come back. How smooth… fluid… and powerful it felt, as you built up your speed on the runway. Let it all come back to you… let it in… know it again… the joy… the power… the pride and confidence... the rush of knowing you were perfection... let it become part of you… part of your spirit... part of your being … Fully connect with it.

Feel the movements that you perfectly executed. How good the pole felt in your hands. How good the start of your run-up felt. The first few steps were right where you wanted them to be. Feel the power that was stored up and then unleashed as you accelerated down the runway. Sprinting and carrying the pole felt effortless as you sped down the runway. Remember the plant. High, early, aggressive. How you smoothly started your plant by moving your pole forward and up… you planted through the box, driving into the pole and staying behind and under the pole. Remember the feeling of the pole and the top hand being high and directly over the takeoff foot, a perfect plant. Remember how good it felt when all the forces came together perfectly as you exploded off the ground on your way to a personal best vault. Remember the knee of the free leg driving hard…quick… forward… and upward. Feel the feeling again as the chest and hips penetrated forward… the left arm keeping the pole away from the body… See yourself in that long vertical position that helped maintain pole speed and helped catapult you to a great vault. See the smooth, fluid action of the swing and rockback. You maintain momentum with your rockback… see the hips between the pole and the head… you remain patient on the rockback… finally see your pole as you pulled vertically through the hips… projecting the hips high. Your pull and turn quick and powerful. You achieved maximum vertical lift as the pole came out of the bend. See yourself quickly lifting your arms over the cross bar. You cleared! A tremendous rush of adrenalin flows through you.

Remember the feeling of flying over the cross bar and the tremendous feeling of satisfaction as you started your downward journey to land on the mat. You knew you had set a personal best. What a satisfying feeling. It felt so good to jump so high. As you walk away from the pit, you receive congratulations from teammates, coaches and friends. What a jump… what a feeling.

While completely involved with this feeling, give yourself a cue word or affirmation that brings all these feelings and pictures into focus… a cue word or affirmation that completely connects you with that time and those feelings when you knew that you were perfect and right on… say the words or words to yourself several times… slowly allow yourself to experience your sense of power and control… feel it in your whole body.

See and feel yourself pole vaulting that day. Higher than you had ever vaulted before and it felt so easy. It felt so good to clear a high height. Everything worked perfectly, just the way you wanted it to.

Activity 15.4
Pole Vault Mental Rehearsal

See yourself arriving at the track meet. You are wearing your competition clothes…your thoughts are focused on pole vaulting…you feel good today… you are looking forward to vaulting high… you have some really good feelings about your performance.

Picture the weather… the sun… the clouds… the wind… the temperature. This is a great day for a P.R. You are excited and ready to jump.

You notice some vaulters you will be pole vaulting against as you warm-up. You remain calm… confident… and relaxed. You feel good and you are ready to vault… you have a deep, calm confidence, yet somewhat nervous feeling inside. Your heart is pounding and the adrenalin is flowing… you say your cue words or affirmations to yourself… what a day this this is going to be for you.

You are looking forward to jumping high and you have a feeling of being well-prepared for your event…you are feeling good both mentally and physical. You feel good because you know that you have been working hard, training well and have made many sacrifices to be the best you can be…think of all the time you have spent vaulting, sprinting, stretching, working on drills… technique… weight training… mental training. All this work is going to pay off today! You are physically and mentally ready to pole vault very high.

See yourself going through your normal warm-up…running… the muscles begin to limber up… the stretching… the sprinting… your breathing hard indicates the muscles are getting oxygen and will be ready to perform when called upon. You prepare mentally as you think about pole vaulting. You loosen up…feel the sweat on your body and your heart pumping…as your body gets warmer and warmer… preparing itself for competition. See yourself going through some run throughs, your steps are right on, you feel fast and smooth on the runway. You pop over the bar at the warm-up heights, you are right on and feeling good. Your warm-up jumps feel easy. You are ready to vault high today.

Your body feels so powerful and explosive today. You are focused and in control. Your warm-up went well…you feel ready …you feel ready for a personal record…just the way you want. You relax while waiting for the competition to start. While waiting repeat your cue words and say your affirmations to yourself… take a deep breath… inhale… exhale… inhale… exhale. Your warm-up and practice vaults felt strong and powerful…your workouts have been going well… you are ready to vault higher than you have all year.

You check in with the head judge. You notice your competitors… see the colors of their uniforms…see all the pole vaulters around you…you acknowledge your surroundings but you remain focused on yourself… You will focus on your pole vaulting. You hear your jumping order… as you hear your name, feel the tinge of anticipation, you hear the official wish everyone "good luck."

You stay loose and confident while you are waiting for your turn to jump… Hear the official call your name and see yourself prepare to vault. As you stand holding your pole you are confident. You are ready! You take a deep breath and gather your thoughts. You exhale and relax saying your cue words or affirmations. Your body and mind responds positively. You have been looking forward to this.

Your grip feels good, your pole is light. See the pole near your hip, you and the pole are one. You feel strong and powerful as you start your approach. Your first few steps are right where you want them to be. Feel the speed building up from a controlled start. Your gradual acceleration is smooth, your pole carry is comfortable. You are sprinting faster and faster down the runway…erect body position. You feel very good as you attain your maximal controllable speed. Three strides out your start your plant. High, early, aggressive. See and feel the pole move forward and up… your bottom arm guiding the pole toward the box… your top arm driving forward and upward in front of the head. A stride closer, feel the top hand moving to the forehead, you plant strongly through the box… shoulders square… your top hand is high… and directly over your take-off foot. Perfect plant… right where you wanted it to be. Feel the drive into the pole… you bring the pole into perfect position. You drive hard and quick with the knee of the free leg in a forward upward direction. Your chest and hips are penetrating forward… your bottom arm is stiff and keeps the pole away from the body… Your body is in a long, vertical position. Your pole speed is fast. Your takeoff is perfect. You feel the transfer of horizontal speed to vertical speed. Like a rod, your upper arms remains straight, your legs come together, synchronized… your hips are in a great forward position. You maintain your momentum on the rock back…your arms working just the way you want them to… top arm straight, bottom arm keeping the pole away from your body. Feel yourself continuing your rock back until the hips are between the pole and the hand. You stay patient in the rock back portion, waiting… waiting… this is a high vault… you are patient…your back is to the bar… the pole straightens out… coming out of it's bend, it is catapulting you to a new PR… Feel the energy coming from the bar… you and the pole are one, working together to achieve a clearance. When the pole is almost straight, you pull vertically through the hips… projecting the hips up high… the legs shoot to a strong upward position. Your movements are quick and powerful. You have a strong push-off… the arms extended straight down the pole… the arms quickly lifting away from the cross bar. You are going to clear the bar… put the final touches on your jump. Feel your thumbs rotate inward and feel the rotation of the elbows away from the cross bar. You are on top of the bar… feel the hips passing over the bar and finally the arms swinging together over the bra. A great vault… a PR… you are filled with a tremendous sense of satisfaction as you fall to the pit in a perfect landing.

You feel great… you have that inner feeling that you've given it your all and have done your best. As you climb off the landing pit you are catching your breath. The adrenaline of success is rushing through your body. You hear friends congratulating you… as you get your pole, people pat you on the back and shake your hand. Feel the exhilaration of accomplishment… the joy of success. As you walk back to put down your pole and put on your sweats, you feel a tremendous sense of accomplishment as you responded to the challenge. You know that you have vaulted a personal best height… you know that you were psychologically and physically prepared. All your training, both physical and mental, has paid off. After you accept congratulations from your coach and friends, take time to thank your body… your legs, your lungs and your entire body… You have achieved your goal!

Begin to let go of this image and this feeling… slowly re-enter your present space…feel your body…move your toes…move your fingers… begin to notice your breathing…inhale…exhale…inhale… exhale… You feel relaxed and filled with a new quiet energy.

To help further develop all of your senses in imagery use Activity 15.5. Certain senses may produce clearer attention than others. Use this exercise to provide direction for extra attention and practices.

Activity 15.5
Sensory Imagery for Pole Vault

Vividness: Imagine the pole. Notice the length of the pole, the roundness of the pole, any markings that are on the pole. Notice the crossbar and the standards that hold up the crossbar. Notice the landing pit. Notice the runway. See the vaulting plant box. Follow the runway all the way to the pit.

Auditory: What sounds do you hear while you are jumping? Hear yourself breathing as you go down the runway. Hear the sound of the pole hitting the vaulting box. Hear the sound as you land on the pit.

Tactile: Imagine the feel of your feet on the runway. What does it feel like? Notice the pit and how it feels to land in the pit. Feel the pole in your hands. Notice how it feels so comfortable as you hold it.

Kinesthetic: Imagine vaulting during warm-ups. Feel what your body is doing during the warm-ups. Feel the muscles in your legs as you run and jump. Note the power in your legs as you do your warm-up jumps. Feel the pole in your hands as you go down the runway. Feel arms and shoulders as you plant. Feel yourself in the air as you leave the ground. Feel the sensation as your body continues to rise in the air. Feel the body go over the cross bar and the body falling onto the mat.

Smell: Smell the pit, the runway, the grass beside the runway, and your shoes. Smell the sweat after a hard practice.

Taste: Taste the salt from the sweat on your lips. Imagine drinking water during a hot day of practice.

Emotion: Experience the confidence you feel when you step up to vault. Experience the satisfaction of jumping high. Experience the pride you feel in achieving a PR. Experience the excitement of being on a successful team.

Vividness Evaluation: What were your strongest images and sensations? What senses do you need to improve?

A Pole Vault Self-Evaluation can be found in Activity 15.6 and can be used periodically to evaluate practice or competition. A general Team Post-Meet Evaluation form can be found in Activity 19.4.

Activity 15.6
Pole Vault Self-Evaluation

Rate yourself on a scale of 1-10 (with 10 being high)

1. Overall Performance _____	11. Ability to push yourself _____
2. Warm-ups _____	12. Contribution to team _____
3. Performance in meets _____	13. Progress towards your goal _____
4. Encouragement of others _____	14. Approach _____
5. My positive attitude _____	15. Plant position _____
6. Use of mental training _____	16. Take off _____
7. Mental training on own _____	17. Pull-turn and rise _____
8. Proper sleep _____	18. Bar clearance _____
9. Proper nutrition _____	19. Landing _____
10. Good hydration practices _____	20. Visualization of jump _____

Activity 15.7
Personalized Guided Visualization

Objective:
To write a personalized guided visualization script. In your own words write a visualization of an upcoming performance. This visualization will let you see, hear, and feel yourself performing your sport.

Directions:
Write a personalized guided visualization script. Be as specific as possible. Include as many senses you can. Write it down as full and complete as you can. Remember to use positive statements and include your affirmations. Use the worksheet to formulate your ideas. Then write out your guided visualization in an essay format. After writing the visualization, I would encourage you to record the script. Find a quiet time to play some relaxation music and then play your recorded script. As you talk to yourself, see the visualization coming to life!

Worksheet for your guided visualization

Day of the Event
- See yourself getting up in the morning with confidence.
- What will you have to eat?
- See yourself dressing for the competition, putting on your clothing.

Arriving at the Site
- See yourself arriving at the site
- See the competition
- See the environment, weather, temperature
- Focus on your goal and the outcome you wish to achieve

The Warm-up
- See yourself doing your general warm-up
- See yourself stretching, drills
- See yourself doing your final preparations
- See yourself putting on your competition shoes

The Approach
- See and feel yourself starting to accelerate
- Feel your self building up momentum
- Feel yourself running under control but fast

The Plant
- See and feel the proper take-off position
- Feel you propel yourself into the air
- Feel the strong pop with the knee

In the Air
- Feel the lay back and wait
- Feel the pull back when the back is parallel
- See and feel the turn and rise
- Feel the hands come off the pole as you go over the cross bar

Landing
- Feel the exhilaration on the way down, knowing you have cleared
- See and feel the landing as you land on your back in the pit

Post Jump
- Feel the satisfaction of jumping high
- See your teammates, coaches, family and friends congratulating you
- When the event is over, you feel great about your jumping

A sample week for a Pole Vault Mental Preparation Plan is provided in Table 15.1. Use the example to help complete the blank form in Activity 19.1 to develop your Mental Preparation plan.

Table 15.1 Sample Weekly Mental Preparation Plan for a Pole Vaulter		
Day	Physical Practice	Mental Practice
Monday	½ mile warm-up Dynamic warm-up 6 x 2 steps, 6 x pop-ups 6 x approach no vault, 6 x full vault ½ mile jog cool down	Incorporate into practice (See Table 15.2) **Outside of practice:** Review weekly goals Positive self-talk Relaxation/Goal imagery
Tuesday	½ mile warm-up Dynamic warm-up Easy strides	Incorporate into practice (Table 15.2) **Outside of practice:** Mental recall/Affirmations
Wednesday	½ mile warm-up Bounding exercises Medicine ball work 6 x approach work-6 x full jumps ½ mile jog cool down	Incorporate into practice (Table 15.2) **Outside of practice:** Develop competition plan Visualize competition plan
Thursday	½ mile warm-up 20 minutes fartlek Team games Character Building Mental Training	Incorporate into practice (Table 15.2) **Outside of practice:** Relaxation Visualize competition plan Visualize mental recovery plans
Friday	Competition	See Table 15.3 and 15.4 for example of meet day mental preparation plan
Saturday	Easy recovery jog Stretch	Complete post-competition evaluation Use mental recall low and highlights Review previous week goal progress Set new process and effort goals
Sunday	Recovery- Walk Bike Swim Stretch	Relaxation Mental rehearsal of next week's goals Positive Self-talk Read about a motivating athlete

Table 15.2 provides ideas to incorporate mental skills into your regular practice. A blank form is provided in Activity 19.6 to help you develop your plan to incorporate mental skills into your workouts.

Table 15.2 Ideas to Incorporate Mental Skils into Workouts		
Physical Activity	When to use	Mental Activity
Approach	Before and during approach	Visualize parts of the approach Cue words
Take-off	Before approach	Rapid energization to achieve proper arousal
Going Vertical	During drills	Cue words Visualization

Use Table 15.3 for ideas on how to develop a Mental Performance Pre-Competition Plan. In Activity 19.2, a blank form is provided to help you develop your plan to incorporate mental skills into your pre-competition warm-up.

\multicolumn{3}{c}{**Table 15.3**}		
\multicolumn{3}{c}{**Example Mental Performance Pre-Competition Plan for Pole Vault**}		
Time Prior to Start	Physical WU	Mental WU
75-80 min	Initial check-in Pick-up number Check flight	Relaxation and cue words
65-75 min	Easy jog to get blood flowing	Go over technical plan Imagery involving jumping with perfect form Confidence card or self-talk script Review back-up plans
50-65 min	Stretching	Focus on breathing, relaxation Positive self-talk Quick imagery of portions of event
40-50 min	Measure in steps Dynamic Warm-up Good form	Cue words Visualization
30-40 min	Drills Proper technique Relax body while doing drills	Positive self-talk Relaxed while doing drills
20-30 min	Jumps	Cue words- to stay fast and explosive Increase arousal if needed to get in proper arousal zone Positive mental attitude high Focus on personal goals and the processes to make it happen
15-20 min	Bathroom Break	Rapid relaxation to deal with pre-race nervousness
10-15 min	Isolation Check final meet gear equipment	Quick review of overall competition plan Vividly see jumping with good form Use rapid relaxation or energization techniques to get in your proper zone Positive self-talk

In Table 15.4, a Pole Vault Mental Performance Plan is provided. The plan is divided into different phases of the competition. To help incorporate your mental skills into your performance, complete Activity 19.3 and develop your Mental Performance Plan

Table 15.4 Pole Vault Mental Performance Plan			
Competition Phase	Physical	Mental	Cue Words
Approach	Consistent, accelerate Pole carry	Positive self-talk Visualization before on runway Energization	Accelerate Quick
Plant	Bottom arm guides pull up Plant through box	Focus on plant box	Float
Take-off	Chest and hips forward	See you and the pole as one	Quick
Lay-back	Top arm straight Bottom hand keeps pole straight	Focus on using the energy of the pole	Away
Pull	Pull vertically Legs shoot upward	Focus	Rise Pull
Turn and rise	Off the pole	Focus on process not outcome	Curl and press Vertical

Table 15.5 provides examples of Mental Recovery Plans for Track Events. See Activity 19.5 for a blank form to complete that will help you develop your Mental Recovery Plan.

Table 15.5 Mental Recovery Plan for Field Events			
Distractors-Field Events	Release	Re-focus	How to prepare for
Wind	Exhale air out, blow the wind away	Focus on process goals not outcome Focus on process cues	Practice vaulting with a cross wind or occasionally into the wind
Rain	Wipe forehead	Positive self-talk Arousal techniques such as energization	Practice on some rainy days
Cold	Rub sweats or clothing	Positive self-talk Imagery of goal achievement	Practice in cold
Weather delays	Relaxation breathing	Relaxation Positive self-talk	Start vault practice and delay it for several minutes to simulate a rain delay
Miss first two attempts	Park mistake in an object	Cue words that focus on process	Simulation vaulting

Chapter 16

Shot Put

Activity 16.1
Shot Put Power Picture

Directions: Find a good picture of when you are competing. Make sure the picture shows you in good form and looking strong. Put the picture on a page (preferably cardboard stock). Place your cue words around the picture. **S**

P
O
W
E
R

E
X
P
L
O
D
E

PUSH

Activity 15.2
Shot Put Affirmations

- I am a shot putter.
- I love to throw.
- I am committed to a thrower's lifestyle.
- I have the power to be a great shot putter.
- Each day I become a better thrower.
- I have great power and technique.
- The shot feels light and flies far.
- My grip is comfortable and relaxed.
- My movements are rhythmic and powerful.
- My shoulders and hips remain separated on my turn.
- I am centered and focused.
- My turn in controlled, fluid and balanced.
- I land in a perfect power position.
- My hips are powerful.
- I want to throw further and further.
- I feel energy ready to explode when I'm in the power position.
- The power travels from my legs, to hips, to chest, to arms, through the shot.
- I drive my legs upward to provide vertical force.
- I feel the torque on my body when I'm in the power position.
- My arm bends to efficiently block the side.
- My shot comes through quickly.
- I enjoy the exhilaration of a great throw.
- I am proud to be a shot putter.
- I am a great shot putter.

Activity 15.3
Shot Put Mental Recall

Begin to think of a time in your life when you knew that you were right on and performed perfectly. See yourself at that time… notice what you look like, what you are wearing, who is with you what sounds are around you, where you are. Feel the environment and the energy. Begin to see yourself putting the shot when you knew you were right on… when everything worked perfectly… when you were in complete control and at your peak. Watch yourself and feel that feeling… connect with all of the feelings you experienced as you achieved at your highest level…. Perfectly…competently… exactly the way you wanted to…what did it feel like?... sound like?…look like?

Remember your thoughts before you threw that day… Remember how the shot felt as you gripped it. A relaxed and powerful grip. Feel the rhythm of that throw come back. How smooth…fluid…and powerful it felt. Let l all come back to you… let it in… know it again… the joy… the power… the pride and confidence... the rush of knowing you were perfection.. let it become part of you … part of your spirit.. part of your being … Fully connect with it.

Feel the movements that you perfectly executed. How good the start felt as you were in control and flowed into a good power position. The first few movements were right where you wanted them to be… consistent… feel the rhythm… starting slow and building up speed… Feel the power that was stored up and then unleashed. Remember the summation of forces that started with the slower and stronger muscles and then shifted to the faster muscles of the shoulder and arms. Remember the strong powerful drive of the legs and hips. The surge of power that went from your leg…to the hips… to the chest… to the arms… and then through the shot as it came off your fingers. All the forces came together perfectly as you exploded with a personal best throw.

Remember the shot coming through in a straight line… see the shot being released at the perfect angle… feel the vigorous wrist snap and your recovery as you check your forward motion. What a throw… what a feeling.

See the shot flying through the air. How it exploded out of your hand and sailed through the air farther than you had ever thrown it before and it felt so easy. It feels so good to throw so far. Everything worked perfectly just the way you wanted it to.

Feel how you threw so effortlessly. Further then you had ever thrown before and it felt so easy. It felt so good to throw far. Everything worked perfectly, just the way you wanted it to.

While completely involved with this feeling, give yourself a cue word or affirmation that brings all these feelings and pictures into focus… a cue word or affirmation that completely connects you with that time and those feelings when you knew that you were perfect and right on… say the word or words to yourself several times… slowly allow yourself to experience your sense of power and control… feel it in your whole body.

Activity 16.4
Shot Put Mental Rehearsal

See yourself arriving at the shot put area. You are wearing your competition clothes…your thoughts are focused on the shot…you feel good today… you are looking forward to throwing far… you have some really good feelings about your performance.

Picture the weather… the sun… the clouds… the wind… the temperature. This is a great day for a P.R. You are excited and ready to throw!

Notice the other throwers…. You are calm, confident and relaxed. You feel good and are ready to throw… you have a deep, calm, yet somewhat nervous feeling inside… your heart is pounding and the adrenaline is flowing… you say your cue words or affirmations to yourself… what a day this this is going to be for you!

You are looking forward to throwing far and you have a feeling of being well-prepared for your event… you are feeling good both mentally and physical. You feel good because you know that you have been working hard, training well and have made many sacrifices to be the best you can be…think of all the time you have spent in the weight room, conditioning, stretching, working on drills… technique… throwing… weight training… mental training. All this work is going to pay off today! You are physically and mentally ready to throw far.

See yourself going through your normal warm-up…stretching…drills… the mental preparation. Feel the muscles begin to limber up… some easy warm-up throws… easy throws to loosen up… feel the sweat on your body and your heart pumping… as your body gets warmer and warmer… preparing itself for competition. Your warm-up throws feel easy and are flying far. You are ready to throw far today.

Your shot feels so light today and your body feels so tuned in and in control. Feel yourself putting more effort into your last few warm-up throws. The movement feels smooth… the power is there today. Feel the pop…. as the shot comes off your fingers in perfect flight and flies and flies. You take your final throw. You feel explosive today. You are focused and in control. Your warm-up went well… you feel ready… you feel ready for a personal record… just the way you want to be… You relax while waiting for the competition to start. While waiting repeat your cue words and say your affirmations to yourself… take a deep breath… inhale…exhale…inhale…exhale. Your warm-up and throws felt strong and powerful… you are ready to throw the best that you have thrown all year.

Hear the official call the throwers together for the final instruction. The flights are announced… as you hear your name, feel the tinge of anticipation, as you hear the official wish everyone "good luck." You take a deep breath and gather your thoughts. You exhale and relax, saying your cue words or affirmations. Your body and mind responds positively. You are ready!

You stay loose and confident while you are waiting for your turn to throw. Hear the official call your name and see yourself prepare to throw. Visualize the shot in your hand… it feels so light… see yourself enter the back of the ring… your grip feels comfortable, you feel the shot resting on the back of the fingers… fingers spread comfortably. Your grip feels good. You feel relaxed, confident, and focused as the shot is against your neck.

As you begin your putting motion, your eyes are focused out the back of the ring. Feel the power as you start, driving hard with the legs, smooth… powerful… the whole body moving powerfully towards the toe board. Feel the separation of the shoulders and hips. The shoulders and the head remain square to back of the circle as you land in the power position. See the hips to the side… the shoulders closed… feel the torqued position. Feel the back foot planted firmly on the ball of the foot. See the front foot near the toe board. Feel your center of gravity over your base as you remain balanced. Your body weight is on a bent back leg. Feel the shot firmly pressed against your neck.

Your movements have given you maximal momentum and you have kinetic energy available to be imparted to the shot. Feel the torque in the power position. Power and energy is stored and ready to be unleashed…ready to explode. Feel the summation of forces from the strong muscles of the leg and pelvis to the fast muscles of the shoulders and arms. As you drive, the back knee drives strong to the front of the circle… feel the trunk pivot powerfully forward and upward behind the hip. Feel the weight transferring from the back leg to the front leg. Feel the front leg brace strongly. The free arm bends and then drives downwards. Feel the front leg and free arm form a solid block and feel the acceleration of the opposite side. Feel the explosive lift of the legs and the trunk. Due to the torque and hip and shoulder separation, you should feel a pre-stretch of the oblique trunk muscles. Feel the power ready to uncoil.

Your throwing arm pushes as the opposite side blocks. Feel the chest forward…be proud... The strike is explosive… upper arm directly behind the shot... driving the shot powerfully. Feel the elbow high, behind the shot until the final flick of the wrist at the release of the shot from the fingers. The wrist snaps powerfully outward, the thumb is down and the little finger is up. When the arm strikes see the head be pulled away from the shot. The shot is directly in front of your shoulder. It feels like a bench press.
Your forward momentum on the explosive release causes you to reverse fast, but you remain under control. You absorb the impact of your body by a slightly bent knee. Your eyes look downward to help lower your center of gravity and stay in the ring, causing your feet to reverse. The fans see the shot released at the proper angle, approximately 42 degrees, and sail and sail through the air. After checking your momentum, you see the shot as it lands… notice the shot hit the landing area with a thud and a roll. This was a fantastic throw.

See the official mark your throw…they reel the tape measure out…reeling more and more tape because your throw is very far… the official calls out the distance… a new P.R!

You feel great… you have that inner feeling that you've given it your all and have done your best. As you walk away from the throwing area to retrieve your shot put you are catching your breath. The adrenaline of success is rushing through your body. You hear friends congratulating you… people pat you on the back and shake your hand. Feel the exhilaration of accomplishment…the joy of success. As you walk over to put on your sweats you feel a tremendous sense of accomplishment as you responded to the challenge. You know that you have thrown far… you know that you were psychologically and physically prepared. All your training, both physical and mental, has paid off. After you accept congratulations from your coach and friends, take time to thank your body… your legs, your muscles, your lungs and your entire body.

See yourself putting the shot again as you continue in the competition…. Each attempt going further and further as your respond to challenges… each time seeing exactly what you want to happen… be as specific as possible… fee the satisfaction of a job well done. You have achieved your goal!

Begin to let go of this image and this feeling….slowly re-enter your present space…feel your body…move your toes…move your fingers…begin to notice your breathing…inhale…exhale…inhale… exhale… You feel relaxed and filled with a new quiet energy.

To help further develop all of your imagery senses, use Activity 16.5. Certain senses may produce clearer attention than others. Use this exercise to provide direction for extra attention and practices.

Activity 16.5
Sensory Imagery for Shot Put

Vividness: Imagine the shot put. Notice the color. Notice how round it is. Notice the landing area. Notice how big it is. Notice the ring you will throw in.

Auditory: What sounds do you hear while you are getting ready to throw? Hear your feet in the ring. Hear the shot land after you throw.

Tactile: Image the feel of your feet in the ring. What does it feel like? Imagine how the shot feels in your hand and fingers.

Kinesthetic: Imagine throwing during warm-ups. Imagine how the shot feels in your hand and fingers. Feel what your body is doing during the warm-ups. Feel the muscles in your legs and arms as you throw. Note the power in your legs and arms as you do your warm-up throws. Feel the sensation of your body from the power position.

Smell: Smell the shot, your shoes, the grass, the ring, and the board. Smell the sweat after a hard practice.

Taste: Taste the salt from the sweat on your lips. Imagine taking a drink of water during a hot day of practice.

Emotion: Experience the confidence you feel when you step up to throw. Experience the satisfaction of throwing far. Experience the pride you feel in achieving a PR. Experience the excitement of being on a successful team.

Vividness Evaluation
What were your strongest images and sensations?
What senses do you need to improve?

A Shot Put Self-Evaluation can be found in Activity 16.6 and can be used periodically to evaluate practice or competition. A general Team Post-Meet Evaluation form can be found in Activity 19.4.

Activity 16.6
Shot Put Self-Evaluation

Rate yourself on a scale of 1-10 (with 10 being high)

1. Overall Performance	_____	11. Ability to push yourself	_____
2. Warm-ups	_____	12. Grip	_____
3. Performance in meets	_____	13. Beginning	_____
4. Encouragement of others	_____	14. Glide in rotation	_____
5. My positive attitude	_____	15. Power Position	_____
6. Use of mental training	_____	16. Hip and leg drive	_____
7. Mental training on own	_____	17. Arms	_____
8. Proper sleep	_____	18. Release	_____
9. Proper nutrition	_____	19. Plant	_____
10. Good hydration practices	_____	20. Visualization of throw	_____

Activity 16.6
Personalized Guided Visualization

Objective:
To write a personalized guided visualization script. In your own words write a visualization of an upcoming performance. This visualization will let you see, hear, and feel yourself performing your sport.

Directions:
Write a personalized guided visualization script. Be as specific as possible. Include as many senses you can. Write it down as full and complete as you can. Remember to use positive statements and include your affirmations. Use the worksheet to formulate your ideas. Then write out your guided visualization in an essay format. After writing the visualization, I would encourage you to record the script. Find a quiet time to play some relaxation music and then play your recorded script. As you talk to yourself, see the visualization coming to life!

Worksheet for your guided visualization

Preparation Period
- See yourself in the preparation phase leading up to the event
- What have you done well?
- Think of some of your best workouts.

Day of the Event
- See yourself getting up in the morning with confidence
- What will you have to eat?
- See yourself dressing for the competition, putting on your clothing

Arriving at the Site
- See yourself arriving at the site
- See the competition
- See the environment, weather, temperature
- Focus on your goal and the outcome you wish to achieve

The Warm-up
- See yourself doing your general warm-up
- See yourself stretching, drills, strides
- See yourself doing your final throws

The Start
- See yourself in the back of the ring
- See and feel the glide or rotation to the power position
- See yourself getting off to a good powerful start

Power Position
- See and feel yourself in control
- See and feel yourself getting into the proper power position
- Feel the torque built up as you are ready to explode

The Release
- Feel the power through your hips, the cores and into your arms
- Feel the shot as it explodes out of your hand and off your fingers
- You remain balanced and in control

Post Event
- Feel the satisfaction of throwing well
- See the teammates, coaches, family and friends congratulating you
- When the event is over, you feel great about your throwing

A sample week for a Shot Put Mental Preparation Plan is provided in Table 16.1. Use the example to help complete the blank form in Activity 19.1 to develop your Mental Preparation plan.

Table 16.1
Sample Weekly Shot Put Mental Preparation Plan

Day	Physical Practice	Mental Practice
Monday	Dynamic warm-up Plyometrics Drills Throws 1/4 mile jog cool down	Incorporate into practice (See Table 16.2) **Outside of practice:** Review weekly goals Positive self-talk Relaxation Imagery of achieving weekly goals
Tuesday	Dynamic warm-up Easy strides	Incorporate into practice (Table 16.2) **Outside of practice:** Mental recall Affirmations
Wednesday	Dynamic warm-up Plyometrics Drills Throws 1/4 mile jog cool down	Incorporate into practice (Table 16.2) **Outside of practice:** Develop competition plan Visualize competition plan
Thursday	Drills Team games Character Building Mental Training	Incorporate into practice (Table 16.2) **Outside of practice:** Relaxation Visualize competition plan Visualize mental recovery plans
Friday	Competition	See Table 16.3 and 16.4 for example of meet day mental preparation plan
Saturday	Easy recovery jog Stretch	Complete post-competition evaluation Use mental recall for low and highlight Review previous week goal progress Set new process and effort goals
Sunday	Recovery- Walk Bike Swim Stretch	Relaxation Mental rehearsal of next week's goals Positive Self-talk Read about a motivating athlete

Table 16.2 provides ideas to incorporate mental skills into your regular practice. A blank form is provided in Activity 19.6 to help you develop your plan to incorporate mental skills into your workouts.

Table 16.2
Ideas to Incorporate Mental and Physical Plan into Workouts

Physical Activity	When to use	Mental Activity
Start	Before throw	Visualize the throw
Power position	Right before position	Rapid energization to achieve proper arousal
Full throw	Before and during	Relaxing breathing Cue words

Use Table 16.3 for ideas on how to develop a Mental Performance Pre-Competition Plan. In Activity 19.2, a blank form is provided to help you develop your plan to incorporate mental skills into your pre-competition warm-up.

Table 16.3 Shot Put Pre-Competition Mental Preparation Plan		
Time Prior to Start	**Physical Warm-Up**	**Mental Warm-up**
60-80 min	Walk to and examine throwing area	Review technical cues worked on in practice Positive self-talk
50-60 min	General WU to get blood flowing and increase body temperature	Positive- Self Talk
40-50 min	Stretching	Visualize achieving goals
30-40 min	Dynamic Warm-up Focus on good drills	Energization
20-30 min	Specific WU Drills Feel the desired body positions	Cue words Visualization
10-20 min	Perform a pre-determined number of warm-up throws	Focus on breathing to re-focus Positive self-talk only
10 min prior	Check-in	Relaxation or Energization to get into proper arousal zone

In Table 16.4, a Shot Put Mental Performance Plan is provided. The plan is divided into different phases of the competition. To help incorporate your mental skills into your performance, complete Activity 19.3 and develop your Mental Performance Plan.

Table 16.4 Designing Your Shot Put Mental Performance Plan			
Competition Phase	**Physical**	**Mental**	**Cue Words**
On deck		Assess environmental conditions	Relax Energize
Enter throwing circle		Positive self-talk Rapid relaxation Narrow focus on throwing circle, and landing area	Ready Go for it
Move to back of circle	Preliminary position	Feel the implement Deep breath	Relax Trust
Initiation of throw	Balanced Control	Focus on cue words	Balance Control
Power position	Feel the torque	Focus on process	Coil Uncoil
Release	Off the finger tips	Feel the spin	Spin Finish

Table 16.5 provides examples of Mental Recovery Plans for Track Events. See Activity 19.5 for a blank form to complete that will help you develop your Mental Recovery Plan.

\multicolumn{4}{c}{**Table 16.5 Mental Recovery Plan for Shot Put**}			
Distractors-Field Events	**Release**	**Re-focus**	**How to prepare for**
Wind	Exhale air out, blow the wind away	Focus on process goals not outcome Focus on process cues	Practice throwing with a cross wind or occasionally into the wind
Rain	Wipe forehead	Positive self-talk Arousal techniques such as energization	Practice on some rainy days
Cold	Rub sweats or clothing	Positive self-talk Imagery of goal achievement	Practice in cold
Weather delays	Relaxation breathing	Relaxation Positive self-talk	Start throwing practice and delay it for several minutes to simulate a rain delay
Foul first two attempts	Park mistake in an object	Cue words that focus on process	Simulation throwing

Chapter 17

Discus

Activity 17.1
Discus Power Picture

Directions: Find a good picture of when you are competing. Make sure the picture shows you in good form and looking strong. Put the picture on a page (preferably cardboard stock). Place your cue words around the picture.

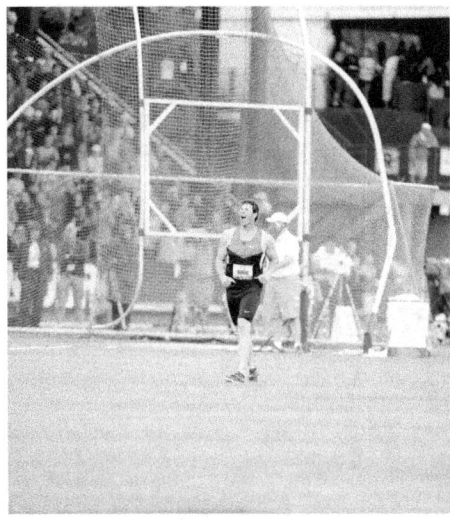

C O N S I S T E N T

R E L A X E D

POWER

Activity 17.2
Discus Affirmations

- I am a discus thrower.
- I love to throw.
- I am committed to a thrower's lifestyle.
- I have the power and courage to be a great discus thrower.
- Each day I become a better thrower.
- I have great power and technique.
- The discus feels light and flies far.
- My grip is comfortable and relaxed.
- My turn is rhythmic and powerful.
- I am in control on my turn.
- My shoulders and hips remain separated on my turn.
- I am centered and focused.
- My turn is controlled, fluid and balanced.
- I enjoy the exhilaration of a great throw.
- I am proud to be a discus thrower.
- I land in a perfect power position.
- My hips are powerful.
- I feel energy ready to explode when I'm in the power position.
- The power travels from my legs, to hips, to chest, to arms, through the shot.
- I drive my legs upward to provide vertical force.
- I feel the torque on my body when I'm in the power position.
- My arm bends to efficiently block the side.
- My discus slings through quickly.
- I relax and let it happen and the discus flies and flies.
- I want to throw further and further.
- I enjoy the exhilaration of a great throw.
- I am a great discus thrower.

Activity 17.3
Discus Mental Recall

Begin to think of a time in your life when you knew that you were right on and performed perfectly. See yourself at that time... notice what you look like, what you are wearing, who is with you what sounds are around you, where you are. Feel the environment and the energy. Begin to see yourself putting the shot when you knew you were right on... when everything worked perfectly... when you were in complete control and at your peak... Watch yourself and feel that feeling... connect with all of the feelings you experienced as you achieved at your highest level. Perfectly...competently... exactly the way you wanted to...what did it feel like?... sound like?...look like?

Remember your thoughts before you threw that day. Remember how the discus felt in your hand. Feel the rhythm of that throw come back. How smooth... fluid... and powerful it felt. Let it all come back to you... let it in... know it again... the joy... the power... the pride and confidence... the rush of knowing you were perfection...let it become part of you ... part of your spirit... part of your being. Fully connect with it.

Feel the movements that you perfectly executed. How good the first part of the discus throw was controlled and flowed into a good power position. The first turn was right where you wanted it to be... consistent... feel the rhythm... starting slow and building up speed. Feel the power that was stored up and then unleashed. Remember the summation of forces that started with the slower and stronger muscles and then shifted to the faster muscles of the shoulder and arms. Remember the strong powerful drive of the legs and hips. The surge of power that went from your legs... to the hips... to the chest... to the arms... and then through the discus as it came off your fingers. All the forces came together perfectly as you exploded with a personal best throw.

Feel the torque built up in your torso...you felt like a coiled spring... just ready to explode. Remember how your body uncoiled...the discus being pulled through, released at the perfect angle. See the discus rotation as it came off your fingers. See the discus sailing and sailing...going further and further.

See the discus flying through the air. How it exploded out of your hand and sailed through the air farther than you had ever thrown it before and it felt so easy. It feels so good to throw so far. Everything worked perfectly just the way you wanted it to.

See yourself receiving congratulations from teammates, coaches and friends. What a throw... what a feeling. While completely involved with this feeling, give yourself a cue word or affirmation that brings all these feelings and pictures into focus...a cue word or affirmation that completely connects you with that time and those feelings when you knew that you were perfect and right on... say the words or words to yourself several times... slowly and allow yourself to experience your sense of power and control... feel it in your whole body.

Remember how you performed so effortlessly. Everything worked perfectly, just the way you wanted it to.

Activity 17.4
Discus Mental Rehearsal

See yourself arriving at the discus area. You are wearing your competition clothes...your thoughts are focused on the discus...you feel good today... you are looking forward to throwing far... you have some really good feelings about your performance. Picture the weather... the sun... the clouds... the wind... the temperature. This is a great day for a P.R. You are excited and ready to throw!

Notice the other throwers.... You are calm, confident and relaxed. You feel good and are ready to throw... you have a deep, calm, yet somewhat nervous feeling inside... your heart is pounding and the adrenaline is flowing... you say your cue words or affirmations to yourself...what a day this is going to be for you!

You are looking forward to throwing far and you have a feeling of being well-prepared for your event...you are feeling good both mentally and physical. You feel good because you know that you have been working hard, training well and have made many sacrifices to be the best you can be...think of all the time you have spent in the weight room, conditioning, stretching, working on drills... technique... throwing... weight training... mental training. All this work is going to pay off today! You are physically and mentally ready to throw far.

See yourself going through your normal warm-up... stretching... drills... the mental preparation. Feel the muscles begin to limber up... some easy warm-up throws... easy throws to loosen up ...feel the sweat on your body and your heart pumping...as your body gets warmer and warmer...preparing itself for competition. Your warm-up throws feel easy and are flying far. You are ready to throw far today.

Your discus feels so light today and your body feels so tuned in and in control. Feel yourself putting more effort into your last few warm-up throws. The movement feels smooth. The power is there today. The turn feels smooth and the discus is just taking off in perfect flight and sailing and sailing. You take your final throw… you feel ready. Your warm-up throws were just what you needed.

Your warm-up went well…you feel ready …you feel ready for a personal record…just the way you want to be.. You relax while waiting for the competition to start. While waiting repeat your cue words and say your affirmations to yourself…take a deep breath… inhale…exhale…inhale…exhale. Your warm-up and throws felt strong and powerful… you are ready to throw the best that you have thrown all year. Hear the official call the throwers together for the final instruction. The flights are announced… as you hear your name feel the tinge of anticipation, as you hear the official wish everyone "good luck." You take a deep breath and gather your thoughts. You exhale and relax saying your cue words or affirmations. Your body and mind responds positively. You are ready.

You stay loose and confident while you are waiting for your turn to throw. Hear the official call your name and see yourself prepare to throw. Visualize the discus in your hand… it feels so light… see yourself enter the back of the ring… your grip feels comfortable, you feel the discus resting in your hand, fingers spread comfortably. Your grip feels good. You feel relaxed, confident and focused as you hold the discus.

Notice the rhythm you gain with your preliminary swing in the back of the ring. Your legs are bent slightly, with the weight on the balls of the feet. Your feet are shoulder width apart…balanced and in control. Your drive begins with the pivoting of the leg… feel yourself on the ball of your foot… feel the foot, the knee and arm all pivot. You have a smooth… fluid start… feel the leg swing wide. The knee drives powerfully forward across the circle… feel the leg now drive toward front of the circle… the hips are ahead of the shoulders as you turn… Feel the stretch on the torso and shoulder as you hold the separation. Feel the discus rise off the shoulder. You land in a perfect power position. Feel the weight on the back of the foot. Your opposite leg is slightly flexed. Feet the torque on your body with the discus back. You feel ready to explode with the throw. The front leg drives hard, driving the hips to the front. The power of the lower body pulls the upper body around. As the discus reaches the low point, the legs drive upwards to provide vertical force. The discus accelerates from the torque of the hips. Feel the surge of power with the upward thrust of the legs. The discus which started far behind the shoulder…is now pulled through…feel the "ripping" in the chest as the muscles are stretched… the feeling of power as you pull through all the way to the fingers… see yourself continuing to pull and accelerate the discus as your chest and arm put the final acceleration on the discus. Feel the arm bend and block. The discus explodes off the index finger… rotating very quickly… what a feeling of power!

As your feet switch positions and you regain your balance notice the discus sailing through the air… perfect rotation. See the discus lift in the wind and sail, seemingly endless through the air… notice the discus begin to stall out…finally, see the discus bounce in the landing area and slide… this was a fantastic throw! See the official mark your throw…they reel the tap measure out… reeling more and more tape because your throw is very far… the official calls out the distance… a new P.R! You feel great… you have that inner feeling that you've given it your all and have done your best.

See yourself throwing the discus again in the competition…. Each attempt going further and further as your respond to challenges… each time seeing exactly what you want to happen… be as specific as possible… fee the satisfaction of a job well done. You have achieved your goal!

As you walk away from the throwing area to retrieve your discus, you are catching your breath. The adrenaline of success is rushing through your body. You hear friends congratulating you…people pat you on the back and shake your hand. Feel the exhilaration of accomplishment…the joy of success. As you walk over to put on your sweats you feel a tremendous sense of accomplishment as you responded to the challenge. You know that you have thrown far… you know that you were psychologically and physically prepared. All your training, both physical and mental, has paid off. After you accept congratulations from your coach and friends, take time to thank your body… your legs, your lungs and your entire body.

Begin to let go of this image and this feeling…. slowly re-enter your present space…feel your body…move your toes… move your fingers…begin to notice your breathing…inhale…exhale…inhale… exhale… You feel relaxed and filled with a new quiet energy.

To help further develop all of your senses in imagery use Activity 17.5. Certain senses may produce clearer attention than others. Use this exercise to provide direction for extra attention and practices.

Activity 17.5
Sensory Imagery for Discus

Vividness: Imagine the discus. Notice the color of the discus. Notice how round it is. Notice the landing area. Notice how big it is. Notice the ring you will throw in.

Auditory: What sounds do you hear while you are getting ready to throw? Hear your feet in the ring. Hear the discus land.

Tactile: Image the feel of your feet in the ring. What does it feel like? Feel the discus in your hand and fingers.

Kinesthetic: Imagine throwing during warm-ups. Feel what your body is doing during the warm-ups. Feel the muscles in your legs and arms as you throw. Note the power in your legs and arms as you do your warm-up throws. Feel the sensation of your body uncoiling from the power position.

Smell: Smell the discus, your shoes, the grass, and the ring. Smell the sweat after a hard practice.

Taste: Taste the salt from the sweat on your lips. Imagine taking a drink of water during a hot day of practice.

Emotion: Experience the confidence you feel when you step up to throw. Experience the satisfaction of throwing far. Experience the pride you feel in achieving a PR. Experience the excitement of being on a successful team.

Vividness Evaluation:
What were your strongest images and sensations?
What senses do you need to improve?

A Discus Self-Evaluation can be found in Activity 17.6 and can be used periodically to evaluate practice or competition. A general Team Post-Meet Evaluation form can be found in Activity 19.4.

Activity 17.6
Discus Self-Evaluation

Rate yourself on a scale of 1-10 (with 10 being high)

1. Overall Performance _____	11. Ability to push yourself _____
2. Warm-ups _____	12. Grip _____
3. Performance in meets _____	13. Beginning _____
4. Encouragement of others _____	14. Sprint _____
5. My positive attitude _____	15. Power Position _____
6. Use of mental training _____	16. Use of hips and legs _____
7. Mental training on own _____	17. Release _____
8. Proper sleep _____	18. Block _____
9. Proper nutrition _____	19. Visualization of throw _____
10. Good hydration practices _____	20. Progress toward your goal _____

Activity 17.7
Personalized Guided Visualization

Objective:
To write a personalized guided visualization script. In your own words write a visualization of an upcoming performance. This visualization will let you see, hear, and feel yourself performing your sport.

Directions: Write a personalized guided visualization script. Be as specific as possible. Include as many senses you can. Write it down as full and complete as you can. Remember to use positive statements and include your affirmations. Use the worksheet to formulate your ideas. Then write out your guided visualization in an essay format. After writing the visualization, I would encourage you to record the script. Find a quiet time to play some relaxation music and then play your recorded script. As you talk to yourself, see the visualization coming to life!

Worksheet for your guided visualization

Day of the Event
- See yourself getting up in the morning with confidence.
- What will you have to eat?
- See yourself dressing for the competition, putting on your clothing.

Arriving at the Site
- See yourself arriving at the site
- See the competition
- See the environment, weather, temperature
- Focus on your goal and the outcome you wish to achieve

The Start
- See yourself in the back of the discus ring
- Hear and feel the initiation of the throw
- See yourself getting off to a good powerful start

Middle of the Event
- See and feel in control as you turn into the power position
- See and feel the proper power position
- Feel the torque built up as you are ready to uncoil

The Release
- Feel the power through your hips, the cores and into your arms
- Feel the discus as it explodes out of your hand
- You remain balanced and in control

Post Event
- Feel the satisfaction of throwing well
- See the teammates, coaches, family and friends congratulating you
- When the event is over, you feel great about your throwing

A sample week for a Discus Mental Preparation Plan is provided in Table 17.1. Use the example to help complete the blank form in Activity 19.1 to develop your Mental Preparation plan.

Table 17.1
Example Discus Mental Preparation Plan

Day	Physical Practice	Mental Practice
Monday	Dynamic warm-up Plyometrics Drills Throws 1/4 mile jog cool down	Incorporate into practice (See Table 17.2) **Outside of practice:** Review weekly goals Positive self-talk Relaxation Imagery of achieving weekly goals
Tuesday	Dynamic warm-up Easy strides	Incorporate into practice (Table 17.2) **Outside of practice:** Mental recall Affirmations:
Wednesday	Dynamic warm-up Plyometrics Drills Throws 1/4 mile jog cool down	Incorporate into practice (Table 17.2) **Outside of practice:** Develop competition plan Visualize competition plan
Thursday	Drills Team games Character Building Mental Training	Incorporate into practice (Table 17.2) **Outside of practice:** Relaxation Visualize competition plan Visualize mental recovery plans
Friday	Competition	See Table 17.3 and 17.4
Saturday	Easy recovery jog Stretch	Complete post-competition evaluation Use mental recall to see highlights Use mental recall to see lowlights-rewind to make it a highlight Review previous week goal progress Set new goals with emphasis on process and effort goals
Sunday	Recovery- Walk Bike Swim Stretch	Relaxation Mental rehearsal of next week's goals Positive Self-talk Read about a motivating athlete

Table 17.2 provides ideas to incorporate mental skills into your regular practice. A blank form is provided in Activity 19.6 to help you develop your plan to incorporate mental skills into your workouts.

Table 17.2
Ideas to Incorporate Mental and Physical Plan into Workouts

Physical Activity	When to use	Mental Activity
Initiation of throw and turn	Before start	Visualize
Power Position	Before position	Rapid energization to achieve proper arousal Image position
Full Throws	Before and during	Cue words Relaxing breathing

Use Table 17.3 for ideas on how to develop a Mental Performance Pre-Competition Plan. In Activity 19.2, a blank form is provided to help you develop your plan to incorporate mental skills into your pre-competition warm-up.

Table 17.3
Throwers Mental Preparation Plan at Meet

Time Prior to Start	Physical Warm-Up	Mental Warm-up
60-80 min	Walk to and examine throwing area	Review technical cues worked on in practice Positive self-talk
50-60 min	General WU to get blood flowing and increase body temperature	Positive- Self Talk
40-50 min	Stretching	Visualize achieving goals
30-40 min	Dynamic Warm-up Focus on good drills	Energization
20-30 min	Specific WU Drills Feel the desired body positions	Cue words Visualization
10-20 min	Perform a pre-determined number of warm-up throws	Focus on breathing to re-focus Positive self-talk only
10 min prior	Check-in	Relaxation or Energization to get into proper arousal zone

In Table 17.4, a Mental Performance Plan is provided. The plan is divided into different phases of the competition. To help incorporate your mental skills into your performance, complete Activity 19.3 and develop your Mental Performance Plan.

Table 17.4
Designing Your Discus Mental Performance Plan

Competition Phase	Physical	Mental	Cue Words
On deck		Assess environmental conditions	Relax Energize
Enter throwing circle		Positive self-talk Rapid relaxation Narrow focus on throwing circle and landing area	Ready Go for it.
Move to back of circle	Preliminary position Swings	Feel the implement Deep breath	Relax Trust
Initiation of throw	Balanced/Control	Focus on cue words	Balance Control
Across circle	Sprint across circle Straight line	Focus on process	Sprint
Release	Off the finger tips	Feel the spin	Spin Finish

Table 17.5 provides examples of Mental Recovery Plans for Field Events. See Activity 19.5 for a blank form to complete that will help you develop your Mental Recovery Plan.

Table 17.5
Mental Recovery Plan for Discus

Distractors-Field Events	Release	Re-focus	How to prepare for
Wind	Exhale air out, blow the wind away	Focus on process goals not outcome Focus on process cues	Practice throwing with a cross wind or occasionally into the wind
Rain	Wipe forehead	Positive self-talk Arousal techniques such as energization	Practice on some rainy days
Cold	Rub sweats or clothing	Positive self-talk Imagery of goal achievement	Practice in cold
Weather delays	Relaxation breathing	Relaxation Positive self-talk	Start throwing practice and delay it for several minutes to simulate a rain delay
Foul first two attempts	Park mistake in an object	Cue words on process	Simulation throwing

Chapter 18

Javelin

Activity 18.1
Javelin Power Picture

Directions: Find a good picture of when you are competing. Make sure the picture shows you in good form and looking strong. Put the picture on a page (preferably cardboard stock). Place your cue words around the picture.

B A L A N C E **C O N T R O L**

POWER

Activity 18.2
Javelin Affirmations

- I am a javelin thrower.
- I love to throw.
- I am committed to a thrower's lifestyle.
- I have the power and courage to be a great javelin thrower.
- Each day I become a better thrower.
- I have great power and technique.
- The javelin feels light and flies far.
- My grip is comfortable and relaxed.
- I am aggressive on my approach.
- I am in control.
- My shoulders and hips remain separated on my transition phase.
- My cross step is controlled and balanced.
- I hit a hard, crisp plant.
- I land in a perfect power position.
- My hips are powerful.
- I feel energy ready to explode when I'm in the power position.
- The power travels from my legs, to hips, to chest, to arms, through the javelin.
- I drive through the javelin.
- I feel the torque on my body when I'm in the power position.
- I release high.
- I relax and let it happen and the javelin flies and flies.
- I want to throw further and further.
- I enjoy the exhilaration of a great javelin throw.
- I am proud to be a javelin thrower.
- I am a great javelin thrower.

Activity 18.3
Javelin Mental Recall

Begin to think of a time in your life when you knew that you were right on and performed perfectly. See yourself at that time... notice what you look like, what you are wearing, who is with you, what sounds are around you, where you are. Feel the environment and the energy. Begin to see yourself throwing the javelin when you knew you were right on... when everything worked perfectly... when you were in complete control and at your peak... Watch yourself and feel that feeling... connect with all of the feelings you experienced as you achieved at your highest level.... Perfectly...competently... exactly the way you wanted to...what did it feel like?... sound like?...look like?

Remember your thoughts before you threw that day. Remember how the javelin felt laying in the palm of your hand...a relaxed and powerful grip. Feel the rhythm of the approach come back. How smooth, fluid and powerful it felt as you built up your speed. Let it all come back to you... let it in... know it again... the joy... the power... the pride and confidence... the rush of knowing you were perfection...let it become part of you ... part of your spirit... part of your being. Fully connect with it.

Feel the movements that you perfectly executed. Feel the cross step that you perfectly executed. How good it felt and set you up in a good power position. Feel the power that was stored up and then unleashed. See the javelin starting to whip through. Remember the strong powerful plant and the drive of the hips. Feel that surge of power that went from your legs... to the hips... to the chest... to the arms... and then through the javelin. All the forces came together perfectly to throw through the point.

See the javelin flying through the air. How aerodynamic it looks as it sails and sails further than you had ever thrown it before and it felt so easy. It feels so good to throw so far. Everything worked perfectly just the way you wanted it to. Remember how you performed so effortlessly.

While completely involved with this feeling, give yourself a cue word or affirmation that brings all these feelings and pictures into focus... a cue word or affirmation that completely connects you with that time and those feelings when you knew that you were perfect and right on... say the word or words to yourself several times... slowly allow yourself to experience your sense of power and control... feel it in your whole body.

Activity 18.4
Javelin Mental Rehearsal

See yourself walking over to the javelin area. ...your thoughts are focused on the javelin...you feel good today... you are looking forward to throwing far... you have some really good feelings about your performance.

Notice your surroundings...the weather... the sun... the clouds... the wind... the temperature. This is a great day for a P.R. You are excited and ready to throw!

Notice the other throwers. You are calm, confident and relaxed. You feel good and are ready to throw... you have a deep, calm, yet somewhat nervous feeling inside... your heart is pounding and the adrenaline is flowing... you say your cue words or affirmations to yourself... what a day this is going to be for you!

You are looking forward to throwing far and you have a feeling of being well-prepared for your event...you are feeling good both mentally and physical. You feel good because you know that you have been working hard, training well and have made many sacrifices to be the best you can be... think of all the time you have spent in the weight room, conditioning, stretching, working on drills... technique... throwing... weight training...mental training. All this work is going to pay off today! You are physically and mentally ready to throw far.

See yourself going through your normal warm-up...stretching...drills... the mental preparation. Feel the muscles begin to limber up... some easy warm-up throws... easy throws to loosen up ...feel the sweat on your body and your heart pumping...as your body gets warmer and warmer... preparing itself for competition... Your warm-up throws feel easy and are flying far. You are ready to throw far today.

Feel the lightness of the javelin as you pick it up... you are strong and confident... your warm-up throws and your body feel so tuned in and in control...Feel yourself putting more effort into your last few warm-up throws. The movement feels smooth... the power is there today. Your approach feels smooth and the javelin is just taking off in perfect flight and sailing and sailing. You take your final throw... your feel ready. You are ready to throw the best you have thrown all year.

You note the wind...you see your strategy starting to unfold... you are powerful and confident. You relax while waiting for the competition to start. While waiting, repeat your cue words and say your affirmations to yourself...take a deep breath... inhale...exhale...inhale...exhale... Your warm-up and throws felt strong and powerful... you are ready to throw far.
Hear the official call the throwers together for the final instruction. The flights are announced... as you hear your name feel the

tinge of anticipation, as you hear the official wish everyone "good luck."

You take a deep breath and gather your thoughts. You exhale and relax saying your cue words or affirmations. Your body and mind responds positively. You are ready.

You stay loose and confident while you are waiting for your turn to throw. Hear the official call your name and see yourself prepare to throw. Visualize the javelin in your hand... .it feels so light. Feel the javelin lay across our palm and feel the fingers curl around the shaft. The grip feels comfortable and relaxed. You are getting ready for your throw... see yourself on the runway mentally preparing for a strong throw. .

You find your starting point on the runway...you feel strong on the runway, your confidence is peaking ... you feel quick and powerful... balanced... centered... and most of all, under control.

Feel the rhythm of the approach as the javelin rests in the palm of your hand... out of the corner of your eye...you see your transition mark, your eyes focus straight ahead. You are being aggressive. Feel the palm up... feel the javelin beginning to come back... You are in perfect rhythm and control...you have good speed as you accelerate and begin your cross-over steps... you feel relaxed as you hit a hard, quick crisp plant...your hips are powerful... see the plant leg...landing heel first with a slight flex... the power traveling from the legs, to the hips, through the chest, to the arm, through the javelin.. the plant leg blocks as the other leg drives through powerfully... driving everything through the point of the javelin....see the elbow come through high over the shoulder. Your throwing shoulder is like a whip handle... you feel the power of your throw, strong, powerful, yet relaxed...the javelin leaves your hands... very high in relationship to your body...you feel the javelin snap off your fingers....a great release... you know this is going to be your best throw ever.

The javelin flies out of your hand as your hand follows through and achieves a thumbs down position... see the feet shift smoothly and feel your center of gravity lower.

See the javelin rotating as it spins, sailing through the air... it seems like it stays up forever....it just keeps on flying and flying....farther than you've ever thrown before... You know it is a great throw. It felt so good.

The javelin finally lands. See the official mark your throw...they reel the tape measure out...reeling more and more tape because your throw is very far... the official calls out the distance... a new P.R.!

Feel the excitement in your body...see the smile on our face... hear your teammates congratulating you... people pat you on the back and shake your hand. Feel the exhilaration of accomplishment... the joy of success. As you walk over to put on your sweats, you feel a tremendous sense of accomplishment as you responded to the challenge. You know that you have thrown far... you know that you were psychologically and physically prepared. All your training both physical and mental have paid off. After you accept congratulations from your coach and friends, take time to thank your body... your legs, your muscles, and your entire body.

Visualize this scene several more times if you wish...each time seeing exactly what you want to happen... Each attempt going further and further as your respond to challenges... each time seeing exactly what you want to happen... be as specific as possible... feel the satisfaction of a job well done.

You have achieved your goal!

Begin to let go of this image and this feeling....slowly re-enter your present space...feel your body...move your toes...move your fingers...begin to notice your breathing...inhale...exhale...inhale... exhale... You feel relaxed and filled with a new quiet energy.

Activity 18.5
Sensory Imagery for Javelin

Vividness: Imagine the javelin. Notice the color and the length. Notice the grip. Notice the throwing area. Notice how big it is. Notice the runway and follow it all the way to the foul line.

Auditory: What sounds do you hear while you are getting ready to throw? Hear your feet on the approach.

Tactile: Image the feel of your feet on the runway. What does it feel like? Notice the javelin and how it feels to hold it.

Kinesthetic: Imagine throwing during warm-ups. Feel what your body is doing during the warm-ups. Feel the muscles in your legs and arms as you throw. Note the power in your legs and arms as you do your warm-up throws. Feel the sensation of your body uncoiling from the power position.

Smell: Smell the javelin, your shoes, the grass, and the runway. Smell the sweat after a hard practice.

Taste: Taste the salt from the sweat on your lips. Imagine taking a drink of water during a hot day of practice.

Emotion: Experience the confidence you feel when you step up to throw. Experience the satisfaction of throwing far. Experience the pride you feel in achieving a PR. Experience the excitement of being on a successful team.

Vividness Evaluation
What were your strongest images and sensations?
What senses do you need to improve?

A Javelin Self-Evaluation can be found in Activity 18.6 and can be used periodically to evaluate practice or competition. A general Team Post-Meet Evaluation form can be found in Activity 19.4

Activity 18.6
Javelin Self-Evaluation

Rate yourself on a scale of 1-10 (with 10 being high)

1. Overall Performance	_____	11. Grip	_____
2. Warm-ups	_____	12. Approach	_____
3. Performance in meets	_____	13. Withdrawal	_____
4. Encouragement of others	_____	14. Cross Step	_____
5. My positive attitude	_____	15. Power Position	_____
6. Use of mental training	_____	16. Hips and legs	_____
7. Mental training on own	_____	17. Arm Action	_____
8. Proper sleep	_____	18. Release	_____
9. Proper nutrition	_____	19. Recovery	_____
10. Good hydration practices	_____	20. Visualization of throw	_____

Activity 18.7
Personalized Guided Visualization

Objective:
To write a personalized guided visualization script. In your own words write a visualization of an upcoming performance. This visualization will let you see, hear, and feel yourself performing your sport.

Directions:
Write a personalized guided visualization script. Be as specific as possible. Include as many senses you can. Write it down as full and complete as you can. Remember to use positive statements and include your affirmations. Use the worksheet to formulate your ideas. Then write out your guided visualization in an essay format. After writing the visualization, I would encourage you to record the script. Find a quiet time to play some relaxation music and then play your recorded script. As you talk to yourself, see the visualization coming to life!

Worksheet for your guided visualization

Preparation Period
- See yourself in the preparation phase leading up to the event
- What have you done well? Think of some of your best workouts

Day of the Event
- See yourself getting up in the morning with confidence
- What will you have to eat?
- See yourself dressing for the competition, putting on your clothing

Arriving at the Site
- See yourself arriving at the site
- See the competition
- See the environment, weather, temperature
- Focus on your goal and the outcome you wish to achieve

The Warm-up
- See yourself doing your general warm-up
- See yourself stretching, drills
- See yourself doing your final throws

The Approach
- See yourself in the back of the javelin runway
- Hear and feel the initiation of the approach
- Feel the rhythm of the approach

Middle of the Event
- See and feel yourself in control on the approach
- See and feel yourself getting into the proper power position
- Feel the torque built up as you are ready to explode
- Feel the transition stages of withdrawal, step and cross-steps

The Release
- Feel the power through your hips, the core and into your arms
- Feel the shoulder like a whip handle with a high release
- Feel the javelin as it explodes out of your hand
- You remain balanced and in control

Post Event
- Feel the satisfaction of throwing well
- See the teammates, coaches, family and friends congratulating you
- When the event is over, you feel great about your throwing

A sample week for a Javelin Mental Preparation Plan is provided in Table 18.1. Use the example to help complete the blank form in Activity 19.1 to develop your Mental Preparation plan.

\multicolumn{3}{c}{Table 18.1 Example Weekly Javelin Mental Preparation Plan}		
Day	Physical Practice	Mental Practice
Monday	Dynamic warm-up Plyometrics Drills Throws ¼ mile jog cool down	Incorporate into practice (See Table 18.2) **Outside of practice:** Review weekly goals Positive self-talk Relaxation Imagery of achieving weekly goals
Tuesday	Dynamic warm-up Easy strides	Incorporate into practice (Table 18.2) **Outside of practice:** Mental recall Affirmations:
Wednesday	Dynamic warm-up Plyometrics Drills Throws 1/4 mile jog cool down	Incorporate into practice (Table 18.2) **Outside of practice:** Develop competition plan Visualize competition plan
Thursday	Drills Team games Character Building Mental Training	Incorporate into practice (Table 18.2) **Outside of practice:** Relaxation Visualize competition plan Visualize mental recovery plans
Friday	Competition	See Table 18.3 and 18.4
Saturday	Easy recovery jog Stretch	Complete post-competition evaluation Use mental recall to see highlights Use mental recall to see lowlights-rewind to make it a highlight Review previous week goal progress Set new goals with emphasis on process and effort goals
Sunday	Recovery- Walk Bike Swim Stretch	Relaxation Mental rehearsal of next week's goals Positive Self-talk Read about a motivating athlete

Table 18.2 provides ideas to incorporate mental skills into your regular practice. A blank form is provided in Activity 19.6 to help you develop your plan to incorporate mental skills into your workouts.

Table 18.2 Ideas to Incorporate Mental and Physical Plan into Workouts		
Physical Activity	**When to use**	**Mental Activity**
Approach work	Before approach	Visualize the approach
Power position	Before throw	Rapid energization to achieve proper arousal Imagery to feel position
Full Throws	Before and during	Cue words Relaxing breathing

Use Table 18.3 for ideas on how to develop a Mental Performance Pre-Competition Plan. In Activity 19.2, a blank form is provided to help you develop your plan to incorporate mental skills into your pre-competition warm-up.

Table 18.3 Javelin Mental Preparation Plan at Meet		
Time Prior to Start	**Physical Warm-up**	**Mental Warm-up**
60-80 min	Walk to and examine throwing area	Review technical cues worked on in practice Positive self-talk
50-60 min	General WU to get blood flowing and increase body temperature	Positive- Self Talk
40-50 min	Stretching	Visualize achieving goals
30-40 min	Dynamic Warm-up Focus on good drills	Energization
20-30 min	Specific WU Drills Feel the desired body positions	Cue words Visualization
10-20 min	Perform a pre-determined number of warm-up throws	Focus on breathing to re-focus Positive self-talk only
10 min prior	Check-in	Relaxation or Energization to get into proper arousal zone

In Table 18.4, a Mental Performance Plan is provided. The plan is divided into different phases of the competition. To help incorporate your mental skills into your performance, complete Activity 19.3.

\multicolumn{4}{c}{**Table 18.4**}
\multicolumn{4}{c}{**Designing Your Javelin Mental Performance Plan**}
Competition Phase	**Physical**	**Mental**	**Cue Words**
On deck		Assess environmental conditions	Relax Energize
Enter throwing runway		Positive self-talk Rapid relaxation Narrow focus on throwing, runway, implement, landing area	Ready Go for it.
Move to back of runway	Preliminary position	Feel the implement Deep breath	Relax Trust
Initiation of throw	Balanced Control	Focus on cue words	Balance Control
Run-up	Accelerate Straight line	Focus on process	Sprint
Power position	Feel torque	Focus on cue	Uncoil
Release	High off the finger tips	Feel the follow-through	Tall Finish

Table 18.5 provides examples of Mental Recovery Plans for Track Events. See Activity 19.5 for a blank form to complete that will help you develop your Mental Recovery Plan.

\multicolumn{4}{c}{**Table 18.5**}
\multicolumn{4}{c}{**Mental Recovery Plan for Javelin**}
Distractors-Field Events	**Release**	**Re-focus**	**How to prepare for**
Wind	Exhale air out, blow the wind away	Focus on process goals not outcome Focus on process cues	Practice throwing with a cross wind or occasionally into the wind
Rain	Wipe forehead	Positive self-talk Arousal techniques such as energization	Practice on some rainy days
Cold	Rub sweats or clothing	Positive self-talk Imagery of goal achievement	Practice in cold
Weather delays	Relaxation breathing	Relaxation Positive self-talk	Start throwing practice and delay it for several minutes to simulate a rain delay
Foul first two attempts	Park mistake in an object	Cue words that focus on process	Simulation throwing

Chapter 19

Activity Forms

	Activity 19.1 Design Your Weekly Mental Preparation Plan	
Day	**Physical Practice**	**Mental Practice**
Monday		Practice: Outside of practice:
Tuesday		Practice: Outside of practice::
Wednesday		Practice: Outside of practice:
Thursday		Practice: Outside of practice:
Friday		Outside of practice:
Saturday		Outside of practice:
Sunday		Outside of practice:

Activity 19.2 Mental Performance Pre-Competition Plan		
Time Prior to Start	**Physical WU**	**Mental WU**

Activity 19.3
Designing Your Mental Performance Plan

Competition Phase	Physical	Mental	Cue Words

Activity 19.4
Post-Meet Evaluation

Name of meet: _____ **Date:** _____ **Weather:** _____

Pre-meet meal:
_____
_____

Pre-meet mental training:
_____
_____

Rate the following on a scale of 1-10 (10 being high)

Your overall performance　　　　　　　　　_____

Proper nutrition　　　　　　　　　　　　　_____

Proper hydration　　　　　　　　　　　　　_____

Warm-up　　　　　　　　　　　　　　　　　_____

Use of mental training before event　　　　　_____

Use of mental training competition plan　　　_____

Start　　　　　　　　　　　　　　　　　　　_____

Middle of event　　　　　　　　　　　　　　_____

Finish of event　　　　　　　　　　　　　　　_____

Mental Toughness　　　　　　　　　　　　　_____

Encouraging teammates　　　　　　　　　　_____

Challenged myself　　　　　　　　　　　　　_____

Accomplished competition plan　　　　　　　_____

Things I did well
1. _____
2. _____
3. _____

Things I contributed to the team
1. _____
2. _____
3. _____

Things I need to work on
1. _____
2. _____
3. _____

Activity 19.5 Your Mental Recovery Plan			
Distractors	Release	Re-focus	How to prepare for

Activity 19.6 Ideas to Incorporate Mental Skills into Workouts		

Resources

Bowerman, B., & Freeman W. (1991). *High performance training for track and field.* Champaign, IL: Human Kinetics.

Burton, D., & Raedeke, T. (2008). *Sport psychology for coaches.* Champaign, IL: Human Kinetics.

Feltz D., & Landers, M. (2007). The effects of mental practice on motor skill learning and performance: A meta-analysis. *Journal of Sport Psychology, 5.*

Freeman, W. (2014). *Track and field coaching essentials, USA Track and Field.* Champaign, IL: Human Kinetics.

Goldberg, A. (2012). *Using your head for championship performance in track and field.* Amazon Digital Services.

Galloway, S. (2007). Consulting with Olympic track and field hopefuls: It can't be this easy, or could it. *Athletic Insight: The Online Journal of Sport Psychology, 9.*

Gilbert, J. (2011). Teaching sport psychology to high school student-athletes: The psychological uniform and the game plan format. *Journal of Sport Psychology in Action*, 2.

Hammermeister, J. (2010). *Cornerstones of coaching, the building blocks of success for sport coaches and teams.* Traverse City, MI: Cooper Publishing, Co.

Hogg, J. (1997). *Mental skills for young athletes.* Edmonton, Alberta, Canada: Sport Excel Publishing Inc.

Janssen, J., & Candrea, M. (1994). *Mental toughness training for softball: A guide and workbook for athletes and coaches.* Casa Grande, AZ: Southwest Campus Publications.

Lefkowits, J., & McDuff, D. (n.d.). Mental Toughness Training Manual for Baseball/Softball players.

Johnson, D. (2012). *Wrestling drills for the mat and mind.* Ithaca, NY: MAG, Incorporated.

Judge, L., Bell, R., Bellar, D., & Wanless. E. (2010). Developing a mental game plan: Mental periodization for achieving a "flow" state for track and field throws athlete. *The Sport Journal, 13(4).*

Murphy, S. (1994). Imagery interventions in sport. *Medicine Science Sports Exercise 26(4).*

Murphy, S., & Martin, K. A. (2002). The use of imagery in sport. In T. Horn (Ed.), *Advances in sport psychology* (2 ed., pp. 405-439). Champaign, IL: Human Kinetics.

Nideffer, R. M. (1989). Psychological services for the U.S. track and field team. *The Sport Psychologist, 3.*

Orlick, T., & Partington, J. (1988). Mental links to excellence. *The Sport Psychologist, 2.*

Reardon, J., & Gordin, R. (1999). Psychological skill development leading to a peak performance "flow state". *Track and Field Coaches Review,* 3(2).

Porter, K. (2003). *The mental athlete.* Champaign, IL: Human Kinetics.

Risk, B. (2009). *Periodized sport psychology-Building the bulletproof athlete.* Fairport, NY: Glass Dragon Digital Publishing.

Rockwood, D. (2011). *Closing the gap: Applied sport psychology for high school.* Provo, UT: Rockwood Publishing.

Smith, D. (1999). *Make success measurable: A mindbook-workbook for setting goals and taking action.* Toronto, Ontario, Canada: John Wiley and Sons, Inc.

Stanbrough, M. (2012). *Motivational moments in men's track and field.* Emporia, KS: Roho Publishing.

Stanbrough, M. (2012). *Motivational moments in women's track and field.* Emporia, KS: Roho Publishing.

Stanbrough, M. (2012). *Motivational moments in Olympic track and field.* Emporia, KS: Roho Publishing.

Townsend, D. (2005). *Mind training for swimmers.* Jamul, CA: Belissima Publishing.

Vealey, R. (2005). *Coaching for the inner edge.* Morgantown, WV: Fitness Information Technology.

Vernachchia, R., & Statler, T. (2005). *The psychology of high performance track and field.* Mountain View, CA: TAFnews Press

Visek, A., Harris, B., & Blom, L. (2013). Mental training with youth sport teams: Developmental considerations and best-practice recommendations. *Journal of Sport Psychology in Action, 4.*

Wann, D., & Church, B. (1998). A method for enhancing the psychological skills of track and field athletes. *Track Coach, (4).*

Weinberg, R., & Gould, D. (2006). *Foundations of Sport and Exercise Psychology* (4th ed.). Champaign, IL: Human Kinetics.

Weintraub, A. (2009). *Coaches Guide to Winning the Mental Game.* Monterey, CA: Coaches Choice.

Woolfolk, R., Parrish, M., & Murphy. (1985). The effects of positive and negative imagery on motor skill performance. *Cognitive Therapy and Research, 9.*

Photo Credits

Treworgy, C. PrettySporty, Graham, NC. http://www.prettysport.com

About the Author

Dr. Mark Stanbrough ran cross country and track and field for the Emporia State Hornets from 1974-1977 and was the head track and field and cross country coach at Emporia State from 1984-1992.

Dr. Mark Stanbrough is a professor in the Department of Health, Physical Education and Recreation at Emporia State University in Kansas. He teaches graduate and undergraduate exercise physiology and sports psychology classes and is the director of Coaching Education. The Coaching Education program at Emporia State is currently one of only ten universities in the United State to be accredited by the National Council for the Accreditation of Coaching Education. He was a co-founder of the online physical education graduate program, the first in United States to go completely online. He received his Ph.D. in exercise physiology from the University of Oregon, and undergraduate and master's degrees from Emporia State in physical education. He has served as department chair and has served on the National Association for Sport and Physical Education National Sport Steering Committee and is a past member of the board of directors for the National Council for the Accreditation of Coaching Education.

Mark has over thirty years of coaching experience at the collegiate, high school, middle school and club level. Coach Stanbrough served eight years as the head men's and women's cross country/track and field coach at Emporia State (1984-1992) with the 1986 women's cross country team finishing second at the NAIA national meet. He has also coached at Emporia High School and Glasco High School in Kansas. He is a member of the Emporia State University Athletic Hall of Honor and the Health, Physical Education, Recreation Hall of Honor and has won numerous coach-of-the-year awards at the high school and collegiate levels.

www.ingramcontent.com/pod-product-compliance
Lightning Source LLC
Chambersburg PA
CBHW081216230426
43666CB00015B/2746